Library of
Davidson College

Politics in Africa

Published for the
University of Rhode Island by
The University Press
of New England
Hanover, New Hampshire
1978

POLITICS IN AFRICA
Dennis Austin

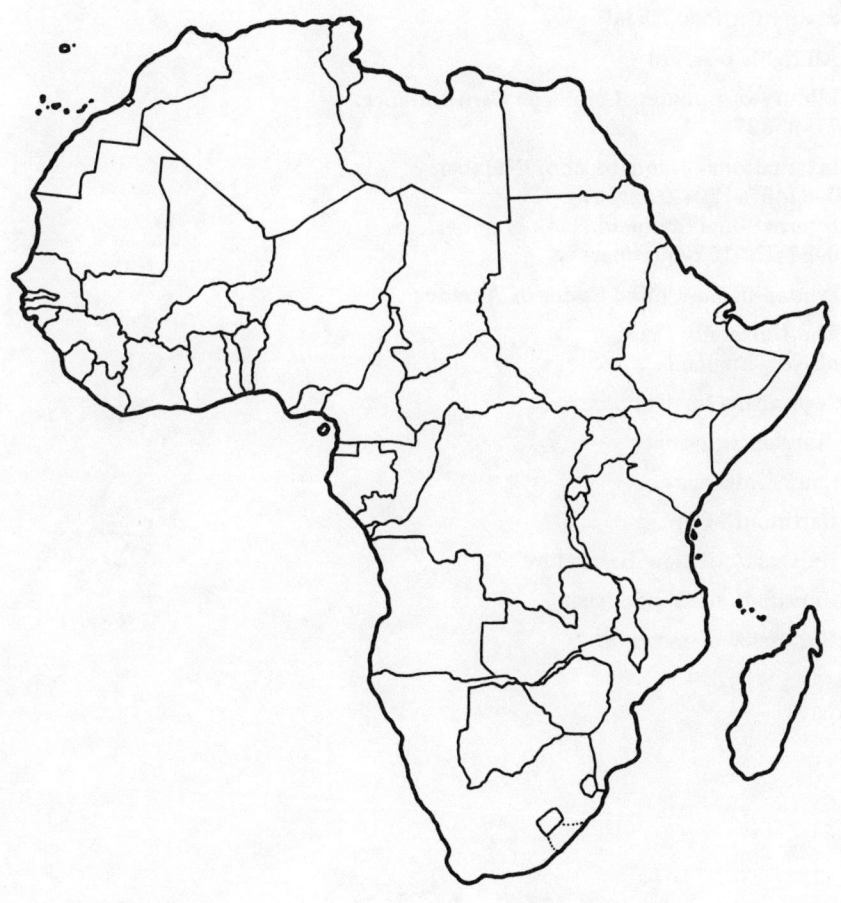

Copyright © 1978 by the
Board of Regents for Education,
State of Rhode Island

All rights reserved

Library of Congress Catalogue Card Number:
77-95397

International Standard Book Number:
0-87451-150-X (cloth)
International Standard Book Number:
0-87451-152-5 (paper)

Printed in the United States of America

The University Press
of New England

Sponsoring Institutions:

Brandeis University

Clark University

Dartmouth College

University of New Hampshire

University of Rhode Island

University of Vermont

Acknowledgments

I very much fear that, in preparing these lectures for publication, I have not succeeded in smoothing away every mark of haste, although I was more than fortunate in being able to turn for advice to colleagues on both sides of the Atlantic. Foremost among them are Keith Panter Brick, Anirudha Gupta, Professor Morris Jones, Valerie and Sid Bennett—Jon Bennett, too. How helpful they have been! Only I know fully the extent of my debt to them, to Newell Stultz also, Virginia and Win Cone, Jack Spence, Nelson Kasfir, Roger Louis, Karl Schmidt, William Tordoff, Marion Doro, Bernth Lindfors and Robbie Wokler, the publishers David Horne and Martin Spencer, and Edgar LeDuc, Chairman of the Political Science Department in the University of Rhode Island. I wish to thank especially Mrs. Marjorie Gray, who helped enormously, at late notice, to type the manuscript for publication: she was unfailing in her patient accuracy. But when all is said and acknowledged, there would have been neither lectures nor book without Josephine and Ron Milburn, Rosemary and Jeffrey, and the comfort of Florence and Margaret Austin, who watched over their preparation with tolerant kindness in Providence, Rhode Island.

D. A.

Manchester, England
October 1977

Contents

Introduction   1

1. The Fallacies of Hope   9

2. No Longer at Ease   35

3. E Pluribus Plures   61

4. The Middle Zone   83

5. White Power: Cohesion without Consensus   109

6. The Darkling Plain: Literature and Politics   135

Appendix   163

Bibliography   165

Notes   171

Index   199

We had fed the heart on fantasies,
The heart's grown brutal from the fare;
More substance in our enmities
Than in our love: O honey-bees,
Come build in the empty house of the stare.

              W. B. Yeats
              Meditations in Time of Civil War

Introduction

The six chapters of this book are an extended version of the lectures given by kind invitation of the University of Rhode Island. The first borrows its title—"The Fallacies of Hope"—from Turner's picture of the West African slave ship, which hangs in the Boston Museum of Fine Arts; but the sentiment expressed there might well be thought characteristic of all six chapters, in the sense that the effort to describe so large a part of the continent within a very narrow compass is certainly optimistic. The first chapter looks at the failure of many of the early hopes attached to the transition from colonial to African rule. Chapters 2 through 5 are concerned with Africa south of the Sahara, and are grouped regionally. The sixth examines the way in which a number of African novelists and poets have taken many of their themes from the political conflicts of the past three decades.

The result is a loose collection of topics spread out across the continent, with no attempt to give them a conceptual unity or model form. I did, however, try to provide a lightly held thread of argument—more theme perhaps than argument—by examining the different ways in which the newly independent African governments have tried to acquire authority, use the structures of power, and adapt to their own purposes the practices of the former colonial state. I thought it a sensible division by which some linked account of the politics of Africa might be rendered to an audience largely unfamiliar with the continent. The only other book of such a kind, to the reading of which this present volume might indeed be seen as a prelude, is Anirudha Gupta's interesting discussion of *Government and Politics in Africa* (New Delhi, 1975). But a preliminary word of introduction was also thought to be helpful, and three primary characteristics—size, complexity and disunity—were singled out for comment.

First, size. It seemed proper, even for an American audience,

Introduction

to stress the immensity of the continent. From the southern shore of the Mediterranean to the Cape, and from the Horn of Africa to the western Atlantic coast, lies a geographical area more than three and a half times the size of the United States—larger, that is, than China, the United States, and western Europe combined. The Sudan alone, its largest state, is almost four times the area of Texas (although there are, to be sure, fewer Texans than Sudanese). Some of the biggest countries are almost empty of people. Mauritania, for example, into which one could very easily fit my small native British Isles many times over, has fewer than a million and a half inhabitants. Namibia, the object of a good deal of current controversy and some guerrilla fighting, is about as large but with under a million people. A few are both large and numerous, Nigeria now being reckoned the eighth most populous state in the world. Many are very small indeed. São Tomé and Príncipe is a tiny independent archipelago in The Gulf of Guinea with fewer than 80,000 inhabitants. The Gambia is scarcely more than two banks of a river which winds its way for three hundred miles into the surrounding country of Senegal. Lesotho is totally enclosed within the territory of South Africa. Botswana, Equatorial Guinea, the central states of Rwanda and Burundi, the newly independent Republic of Djibouti, and the West African states of Guinea Bissau, Togo, and Liberia are all under or a little over the million mark.

Taken together, north and south of the Sahara, there are said to have been about 350 million people within the continent at the beginning of the present decade, of whom 90 million or so lived in "Arab Africa." Without allowing for the extended, inhospitable regions of desert and savannah it might be thought that there was room for many more in so large an area of the world. Yet the overall rate of growth has conjured up contrary fears. The percentage increase of population is now slightly above the rate for the developing world as a whole and may reach the very high figure of 3 percent per year by 1981. Not only will the birth rate be high, but, if medical provision improves, fewer children will die. And although the expectation of life is still low, it is thought to be rising. Throughout the continent, therefore, from the crowded Nile Delta to the peasant societies of tropical Africa and the urban slums of South Africa, the growing number of young and old alike places a heavy burden on society and the state.

The enormous scale of Africa, north and south, east and west, has itself brought political problems for many of these independent states. Airways span the continent for those who can afford to use them, while at a popular level roads and railways have recently begun the task of linking countries on a trans-Saharan and transcontinental base; but the pattern of communication is still largely that devised to serve an export-based economy—cash crops and mining—under colonial direction. The effect is looked at (in Chapter 4) in central Africa, where political control has been made extremely difficult by the pull of railroads and economic interests in one direction and that of ideology, race, and politics in the opposite direction. The huge, often empty map with its poor communications has also had its effect on local wars, minimizing them in one sense, perpetuating them in another. There has not as yet been any sustained international conflict between African states if only because of the difficulties in many instances (between Uganda and Tanzania, for example) in keeping a small army in what is likely to be a large field of operation. On the other hand, the empty tracts of land and inadequate security forces have enabled small guerrilla campaigns to continue almost indefinitely, as by the Eritrean Liberation Front in Ethiopia, or by anti-MPLA forces in southern Angola or similarly discontented groups in Chad, Rwanda, and a number of other states. Distance and poor communications have also worked against notions of pan-Africanism. The leaders can meet together by air, but the size of the continent makes joint policies extremely difficult. Africa is not at all like its most familiar symbol, the elephant, which can at least move quickly when it wants to; it is like a stranded whale. For example, those who talk of the necessity of an all-African attack on white rule in South Africa fall silent when faced with the logistics involved in such plans. In 1976 the largest African army was Nigerian, but it lacked any air command system, and it was over 1,500 miles from the Zambesi. The most efficient army was Egyptian, 3,000 miles distant and facing not Africa but the Middle East.

Second, complexity. The variety of the fifty or more states, in not only size and wealth but also political belief and social

Introduction

custom, makes something of a mockery of the cartographical unity of the continent. Africa can be framed easily as a single map. Neatly ruled into states, the familiar shape of the continent is displayed in most African captials, and its leaders often say, "we are all Africans." They meet together within the framework of rules devised in 1963 for the Charter of the Organisation of African Unity but, within the map, and within the OAU, there are the immense distances and the great differences. There are monarchies (Morocco, Swaziland, Lesotho)* and republics, military rulers and party-controlled governments, Islamic states, Christian societies, and pagan beliefs. There are the "imported languages"—English, French, Spanish, Portuguese, Afrikaans, and Arabic; widely spoken African languages—Hausa in the west, Swahili in the east; and a large variety of regional and local languages. There are also Marxist, capitalist, and mixed economies, fervently ideological and mildly pragmatic regimes, murderous governments—those of Equatorial Guinea and Uganda might be held to be pre-eminent—and no more than semiauthoritarian governments, for which that of Tanzania (mainland) is a good example. Even the common badge of poverty—the portrayal of Africa as a third-world continent of the dependent poor—is not unambiguously true. Some states and most peoples are very poor indeed, but others are far from that. Libya, which has oil, is rich beyond the dreams of Lesotho, which has nothing, just as within many even of the poorest countries there are gross inequalities of income and possession. Arguments that see Africa as part of a third world are true only in a very general sense, and when true they may be said to extend the element of sameness beyond the continent, as between, say, Zambia and Chile in relation to copper (though not to much else), Kenya and Colombia in respect of coffee, Nigeria and Iran as members of OPEC, or between the very poor in Africa and those similarly disadvantaged in central and South America and Asia. It seems sensible, therefore, to be aware of these complexities when one talks in general terms about "African politics."

It may be asked whether there is a common reference point in the African experience of colonial rule. Africa is certainly very

---

*And presumably the Central African Republic, where Emperor Bokassa —that "army sergeant, tyrant and buffoon"—has now been enthroned.

Introduction

much the excolonial continent. It had been totally divided between the European powers at the end of the nineteenth century, and the period of decolonization is very recent. In 1950 there were still only four sovereign states within the continent: Egypt, Ethiopia, Liberia, and South Africa. A decade later there were ten, following the independence of Libya, Sudan, Morocco, Tunisia, Ghana, and Guinea. By the end of 1960 the number had risen to over thirty. The whole of north Africa other than Algeria was now free of colonial control. So was western Africa, from Mauritania to the Congo River, except Portuguese Guinea and the small Spanish colony of Rio Muni. Within a further decade the British had extracted themselves painfully from east and central Africa and had been thrown off by Rhodesia. The Portuguese and Spanish had also begun to withdraw, freeing themselves at last of Guinea-Bissau, Angola, and Mozambique, and of Ifni, Equatorial Guinea (Rio Muni), and the Spanish Sahara. By 1977 nothing north of the Zambesi remained of the once familiar colonial map save the twin Spanish cities of Ceuta and Melilla on the coast of Morocco. It is a remarkable transformation of the African scene, and the coincidence in time of the retreat of European rule may easily be thought to have given the politics of the independent states common characteristics derived from either their colonial past or, more fashionably expressed, a "neo-colonial dependency."

There are difficulties, however, about such assumptions. I had to confess that I was skeptical about the utility of labels that tried to push all the African states into one category. Only from the commanding heights of a very general Marxist theory, or from the former vantage point in the United States of a simple morality, could colonial rule (as it once existed) be seen as an undifferentiated system. Colonies had varied a great deal as colonies even within the same empire. Not only had the European powers followed different policies from one another, they had also governed in different ways according to local circumstances. The politics of colonial rule in the former British Gold Coast were unlike not only those of the Belgian Congo or Portuguese Angola, but also those in British Kenya. The absence or presence of white settlers had made a very big difference, quite apart from contrasts between the African communities themselves, as (for example) between the kingdom of Ashanti in the Gold

Introduction

Coast, the powerful Muslim Emirates in northern Nigeria, and the clan societies of the Masai or Kikuyu in Kenya. Colonialism has also been domination of a distinct kind. It had been "imperialism with empire." It had meant direct political control. And the differences of language, administration, political style, and elite behavior between the metropolitan countries had left their mark on the territories they governed.

There were substantial differences, too, in respect of the degree of their dependency on the outside world. Dependency was itself, to use the jargon, a dependent variable: it depended on the dependent as well as on the actual situation of dependency. Kenya was one example in relation to its industrial, manufacturing base and outside interests; but so, too, were Lesotho and Mozambique in their dependency on the South African labor market. Egypt was heavily dependent on finding a donor to take up its debts. Nigeria was solvent, but still dependent on the import of foreign skills. General arguments about "neocolonialism" and dependency which drew on the disparities of economic power between strong and weak states in relation to a global capitalist economy, or to the regulated economies of the communist world, might be helpful if one wanted to mark out the working limits to independence. They might help as a mode of inquiry for specific purposes. But they did not help very much toward an understanding of the very distinct politics of particular countries. It was not sensible to put Field Marshal Idi Amin of Uganda and President Houphouët Boigny of the Ivory Coast, or President Kaunda of Zambia and Grégoire Kayibanda of Rwanda, all in one box, label it "dependency," and then say, "that is all that needs to be said about the political structure and economic texture of their rule."

One last point in this connection is also worth making here, although the first chapter takes up the argument in a larger context: namely, that the former colonial powers are by no means as important today as they were even ten years ago. They have been displaced, though not in equal measure: Britain perhaps more than France, Portugal more than Belgium. Many African governments are still dependent on the outside world for aid, weapons, markets, manufactures, even (it might be said) for ideologies of one kind or another; but the former metropolitan countries are by no means the sole or, in many instances, the

Introduction

dominant supplier. New forces are abroad and at work, directed from Moscow or Washington or Peking, much less direct, very often subtle, though hardly less powerful as instruments of an "imperialism without empire" than the colonialism of European rule. That, too, may help a little to explain some of the differences which now divide the African states.

Third, disunity. Between 1960 and 1977 the African governments fell out among themselves over many issues. I have no wish to be misunderstood: disunity is not total opposition and separation, any more than complexity means the absence of similarities. The independent governments still cling to the concept of "being African." They have tried to give it more than token meaning, and there is still a sense in which it is possible to talk about "African politics" (or what point is there to the book?) as one might talk about "European" or "Latin American" politics. It would be silly to move from too grand a notion of the unity of Africa and its affairs to an opposite view in which the African states are seen as isolated countries of what is simply a geographical area. Nonetheless, the melancholy fact remains that quarrels have arisen, and have brought disunity. There have been disputes over territory, as between Morocco, Algeria, and Mauretania in the once Spanish Sahara; divergent policies over fundamental issues, as in the recognition of "Biafra" by Tanzania, Zambia, the Ivory Coast, and Gabon during the Nigerian civil war; opposition over attitudes and policy toward South Africa between the now conservative Dr. Banda in Malawi and his more radical neighbors—the Marxist Dr. Machel in Mozambique, the humanist Dr. Kaunda in Zambia, and the socialist Dr. Nyerere in Tanzania; a fluctuating series of quarrels and rapprochements over the form that African cooperation should take; postures of war between Amin's Uganda and both Kenya and Tanzania; and heavy fighting between the Ethiopian army and Somali-backed forces.

Disunity was not surprising over a very troubled decade and a half, although there was little profit in it for the African governments themselves, the beneficiaries very often being outside interests which found an entry into Africa by backing one side against the other. But much of the discord has also been a reflection of the uncertainty and fears of the leaders, heightened by bewildering changes in the political map of Africa. At this point,

Introduction

we are back at the beginning: an immense continent, great variety and complexity, and a widening disunity among the independent states. Such is the background for this volume.

1. The Fallacies of Hope

It cannot be said that all the political hopes entertained in recent years in relation to Africa have been illusory. The early expectations among African nationalists of independence as a movement away from colonial rule were abundantly realized in the 1960's, and in one particular respect—the upholding of the colonial state—the measure of African success might well be thought to have been substantial. But behind the expressions of many of the beliefs about the end of colonial rule were optimistic assumptions which one can now see were grossly misconceived. Such is the theme of the opening chapter, which looks at some of those hopes, under four different heads: the attitude of the colonial powers as they began to surrender control, the fate of the early party leaders, the experience of the ordinary citizen, and the brief history of the African states as political entities since independence.

The observation that colonial rule was neither wholly good nor entirely bad in its effect is now commonplace. Everyone can recite its evils and (almost) everyone its advantages—Marx did for India, Mao for China, and western academics continue to add up the balance sheet in rather more complicated language. J. A. Hobson, in London, in the early years of this century, argued that imperialism was bad for the exploiter as well as for the exploited. Lenin, in Zurich, thought that the growth of capitalism-as-imperialism was bound to lead to world revolution. And there has been a good deal of loose talk in recent years about the danger of "neocolonialism," or of "postimperialism," much of it arising from confusion between old-fashioned colonialism (imperialism with empire) and less formal modes of domination (imperialism without empire). But the colonial governments, too, were well aware that in Africa in particular they had broken into societies which were much weaker than the technically advanced and culturally distinct civilizations of which they were the outposts. Like the trader and missionary, the administrator had arrived from a world of which the African kingdoms and communities were for the most part ignorant. But it was believed that the impact might be lessened if the colonial powers, once they entered directly into the continent, were able to provide a framework of control—the colonial state—within which African societies could be remolded and recast. The most familiar parallel was that of Prospero and Caliban: so many colonial Prosperos who would govern, so many subject Ariels and Calibans to be rewarded and admonished. It was confidently assumed that Africans were biddable, and might one day (though the Administering Powers were not in agreement among themselves in this respect) be enabled to stand up by and for themselves—by the end of this century or at some time in the next hundred years or so.[1] Meanwhile there was a profit to be made (and on this, agreement was more general), since colonial rule ought not to be a free good.

Such comfortable beliefs about the possibilities of control were by no means groundless. Prior to 1939 there was little overt expression of anticolonialism among the African populations. Protests were confined to particular injustices, they were not voiced against the totality of foreign rule. The error behind such optimism, however, was twofold: first in the assumption by Britain and France, Belgium and Portugal, that there was unlimited time available for peaceful change, second in misjudging the degree of transformation that was likely to be achieved within the colonially fashioned state. Had the European states not engaged after 1914 and 1939 in destructive wars among themselves, they might perhaps have been able to rule their African territories for a longer period. Yet one may still doubt their capacity to play the role of pattern-maker. Very possibly the fault lay deeper still. The European rulers of these colonial states tried gropingly to uphold the advantages of universality, and there was a time when the British and French empires, despite the exploitation and greed and the more extreme manifestations of racial superiority, were seen by their subjects as well as by their rulers as a protective framework of law and peace. It was not unreasonable to see European rule, like the empires of the ancient world, as enabling a canopy of civilization to be spread across local cultures and peoples. But by the middle years

The Fallacies of Hope

of the present century the persuasive force of a *pax Britannica* or of *La France d'Outre-mer* had diminished sharply. It was out of keeping with the times. Very powerful emotions were stirring among non-European peoples, borne by the winds of history, carried forward by a rising tide of nationalism. And it was right in a sense to use such phrases as tides and winds and natural forces of change, since they properly conveyed the notion of inevitability, of an irresistible compulsion which the colonial governments seemed powerless to gainsay.[2]

It seems to be in the nature of such changes, however, that those most likely to be affected by them are often the least able to foresee their consequences. The British record is particularly illuminating in this respect. They were the first to move away from colonial rule. Indeed, by agreeing to political reforms that became successive stages toward full self-government, they gave the movement for colonial independence a respectability, and even legitimacy, which forced a parallel acceptance of similar demands in the non-British territories. They had tried at first to construct a protective framework of indirect rule from the structure of traditional government under chiefs and elders, but by the mid-1940's they were moving cautiously (starting in West Africa) in what was for them the familiar direction of the transfer of power from colonial to local hands wherever they could find acceptable collaborators and heirs. British Africa, it was then hoped, would achieve independence through the traditional gateway of parliamentary government by turning colonial legislative councils into national parliaments within a Commonwealth of former colonies.[3] Ceylon in South Asia—a third-world parliamentary democracy—would thus have its counterpart in West Africa, and for a time Kwame Nkrumah was seen (rather uncertainly) as playing that role in Ghana when independence was granted in 1957. Nigeria followed in 1960, Sierra Leone in 1961. Of course there were difficulties. Sierra Leone had to face an internal shift of power from the Creole-dominated area of Freetown to Protectorate leaders. Kenyatta had to be set free from detention after the Mau Mau Emergency, and the European settler and Indian trading communities in Kenya had to give way to African majority rule. Uganda needed help to compose the historical rivalry between its local kingdoms, and both Malawi and Zambia had to be released from the 1953 Central African

The Fallacies of Hope

Federation. There was no shortage of problems during the transitional stages. But the British comforted themselves with the hope, doubly fallacious, not only that the governments of Commonwealth Africa, like those of Asia almost a generation earlier, would retain the parliamentary structures devised for independence, but that the relationship between Britain and its former dependencies, including economic relations of mutual advantage, would not be disturbed.

Neither hope was realized. It is true that trust in the survival of democratic institutions had always been held more confidently the farther one moved from the colonial capital, where local officials were never very optimistic about the survival of parliamentary institutions which they themselves had scarcely understood as they presided over their hasty construction. The melancholy case remains, however, that the Westminster model of British government has almost everywhere been abandoned or distorted, and there are few if any African leaders, whether in military or in party uniform, who believe that it should be reassembled. Indeed, in many former British territories, in place of the Speaker with a wig, there stands a soldier with a gun. The scale of hopes unfulfilled can be seen at its fullest extent in Uganda, where so much effort was spent by able Governors and clever advisers to gain agreement at independence on a constitutional formula for restraint only to see the entire framework set aside, first by Obote under single-party rule, then by Amin under military decree, leading to the severance of diplomatic ties by Britain. From a more narrowly British view, the erosion of economic ties has been more grievous. It was certainly unexpected, for there was a confident feeling in London that British trade and finance would continue to be the dominant influence in Commonwealth Africa. The present position is quite different and can be simply if crudely described. It is sometimes said that Africa as a whole, including the substantial areas formerly under British rule, is in the beneficent or malevolent grip of international capitalism—the epithet is usually one of moral interpretation—but whatever the morality, the fact is that there are far fewer British fingers today in the till. Although British interests in Africa are still substantial, there has been a noticeable shift of economic influence over the past two decades not simply from colonial to nationalist hands but from British to Japanese,

The Fallacies of Hope

German, American, and even Soviet interests. Similarly, one may note that whereas the United Kingdom was dominant in the East African market at the end of the 1950's, the value of British imports as a percentage of total imports into Kenya and Tanzania, as into the greater part of Commonwealth Africa, declined by 10 to 15 percent over the fifteen-year period between 1959 and 1974.[4]

By the end of the 1950's, the French, too, had been obliged to surrender a large part of their national beliefs. More romantic of vision, and committed after 1945 to the fraternity of a greater *France d'Outre-mer*, successive French governments declared their opposition to any form of independence. "The aim of the civilising labours of France in the colonies excludes all possibilities of development outside of the French imperial system; the eventual formation even in the distant future of self-government in the colonies must be dismissed."[5] The French had suppressed an armed rebellion in Madagascar in 1947, and they fought in Algeria (as in Indo-China) in the 1950's, not as the British did in Kenya in order to quit, but to try and stay. They also extended the practice of African representation in Paris in an attempt to stop the drift to independence. Yet they, too, were forced to move in that direction not only in North Africa but throughout *L'Afrique noire.* In September 1958, in one of those abrupt reversals of policy that often marked French attitudes, de Gaulle held a single referendum throughout French West and Equatorial Africa and in Madagascar, compelling a choice between "yes" and "no" on the issue of continued association with France. Remarkably, each of the territories (with the sole exception of Guinée under Sekou Touré) voted "yes"—that is, against separation. Yet within two years they had changed round, to move forward into independence in 1960 under a series of agreements amicably arranged in Paris.

If the French lost on the political swings, they were considerably more successful on the economic roundabout. Because of the relatively closed nature of the French-speaking world and its focus on Paris, the French were able to retain a close financial and economic hold on their former colonies within the franc zone. Although they agreed to widen the relationship in 1957 under the Treaty of Rome to embrace the European Economic Community as a whole, opening the markets of the Six (and later the Nine) to African produce, they did not concede very much, except the full burden of aid, to their European associates. In this respect the equation *après l'indépendance = avant l'indépendance* has been much closer to the truth for the French than for the British. Yet it seems doubtful whether successors to the present French-educated elite, most fully represented by Léopold Senghor of Senegal and Houphouët-Boigny of the Ivory Coast, will be so strongly men of two cultures, as comfortably at ease in Europe as in Africa. Even in the early 1950's the dominance of France evoked its counter demand (admittedly in French) for a *Présence Africaine*.[6] True, there is still the expectation of a postcolonial relationship under French leadership—*La Francophonie*—reminiscent in attenuated form of the much older structures of a once British Commonwealth, but it is hard to believe that it will not become, like its larger Commonwealth counterpart, one more fallacy of European hope unrealized.

Once the British and French had transferred power to local leaders, the remaining colonial powers were unable to retain control for any length of time. In 1960 the Belgians abruptly abandoned their rule in the Congo (now Zaire) and in Rwandi and Burundi. The Spanish gave up control of Western Morocco, Rio Muni, and—after some hesitation and resistance—Spanish Sahara. By then the Portuguese had also begun to be forced out of their African possessions. The once exotic dream of a Lusitanian Empire within which the African territories would remain as overseas provinces of Portugal began to be lost amid the onset of revolution in Lisbon and guerrilla warfare in Guinea-Bissau, Angola, and Mozambique. By 1976 all three areas were independent.

The phenomenon of European withdrawal was truly remarkable. Whereas in 1945 colonies were part of a familiar world order, within a generation they had become anachronistic. Who can say how the impetus for change came about? Looking at the persistence of white minority rule in Rhodesia and South Africa, I am inclined to argue that the end of the European empires came as much from a slackening of the will to maintain control as from the upsurge of African demands. But no doubt the fullest explanation lies in a combination of the two. Both were needed—the European willingness to concede, and the African determination to oppose. The willingness to concede, however, like that of the nationalist to demand, was (I suggest) confused, and camouflaged in self-deceit, by hopes entertained on both sides—by the European governments, which believed that nothing very important would be lost, and by the African nationalists, who believed that there was everything to gain. Both such expectations were illusory. The disparity of power between the African states and the external world is there still, and new empires—located outside Europe—are enlarging their frontiers, which are nonetheless real for being informal or denied. Africa has not yet had to endure the full imposition, as has Southeast Asia, of American protection or communist control; but that both the USSR and the United States are being drawn closer in their interests to Africa is now very clear. Theaters of war beyond the continent have become dangerously joined to local conflicts, not only in the Horn of Africa along the shores of the Red Sea, but across the broad central zone from Zaire to Mozambique. Wars are beginning to be fought by proxy and financed by covert intelligence operations in what often appears to be a new partition of Africa not by conquest but by stealth.

When we turn to the nationalist inheritors of the European empires, the picture becomes very complicated. Many more figures crowd the canvas. Four or five large empires were transmuted into fifty sovereign states under a variety of governments each of which was initially determined to strike out an independent path. But it was also clear that they had one primary aim in common: to stay in office as long as they could by whatever means were available. Some turned for help to phrases of an earlier age in relation to "becoming a nation" or "furthering the revolution"; but whatever solace they might derive from Mazzini to Marx, all of them have been ready in practice to use to excess the powers of the colonial state while laying claim to its authority. What else could they do? Whereas at a local level in most African states there is still a deeply-felt sense of belonging to a community based on kinship and allegiance as a residual inheritance from the former exercise of chiefly power, there is no parallel to such modes at the national level. As Meyer Fortes observed,[7] there was once a delicate balance between consent and authority within a "fine spun web of kinship," sustained by unifying symbols "in the form of myths, fictions, dogmas, ritual, sacred places and persons," and these sacred symbols endowed

The Fallacies of Hope

traditional African society with "mystical values which evoked acceptance of the social order ... far beyond the obedience exacted by the secular sanction of force." But matters have been very different in respect of the central government. The symbols and myths of the nationalist period were still painfully being assembled at independence, and the new party leaders soon began to understand that the structure of power they had put together to force the colonial regime to quit was extremely precarious. It could fall apart very easily while they themselves, heroes today, could be on trial as failed villains tomorrow.

The danger had not been foreseen. On the contrary, there had been a jubilant assertion of nationalist demands. But in retrospect—looking back over the period of independence—one can begin to understand the failure among the nationalist leaders of so many misplaced hopes. They were in essence threefold: an exaggerated belief in the strength of their own achievement, a corresponding disbelief in the enduring force of subnational and sectional loyalties, and (very often) a lack of common sense about the limits of what they could or could not do in relation to resources and skills.

For example, there was the belief that control of the newly independent states would not be difficult. The colonial governments had ruled quite easily for a long time with a minimum of men and measures. Their nationalist successors, it was assumed, would have the added dynamic power of popular support. But there lay the fallacy of many hopes, which failed to understand the mystique of European rule in its early years, or its prudent retreat—at least in respect of Britain and France—once popular pressures appeared. When they did begin to be exerted, the colonial powers allowed the use of the suffrage in order to muffle or divert discontent, but in effect the ballot became a Pandora's box, without the final comfort of hope. It released all manner of plagues—ethnic, elitist, and radical demons—which the independent African governments have since tried to suppress.

A second mistake followed from the first, namely, a misplaced confidence in the staying power of what had been an anticolonial nationalsim which then either faded (withered by success) or, what was worse, adopted new forms masked by "tribalism." The party leaders tried to extend their appeal in ideological terms—"the struggle still continues to build an African socialist state" and similar sentiments—but the expectations aroused by independence were not so eaily diverted. Competing local interests of many different kinds, more often than not ethnic or "tribal" in character, put forward claims on the central government—the Buganda chiefdom in Uganda, the Ibo peoples in Nigeria, the Ewe in Ghana and the Fullah in Guinea, or the Lozi, Bemba, Nyanja and Ila-Tonga in Zambia—their leaders arguing the case for a distribution of resources rather different from the continuation of colonial rule by nationalist politicans. The effect was pervasively and continuously disruptive. At different levels of intensity such claims led to civil war in Nigeria, the suppression of local kingdoms in Uganda, Ghana's closing of its frontiers with neighboring states, and the imprisonment of factional leaders, including such notables as Diallo Telli (to give only one example of a great many), who was once a close associate of Sekou Touré and a former Secretary of the Organisation of African Unity (OAU) but is now in prison in Guinea accused of the double crime of being "a CIA agent and a Fullah secessionist."

The familiar phrase "tribalism" has been put in quotation marks if only because, whatever it may have been in the precolonial past, it is now a modern phenomenon. It is grounded, of course, on tradition, but like much else it is also a reaction not only to colonial rule but to the end of colonial government. Party and military leaders alike have had to face the drawing together of local interests of a territorial or communal kind. The general effect has been to create rival networks of political bosses and their local clients—patronage in exchange for support, support in return for patronage—constructed very often on an ethnic base.[8] Some party leaders built their support initially on their fellow kinsmen—Kenyatta, for example, on the Kikuyu, and the former President Alphonse Massamba Débat on the Bateke tribe in the Congo (Brazzaville)—but national interests of that kind quickly evoked rival claims, with the result that traditional communities which had hardly known of each other's existence in the past began to compete against each other—Hausa against Ibo in Nigeria, Luo against Kikuyu (whose traditional enemies had actually been the Masai) in Kenya, Lozi against Bemba in Zambia. It can hardly be said that tribalism was created by colonial rule, but it was certainly evoked by its passing. European control put a boundary around culturally disparate entities that have now become powerful ingredients of rivalry in almost every aspect of the state: in the army, in party politics, in the trade unions, in the universities, and in the public service. They are the ethnic solidarities that form the slopes of the social pyramid. But the party leaders who stood so confidently by the side of the retiring colonial power at independence could scarcely believe that the nationalist loyalties they had evoked were so delicately compounded.[9]

Not only did the early party leaders misjudge the extent to which the excolonial state was still a mosaic (not fully cemented together) of local communities. They also failed to see how easily it could be captured by rival structures of power distinct from that of the nationalist party. There the presidents or prime ministers sat, enthroned in office as high successors to the colonial regime. But they were very vulnerable to attack from those they offended. Sometimes the challenge came from the growing labor force through the unions (whose members were not, however, powerful enough as yet to enforce their demands); more dangerously, the threat came from those in the army and the police who had once loyally supported the colonial administration but who were now disposed to act politically, either as armed malcontents in their own behalf or as military guardians of what they perceived to be the national interest. In the ten years after 1960 there were over fifty coups d'état across the continent (the little Republic of Benin—formerly Dahomey—suffered at least five armed palace coups between 1960 and 1970) and there were no protective barriers of civilian interest which the postindependence parties could use to prevent them.

Along with the domestic failure of many nationalist governments went a grossly misplaced confidence in their ability to act decisively abroad. The first meeting of the Heads of Independent African States in Accra, in April 1958, was proclaimed as the revival in sovereign form of the early pan-African meetings in London and Paris, and enormous enthusiasm was voiced. The Heads of State—eight in all—announced with assurance that Africa was to become a powerful force in a third world of nonaligned countries, that the Sahara had become a bridge replacing the barrier between Arab and black Africa, that all the colonial frontiers would be abolished or at least minimized, and that the rest of the continent, including "white southern Africa," would be liberated. The great African ship of state, with unity at its prow, was to be launched upon the waves toward the open and turbulent sea of freedom, able once again to seek its destiny wherever it led.[10] And for a brief period all went with a leap and a bound in the right direction. The French withdrew, the Belgians collapsed, the British continued to retreat. But then the pace slackened, and the newly independent states began to divide not only internally but among themselves. There had actually been a formal surrender of sovereignty by Senegal and the Soudan to a new Mali Federation and by Ghana and Guinea to a new African Union: but within a couple of years they lapsed, and when the Organisation of African Unity was brought together in 1963, the leaders stressed the need to preserve the colonial state and its boundaries in order to safeguard the national existence of its member countries. Pan-Africanism had declined into diplomacy. The OAU has since struggled to keep a common front of negotiations at the United Nations and in its several relations with the European Community: it can muster a large vote against apartheid, and it can argue a collective case for economic help. But in almost every major crisis within the African states, outside help has had to be solicited: the United Nations in the former Congo in 1960; the British in East Africa when the armies of Kenya, Tanzania, and Uganda mutinied in 1964; the British, Russians, and French in Nigeria during the civil war in 1967; the Cubans and Russians in Angola; the Americans and British in Rhodesia; the French, Russians, Americans, and Chinese as well as Moroccans, Egyptians, and others in Zaire. Looking back from 1976 to 1960, it is difficult not to be impressed by the swift unrolling of European power from Africa, and easy to believe that very great historical forces were at work. Yet the powerlessness of virtually every African state is also there: sovereignly independent, they are still largely helpless to help either themselves or their neighbors.

There is perhaps a double mystery in this collapse of so many nationalist hopes. There is the mystery—familiar enough and yet puzzling—of political survival and nonsurvival.[11] Why have some leaders succeeded and not others? And there is a further mystery: the demise of a revolutionary impulse of which African nationalism was very properly seen as a notable example. It is

The Fallacies of Hope

worth spending a little time trying to understand both in order to see why there has been so general a loss of confidence among the nationalist leaders.

Why have some survived in office and others not? Most were overconfident at first, then excessively nervous, moving uneasily from being sure of their victory to uncertainty about what might erupt to rob them of their new wealth and power. Nervousness bred doubt, and doubt turned often enough into a paranoia of suspicion. They became divided among themselves—Senghor against Mamadou Dia, Nkrumah against Gbedemah, Nyerere against Kambona, Banda against Chipembere, Kaunda against Kapwepwe. There was nothing particularly unusual in this falling out of revolutionaries, except that none of the African states had experienced anything like the massive upheaval which destroyed the *ancien régime* in France or Russia or China. For the most part, the leaders had inherited a colonial apparatus of control which (except in Angola and Mozambique) was in good working order. Yet still some governments have survived, others have not. Why?

I can think of half a dozen possible explanations: interference from outside, either supportive or hostile; the effect (harmful or beneficial) of the route to independence; the character of the nationalist movement; the sociopolitical and military makeup of the former colonial state; the lack of material resources; and the political skill of the leaders. It is a formidable list, and one could argue about it.

One can quote examples of interference (some were noted earlier)—as by the French, when they tried unsuccessfully to hamper Sekou Touré after the abrupt granting of independence to Guinea in 1958 or when they rescued President M'Ba of Gabon in 1963 after a coup against his government; by the British in East Africa in 1964; by the Americans and the United Nations in the Congo in 1960; by South Africa (unsuccessfully) and Cuba (successfully) in Angola; by non-African-Arab as well as some African-Moslem states in Ethiopia; and several foreign governments as suppliers of aid or arms or guerrilla training. Yet when all these occasions are taken into account and the help or hindrance given by African leaders to fellow African governments is included,[12] I do not think they offer a sufficient explanation of, say, the downfall of the government of Nigeria under Alhaji Abu Bakar in 1966, or the survival in office of President Ahidjo in the Cameroun Republic since 1960. It would be sensible to acknowledge that in many African states sinister forces are at work, financed by outside powers; but with the possible exception of Angola I cannot see any of the governments as totally dependent puppet regimes.[13]

Second, the route to independence. To have fought valiantly against the imperialist might be thought better than to have collaborated with the retiring colonial power. Or to have experienced the collapse of Belgian rule in Zaire might be thought a heavier burden to carry into independence than the experience of British rule in Nigeria, the former ending in chaos, the latter lapsing peacefully into a negotiated settlement. But that is too simple a correlation. Indeed it is quite wrong. Between 1960 and 1970 Zaire recovered from almost total breakdown and Nigeria was divided by civil war, although the balance between order and chaos is always dangerously at risk in Zaire. Nor have the heroes of the revolution fared better or worse than the nonheroes. Milton Margai (an unheroic moderate) worked closely with the British to bring about self-government in Sierra Leone, and then remained in office until his death in 1966. On the other hand, Alhaji Abubakar and Chief Festus Okotie Eboh, after an equally peaceful transition to independence, died violently in a ditch when the first coup took place in January 1966. North of the Sahara, Ben Bella was a hero of the long struggle against the French in Algeria, only to be overthrown by the army under Boumedienne, whereas Bourguiba of Tunisia, a "man of the center," is still in power. Radical socialists like Nkrumah in Ghana or Modibo Keita in Mali were dislodged by the army, whereas Houphouët-Boigny (on the right) and Sekou Touré (on the left) have both survived to date. Jomo Kenyatta and Hastings Banda in Malawi were once the heroes of the anticolonial movement by their opposition to white settler rule in Kenya and to European control of the Central African Federation, only to move out of favor with the radical left because of their conservatism in office; yet both have remained in power. There is no discernible pattern of explanation in this ebb and flow of political fortune.

Third, the character of the nationalist movement. It used to be argued that the mass parties which directed the agitation against colonial rule were there to stay as instruments of social transformation. Mass parties were good and durable; other kinds of organization were archaic and doomed.[14] But that was much too indulgent. In effect, some mass parties have survived—the Partie Democratique de la Guinée and the Tanganyika African National Union,[15] for example—whereas others (the Union Soudanaise in Mali and the Convention People's Party in Ghana) have not. Moreover, the rather shaky governments put together by Senghor in Senegal and Seretse Khama in Botswana have held together. At extreme ends of the spectrum, and of the continent, the former National Liberation Front (FLN) in Algeria has disappeared, whereas the very conservative Botswana Democratic Party has held onto office. Once again, therefore, there is no simple relationship between mass-populist versus elite-dominated regimes and survival versus nonsurvival.

Fourth, the makeup of the former colonial state. One might readily assume that some African states are easy to govern, others difficult. Is there not an important ethnic factor of uniformity and diversity? Tanzania has few major opposed communities—Nyerere is still there; Uganda has too many and, like Nigeria, has struggled constantly to reconcile historically separate peoples; both have experienced violent changes of regime. In Swaziland, which is homogeneous, King Sobhuza rules still; in Ethiopia, which is ethnically divided, His Imperial Majesty Haile Selassie died a prisoner in his own palace. There is surely some political clue here. Yet there are exceptions: Ghana is hardly a difficult country to govern—certainly the British never thought it was—yet it has suffered two coups and two very different civilian regimes. Zambia is divided ethnically to a greater degree than Ghana, yet Kaunda has been in office since independence—for a longer period than either Nkrumah or Busia or the two military junta.[16] Ethnic conflict is certainly an important (probably the most important) source of diversity, particularly when the legacy of unity from the colonial past is feeble or (as in Ethiopia) nonexistent. But there is no simple rule of thumb by which one can measure the governability or nongovernability of a particular state. All manner of ills are growing—social factors of class, the corrosive effect of poverty and wealth, religious differences between Islam and Christianity, and the spread of military rule as soldiers seize the opportunity to intervene and become part of the political structure of control.¹⁷ It is true, however, that most African states are not only divided but poor. How important is that?

Fifth, therefore, resources. Does wealth equal stability, continuity, and happiness; does poverty produce instability, breakdown, and misery? How easy it would be to understand the ways of African politics if that were so. But, as in private life, wealth can confuse, poverty may stabilize. There is simply no direct correlation between GNP/per capita income and political fortunes. Nor do I believe that African politics are little more than primary extensions of economic relations, the idols of the tribe giving way to the idols of the marketplace.¹⁸ Tribal idols are too strong for that. Of course it is true that African governments are more at ease where they can keep up the political dividends of rewards and goods. Most politicians are happy in that vein. We shall see later how critically dependent on external markets and prices many African states are, but the variety of wealth and the variety of poverty are as great and as different as the variety of political life. Nigeria, for example, has rightly been described as a "poor oil-rich" country as against a "poor oil-poor" state like Niger, but although such categories may help one to understand in a general way the politics of both countries, they can hardly be said to explain the particular differences between the military regime in Niamey and that in Lagos.¹⁹ It is also fairly clear that Kaunda and his party in Zambia have coped more successfully (or less dismally) with the fluctuating market for copper than the more radical Nkrumah, or his much less radical successor Busia, was able to do in relation to cocoa.

Perhaps the last possibility—in itself a mystery within a mystery—is the most critical: political skill. Has Houphouët-Boigny been more skillful than Nkrumah, Nyerere cleverer than, say, Obote in Uganda? Houphouët-Boigny is said to have remarked, "I am like the crocodile, I sleep with one eye open." Is that indicative of something? Nkrumah, one might add, often seemed to have both eyes shut when he was awake. It is certainly arguable that Gowon, who led Nigeria successfully out of the civil war, had lost some of his earlier deftness by 1974 when he was peacefully removed by a further coup. And Albert Margai in Sierra Leone was certainly a less able leader (though much noisier) than his elder brother. Political skill is not necessarily admirable, nor is it an attribute of the left or the right (though it may more often be found perhaps at the center). A list which, for Africa alone, included Kenyatta, Tubman in Liberia, Habib Bourgiba in Tunisia, Banda in Malawi, Ahidjo in the Cameroun Republic, or Chief Jonathan in Lesotho would be a very mixed group of skillful survivors. There is also, unfortunately, a large element of circularity about such assertions: success defines itself—unless it fails; failure reveals itself only by its failure.

The second puzzle was that of the demise of the nationalist revolution. Perhaps that, too, can be explained, or explained away, by its success? Perhaps we need to see the removal of colonial rule as a self-sufficient end, of which nothing much should have been expected except the fact itself. But is that really the case? Can so broad a movement of emancipation come to an end so quickly and finally? Or is there a sense in which the force of African nationalism has gone underground—is lying fallow, so to speak—to spring to life under new forms at some distant time? No independent African country has yet experienced a large-scale rural uprising of the kind that took the Socialist/Marxist government of Sri Lanka by surprise in 1971, but the nationalist expectations disappointed by the dismal record of postindependence politics might take on a social revolutionary form if it could find a lodging among the urban poor or within a jobless educated stratum with strong rural ties. Whether such conditions exist in any African states is unclear; and if nationalism does still have to run its course, it may be as likely to find outlet in secessionist demands (as among the Galla or Eritreans or Tigre in the divided Amharic-imperial state of Ethiopia) as in revolutionary slogans among Marxist soldiers or politicians. Or might it not move from the assertion of nationalist pride to racist sentiments, of the kind already seen in Central and East Africa—European against African, African against European and Asian? Conceivably, too, nationalist zeal could rekindle a religious revival, as in Libya under Gaddafi, although it is difficult to foresee what form it could take south of the Islamic African world.

In brief, it is much easier to raise such queries than it is to resolve them. At the heart of the problem, whether it is one of political survival or the transformation of nationalist sentiment, there are difficulties central to the notion of politics itself, those of allegiance and identity and obligation on the part of the

The Fallacies of Hope

ordinary citizen in his relationship with the state and its government. And it is when we turn to the third of our main categories of faded hopes and look at the fortunes of the general population since independence that we find the largest and saddest of our examples. So many hopes have been disappointed which were once held out to and entertained by the ordinary public. Adult suffrage, national assemblies, populist parties, military councils, African socialism and related ideologies of one kind and another—each has been used to claim a popular support that was often granted in large measure. But still the major divide has been between the educated few and the illiterate or scarcely literate majority; the greatest betrayal has been the misplaced trust of peasant farmers and the urban poor in their educated leaders. Kinship ties have helped a little to bridge the wealthy and the poor—there is a trickle down of benefits through communal obligations—but the fact remains that in African state after state the bulk of the population has labored to enrich the minority. The effect, so far as one can tell, has been a sharp disappointment and the loss of hope. The growth of a greedy acquisitive class in Nigeria, the party state direction of farmers in Tanzania, and the alternation of party promises and military exhortation in Upper Volta or the Congo (Brazzaville), or Ghana or Sierra Leone, has left the African village in no mood for hope. At best there is a patient resignation to fate—the note struck by Chinuah Achebe in *A Man of the People*:

"Let them eat", was the people's opinion. "After all, when white men used to do all the eating did we commit suicide?" Of course not. And where is the all-powerful white man today? He came, he ate and he went. But we are still around. The important thing then is to stay alive: if you do, you will outlive your present annoyance. The great thing, as the old people have told us, is reminiscence; and only those who survive can have it. Besides, if you survive, who knows? It may be your turn to eat tomorrow. Your son may bring home your share. (p. 161)

A resigned waiting for each turn of Fortune's wheel has replaced the high nationalist expectations held prior to independence by many thousands of voters in each country—numbered in their millions across the continent—who waited in line under a tropical sun to record their vote for this or that nationalist party and its leaders. What motives led to a demonstrative mass support for the anticolonial movements of the 1950's and '60's can only be guessed at: perhaps the hope of economic betterment, or the assertion of racial pride, or the coalescence of individual ambition and new social identities. But whatever psychological satisfaction there may be for the ordinary citizen in being governed by black rather than European rulers, it is difficult to see what material advantages have been secured for the peasant farmer or the urban poor. Individuals have become rich, often grotesquely so, as inquiry after inquiry (invariably conducted by new governments into the corrupt ways of those they displaced) has shown; but the poor have remained very poor. Most regimes have also advertised their devotion to economic development under a variety of banners: African Socialism in Tanzania via the party; African Socialism in Kenya through the administration of development; the encouragement of foreign investment and even expatriate entrepreneurs in the Ivory Coast; a call for self-reliance in Ghana under the military and for local adaptations of a Cuban Marxism in Angola and Mozambique—there has been a great variety of endeavor. But by and large, the rich have become richer and the poor poorer. Few governments seem capable (if recent evidence is accepted as valid) of escaping the restraints of scarce resources and a shortage of skills; fewer governments still (if the comments of both liberal and Marxist critics are taken into account) have been morally equal to the task of distributing what wealth exists.

We have reached the last category of the fallacies of hope—in relation to the construct, powers, and modus operandi of the state itself. It might be thought that we should reject out of hand the notion that the excolonial state has failed to do what was asked of it. It has at least survived. The OAU gave particular emphasis in 1963 and in 1964 to the need to protect its separate existence.[20] Nor was it difficult to understand the sensitivity of the African Heads of State and Governments at that time. The earlier dream of unity of the pan-Africanists having faded, the need of fearful politicians was the prosaic one of how best to keep the state going. Prudently and realistically, it could be argued, have they come to terms with their colonial past, not least because any alternative to the existing pattern of states was at first hardly conceivable and then dreadful to contemplate when, as in Zaire and the Sudan and Chad and Nigeria and Ethiopia, it did appear in the demand for secession.

Look closer at the map. As we have seen, it is almost as it was prior to independence. The colonial frontiers drawn by the European powers at the end of the nineteenth century and amended in 1919 after the defeat of Germany were gradually seen to have at least the merit of certainty about them. They exist and are recognized internationally.[21] One might add, too, that the record of wars in Europe over the territorial definition of Poland or the Balkan states or the Low Countries, or in Latin America over boundary disputes, or (more recently) over partition in South Asia, has scarcely provided an attractive precedent. Nor are there any powerful historical identities waiting (so to speak) to be given new form. The precolonial tribal societies and kingdoms do not have the attractive resonance of older cultures and civilizations in Asia. They are too small, too blurred in their appeal, to become the focal point of new states, as in Pakistan and Bangladesh. It is true that the colonial state was imposed on traditional African societies which had evolved various forms of political organization satisfactory for the arrangement of their affairs. But the intrusion of direct European rule gave political life to much larger entities—Nigeria, Senegal, Kenya, Ghana, Zambia—none of which had existed under that name or in that context until colonial rule enfolded together Yoruba, Hausa, Fulani, Ibo, and Tiv as Nigerians, or Luo, Kikuyu, Kamba, and Masai as Kenyans. The colonial state then drew to itself—into its form and power and associations—new interests under new leaders through the use of a common (European) language, an enlarged market economy, and a colonially designed structure of administration. Almost by definition, too, the nationalist leaders became committed to an anticolonialism which had as its aim the capture of the colonial state, and, after the capture was made, the castle keep was quickly defended under the nationalist flag. Only a minority of governments (notably that of Somalia) and of ethnic groupings whose members straddle a particular frontier (notably the Ewe between Togo and Ghana) have tried to argue the case for revision. It is worth noting that even the regional associations which have tried since independence to bridge two or more territories have usually had a particular excolonial identity, as in the Organisation Commune Africaine et Malgache (OCAM) between the ex-French colonies, or the East African Common Services Organisation (and, later, the East African Community) between Kenya, Uganda, and Tanzania, or the Commaunité Economique des Pays des Grands Lacs between Zaire, Rwanda, and Burundi. Neither has it escaped comment that a large residue of colonial practice, whether British or French or Belgian, is still at work in the administration of many African countries. Generally speaking, the instruments of *control*—the civil service, police, and armed forces—have been strengthened and expanded; those with any degree of *autonomy*—universities, newspapers, the courts, and the constitution—have been curbed; and those of a *representative* nature—parliaments, trade unions, local councils—have been minimized or put into recess. It is as if the independent governments, almost without distinction of kind, have been trying in very different circumstances to reconstitute the colonial state in its pure form as a framework of control. Such has been the prestige and power of the colonial state, which surely cannot be seen to have failed.

But if the form and number of these excolonial states have remained remarkably constant, that cannot always be said unequivocally of the content of their rule. Whatever the similarities, there was after all a major political difference between the colonial government and its nationalist successors. The former was an intrusion, however locally devoted its officers might be to those over whom they ruled. They were always a foreign elite, banded together under the governor as much by a code of colonial behavior as by instructions; and although there might be some backsliding ("going native"), they were—as Kipling portrayed them in India—always a disciplined hierarchy. It was not the lawlessness but the law of the jungle which ruled their conduct as a set of guardians whose stength lay in the pack.

> *Now these are the Laws of the Jungle, and many and mighty are they;*
> *But the head and the hoof of the Law and the haunch and the hump is—Obey!*

Their African successors have no such code of ethics or surety of racial solidarity. They are party or military leaders who retain control by exercising power over their own kind. The difference can be sharply expressed at its extreme by noting that no governor ever hanged one of his colonial officers, whereas Nkrumah in Ghana imprisoned his own party colleagues, and Idi Amin in Uganda beats to death civil servants, judges, university teachers, and his fellow army officers alike. We must be careful, therefore, when looking at the persistence of colonial traits to note also the interruption of the legacy or, more accurately, the new departures as well as the old continuities.

Indeed, it has not been easy to describe what the newly independent states are like. The confusion of categorization in academic accounts has been confounded by the variety of interpretation. Yet one aspect is commonly noted. At almost every level of analysis they are seen as being governed by insecure regimes uneasily in control of unsettled societies. Power has moved uncertainly, sometimes very bloodily indeed, in a frenzy of killing from one community to another, as between the Tutsi and the Wahutu in Rwanda and Burundi,[22] or from party leaders to military commanders, or from one section of the civilian elite to another. What kind of states, then, are they?

There is no shortage of analysis. It has been attempted from many standpoints, each interesting though often distorted because of its single perspective. A good deal of effort, for example, has been expended by political sociologists in talking about loads and the capacity to sustain them when trying to portray the African state as weakly articulated in that its component parts are poorly knit together and its collective interests feebly voiced. Each state, it was said, is involved in a painful progress toward modernity. Some, however, become overloaded, not least by promises and expectations, to the point where their institutions cannot sustain the burden placed upon them: too many inputs of demand, too little capacity to absorb, and too few outputs to meet such demands. The level of institutionalization is low and the resources are inadequate. We should not be surprised at the incidence of breakdown, since they are (like the ass) overburdened or (like the electrical circuit) overcharged. Leaders, parties, parliaments, armies, administrative structures, and local institutions all tend to crack under the strain. There is no binding philosophy of government, only competing sectional interests to placate.

The arguments are interesting, although it is not always easy to see what it is that determines the level of capacity within a state or what the degree of capacity is needed *for*, since the ability to coerce in, say, a murderous little state such as Equatorial Guinea, or a technically advanced state like South Africa, may be very different from the capacity to mediate between competing interests in, say, the Ivory Coast or Tanzania. Marxists, however, and those concerned with theories of dependency, have produced a rather different explanation of the difficulties encountered by newly independent governments. They have stressed the extent to which many African states are still dependent categories, at the mercy of forces located outside the continent in the capitalist world of the developed nations from whom, it is asserted, they cannot escape, since the elites who run the state profit from the relationship: indeed, it is the basis of their rule. The states are prisoners of the outside world, the elites their jailers. The elites themselves are seen disparagingly as a bureaucratic bourgeoisie because of their reliance domestically on state power, or as representing the emergence of a neocolonial petit bourgeois state which is busily engaged in converting the surplus wealth extracted from the peasantry or urban workers into the economic foundation of a new ruling class. Where there is a heavy dependence on mining, or the export of primary produce, or the production (under foreign control) of manufactures, the state is said to be "rooted in the international relations of exchange rather than in the social organisation of production in the country itself."[23] Phrases abound to describe their plight. There is an "under-development of private capitalism" and an "over-development of the state apparatus," both being part of the colonial legacy. "The colonial export economy," writes Beckman in his study of Ghanaian cocoa farmers, "had created favourable conditions for the growth of an advanced state apparatus but not for the growth of a nationalist capitalist class."[24] Such states, it is argued, tend to be unstable, since they have no firmly rooted class to manage their affairs.

The literature of dependency theory is now extensive and often persuasive, although the reservations expressed in the introduction still seem cogent—namely, that dependency is itself a variable factor, by which even those African states which could be said to fit politically into that category differ considerably among themselves. Nigeria, for example, is likely to become dependent on oil exports for up to 90 percent of its revenue, and one can see a growing involvement by the government, whether it is military or civilian, in the operation of the oil companies. A broad class of businessmen has already emerged as intermediaries between the government and the companies, although whether such a development is likely to make Nigeria more or less stable no one can say. But the enormously complicated politics of Nigeria cannot be explained simply by that one phenomenon. Nor are the Nigerian politics of oil dependency at all like Ghana's dependency on cocoa, or Lesotho's and Mozambique's dependency on the export of labor to South Africa. The very literature of dependency itself, and of development and underdevelopment, is beginning to grow rather like its subject matter. Liberia, for example, was labeled the great example of "growth without development," since it was argued that the undoubted increase in its wealth had been "generated primarily in the rubber and mining enclaves which sold their products abroad, imported capital equipment and skilled labour from abroad, and did not create linkages with the rest of the economy or increase the level of well-being of the average citizens."[25] More recently, however, Ghana was described as having accomplished the still more remarkable phenomenon of "development without growth."[26] The debate grows wilder, but it is not one into which I wish to enter. There is also the undisputed and growing dependence by many African governments—very much in the category of growth without development—on the purchase of weapons from the developed world. The problem has begun to attract comment. And although the African states are among the least profligate in this respect, nearly 2½ billion dollars' worth of equipment was sold to the continent between 1965 and 1974.[27]

Implicit in many of these descriptions are moral imperatives. More than a decade ago René Dumont pointed to the worship of riches and the worship of power in the then newly independent states, the former based on a privileged elite, the latter leading to tyranny.[28] And tyranny is certainly not an exaggerated term, as in the dreadful uncertainty of political life under Idi Amin, where the fate of missing persons is explained by saying that they "have gone the way of those who foolishly opposed authority."[29] The shift toward coercion is plain across the whole continent. It is a singular fact that, with one exception only, no independent government in Africa in all the fifty or more states has been removed from office by an election: only by the army or an assassin.[30] More specifically, moral criticism is directed at the new African elites. They are seen at best as victims of circumstances, at worst as a parasitical class. Frantz Fanon, for example, writes: "Before independence, the leader generally embodies the aspirations of the people for independence, political liberty and national dignity. But as soon as independence is declared, far from embodying in concrete form the needs of the people in what touches bread, land and the restoration of the country to the sacred hands of the people, the leader will reveal his inner purpose: to become general president of that company of profiteers, impatient for their returns, which constitutes the national bourgeoisie."[31] Of course such criticisms are not new, nor confined to Africa. They were expressed movingly—and much more gently—by writers like R. H. Tawney, who used to argue that "a conception of Socialism which views it as involving the nationalisation of everything except political power, on which all else depends, is not, to speak with moderation, according to light. The question is not merely whether the state owns and controls the means of production. It is also who owns and controls the State."[32] Within Africa today, however—or, more prudently, from outside the continent—criticism has taken on a much harsher note. When pessimism is foremost, Africa is seen as moving in the direction of Latin America: corrupt regimes, praetorianism, the use of state violence to suppress dissent, and the beginnings of a comprador class, or even of a Demo-Bourgeois-Fascism—that is, a "bourgeois regime without a bourgeois class."[33] Even when optimism asserts itself, it still brings a demand for restructuring the excolonial state by way of "a social revolution [involving] necessarily the destruction of the existing power structure in the African states."[34]

The difficulty about such criticisms, whether condemnatory or programmatic, is not only the enormous problems involved in trying to bring about such a revolution (whether agreeable or disagreeable in the result) but the fact that they are too sweeping. Just as some states are more dependent than others, or are dependent in many different ways, so some governments are morally not too bad, while others are atrocious. Are Uganda and

Kenya both bourgeois regimes without a bourgeois class? Surely not of the same kind. Nor are such phrases a very helpful description of the politics of either country. Are all the African leaders committed to the worship of riches and power? Very likely. But I would still want to draw a moral distinction between the mild unpleasantness of, say, Zambia or the Ivory Coast and the cruelty of Uganda and Equatorial Guinea.

I turn to one last, and very interesting, interpretation of the difficulties faced by many of the new regimes. If questions of political obligation and consent are raised, many African states appear indeterminate, lacking any clear shape of authority, uncertain in their powers, shifting from one form of association to another and unable even to be fully totalitarian. It is perhaps this indeterminancy which explains the rapidity of constitutional change and the quick turnover of leadership. Rulers and citizens are inclined therefore to look upon the state as an object of plunder, since their affections and loyalties are chiefly engaged at a more familiar level of attachment. There is no clear center of national allegiance, since to be a Zairean or Zambian or Angolan is to be much less, in respect of the identification of the citizen with the state, than the proclaimers of national unity care to admit. And because the state is of blurred identity, its leaders lack confidence in their own office of authority. No wonder, then, that many of them—party leaders and military junta alike—move as boldly as they dare toward the increased use of state power in order to stay in control. Ethiopia, the only noncolonial African state, is a case in point, unable to sustain a sense of Ethiopian nationality among its own non-Amharic peoples: hence the terrible disarray of both government and people at the present time.[35] Some—Angola, Mozambique, Benin—turn to Marxist programs and outside communist help in the general hope of inculcating a national sense of revolutionary transformation; but who can doubt that such hopes too will be fallacious?

From almost every standpoint, therefore, the excolonial state makes a poor showing. Ideally, no doubt, what would be desired are ancient traditions harmoniously related to the present, a benign and long period of colonial rule, adequate resources (assuming there are such assets), a clear location of power, skillful leaders of clear moral perceptions, and a close identity between citizens and state. The African world is, unfortunately,

The Fallacies of Hope

not at all like that. Yet the colonial state in African guise seems certain to continue, both as a territory which is accepted internationally and as a society within recognized frontiers. Even for those who wish to see a structural shift in the location of power locally, or an awakening of conscience globally from indifference to concern, the matrix of change will still have to be the former colonial state. And even if a number of African countries were to become a good deal more pleasant than they are now—a prospect that does not seem very promising—it is likely that they would still be the recognizable descendants of the colonial past as a territory, as a society, and as a framework of administrative control. The whole history of the past two decades suggests that would be the case. If, as John Dunn has observed, the dreams of Frantz Fanon could not be realized by the Algerian war of national liberation, they are certainly in no danger of being fulfilled by governments that owe their identity and existence to much less militant origins.[36] It is easy enough to understand why the African states are criticized. Many fail to dispense justice and hence appear as a band of robbers. Most of them fail to deliver the goods and thus appear incompetent. Some are capriciously cruel. But, setting aside the worst and recognizing all the fallacies of hopes not achieved, the adaptation to independent life of the excolonial state may still represent something substantially better than the alternative of breakdown and the consequent banditry of collapse. At that rather despairing level of interpretation, it seems sensible to draw the conclusion that the map of independent states throughout the continent is not only the clearest definition of African success so far achieved but the one that is most likely to endure.

2. No Longer at Ease

The title is taken from Chinua Achebe's novel of a would-be idealist, a member of the new elite in Nigeria who, returning from England to become an Education Officer, grows increasingly uneasy under pressure from his relatives and friends to repay the debt he has incurred by becoming educated. Eventually he is disgraced. He is trapped into corruption and caught being corrupt. Is it his fault, as a corruptible civil servant, or do the circumstances force him into deceit? The story describes a familiar situation in any one of the West African republics, of a hero bewildered, politicians on the make, an uneasy administration and bemused citizens. The intelligentsia are no longer certain of their past or their future. There is a sense of values falling apart, and of loyalties no longer holding together.

No longer, then, at ease. But when *were* these societies at ease in West Africa, the most divided part of the continent? Partitioned by the French and British who bought or forced out the Dutch and the Danes and the Germans, it was once the catchment area of the transatlantic slave trade, profitably transacted between local African chiefdoms and European merchants. Then colonial rule was imposed, and by 1900 division between the European powers was virtually complete: four British colonies and protectorates (the Gambia, Sierra Leone, Ghana, Nigeria), twelve French *territoires d'outre-mer*, the Portuguese colony of Guinea-Bissau, the Spanish colony of Rio Muni, and the independent republic of Liberia.[1] By 1919 there were also two League of Nations mandated territories, Togo and Cameroons, both taken from the Germans and divided administratively between France and Britain. (Each became a United Nations Trust Territory in 1945.) There were uncertain attempts later, in the 1960's, to alter some of the boundaries, but the present pattern is much as it was before decolonization. The Gambia is still not part of Senegal despite a number of schemes to join them together, the Ewe are still divided between the Republic of Togo and Ghana, and the French-speaking countries still keep separate identities despite mutual efforts at closer association, including for a time in the 1950's an interterritorial political party —the *Rassemblement Democratique Africain*. The only major alteration came in 1960 after a majority of the population in the southern area of the (British) Cameroons voted not to remain with Nigeria but to become part of the about-to-be independent Republic of Cameroun. In other respects, despite civil wars and international quarrels, the West African states have remained within their colonial boundaries and have had to live with the absurdity of the mosaic into which the region is divided. But was there ever a time, one might ask again, when political life in this part of the world was under the direction of "men at ease"?

I am old enough to have talked with those who still remembered the coming of the white man, and young enough to have been drawn into the nationalist excitement of the 1950's. I suspect that only for limited periods under traditional rule, and only during the middle years of colonial government, was there any degree of continuity—of a sense, that is, of the present and the future as related peacefully to each other—and an understanding of where power and authority reposed, sanctioned by habit, custom, and ceremony. Very often in precolonial times, calamity ruled people's lives—smallpox or famine or conquest— while colonialism established a steady state only during the interwar period when it was at its fullest and most confident extent. Moreover, even during that colonial paradise of paternal government there were serpents of knowledge and temptation, more disturbing to West African society as a whole than even smallpox or famine or foreign rule. Colonialism not only pushed together local emirates, kingdoms, and clan societies into novel groupings as states; it also dragged them into the market economy of the world. The expansion of European society under the immense power of capitalist forces—in familiar words never again to be expressed with quite so assured a sweep of argument— brought about what may readily be observed in West Africa today, namely, "the revolutionising of production, uninterrupted disturbance of all social conditions, everlasting uncertainty and agitation... Fixed, fast frozen relations, with their train of ancient and venerable prejudices and opinions, are swept away, all new ones become antequated before they can ossify. All that is solid melts into air, all that is holy is profaned." But colonial rule also brought "the rapid improvement of all instruments of production [and it] immensely facilitated means of communication [which] drew all, even the most barbarian, nations into civilisation." In short, it attempted abroad what it succeeded in doing at home, to "create a world after its own image."[2]

The quotation is from Marx's description of the growth of capitalist society in Western Europe. The impact of that society overseas was immensely complicated by being exported. Indeed, there were at least four transferred images of Europe in West Africa: British, French, Portuguese, American, and, for a time, German. In 1945 there were four currency zones and three metropolitan administrations. Much the greater part of the region was divided between the two main empires, the British and the French. But that was considerably better than the present position. Since 1960 the former colonial states have lost most of the advantages of a regionalism they once possessed. There are ten or eleven currencies (many unusable beyond their own country) and very few common institutions such as the old West African Airways, research institutes, currency boards, consultative assemblies, and so forth; the frontiers are patrolled, governments eye each other more suspiciously than ever before, and there is a constant pressure toward a national indigenization of cultures and the economy. Neither Pan-Africanism nor socialist proclamations nor joint economic interests can fill the void left by colonial rule. It is fashionable to talk of the Balkanization of West Africa, and that has certainly been the consequence of the end of colonial rule, but it was the anticolonial nationalism of the postwar years which deepened the colonial divisions into residual states. In 1944, for example, the Asquith Commission proposed the establishment of a West African university for the four British colonies. There was an immediate outcry—in which country should it be sited?—and eventually separate universities were founded. Even so, argument did not stop there. Regions and states within each country began to insist on asserting their interests against the center, and there are at present two universities in Sierre Leone, one on the coast, one up-country; three in Ghana; and almost one to each of the nineteen states in Nigeria.

In following such a path, the former colonial territories were following a well-established phenomenon: nationalism is like an amoeba—it grows by expansion and fission. But there are special features of the West African scene that we need to note. They are grouped under three broad headings: disunity, disparity, and dependence. By disunity is meant the unsettled postcolonial pattern (nationally) of authority and power, by disparity the inequalities of wealth and standing (regionally) between the twenty or more states. But first we need to look again at dependence, or the need of all the West African governments to draw help from the outside world.

The plain fact of dependence, whether it is of a diplomatic or military or economic kind, is not at all unusual. All but a handful of states in the modern world are in that broad category. Only the extremes of total isolation, as Burma tried to achieve, or total self-sufficiency (China?), can abstract themselves from the world. The United Kingdom, for example, is absolutely dependent for its livelihood on external markets and for its security on external alliances. It was also financially dependent to the tune (in 1976) of $14 billion to the International Monetary Fund and other creditors. Why should we single out for comment the dependence of the West African states? Well, there is a distinctive feature: the almost certain fact that the capacity of all the West African governments, other than Nigeria, to moderate their dependency is extremely limited, if indeed it exists at all. Nigeria has the unexpected good fortune of manna from the underworld in the oil fields of the midwest and the offshore delta fields to rescue it from financial dependence. So, too, has Gabon. But nearly all the remaining states are locked into a relationship with the outside world from which they cannot apparently escape.

It is time to narrow the focus to one or two examples. I turn first to Ghana and cocoa. The crop is exported to be turned into chocolate by the United States, western Europe, and the communist countries, much as other African states export tea, coffee, sisal, or bananas. Cocoa began to be widely grown during the early years of colonial rule and it has dominated the economy ever since. It has also transformed social and political relationships within the country by stratifying the rural and urban population into rich and poor, laborers and farmers, large and small peasant holders, middlemen, government marketing officials, and the very large number who are dependent on the wealth generated by cocoa sales. The value of this unusual crop has been roughly 60 percent (plus or minus 5 percent) of all exports since 1945. It has engaged over half a million farmers and farm laborers in a complicated tenurial relationship, and it has supplied the base of modern government in Ghana. Colonial, traditional, nationalist, party-dominated, military, reformist, socialist, and conservative regimes—each has had to depend on cocoa and the surplus wealth extracted by the government, through a state monopoly—a marketing board or a farmers' council—on the basis of the difference between the world price and domestic payments to the farmer. In 1948-49, for example, the total harvest was 278,000 tons. The world price was $456 a ton: the colonial government authorized payment of $288 to the farmer, and the Cocoa Marketing Board put the difference of $168 into reserves both for general development and with the hope (once again fallacious) of stabilizing the domestic price. In 1956-57, the year before independence, the figures were: a harvest of 264,000 tons; world price, $530 a ton; payment to farmers, $355. In 1965-66 the world market fell catastrophically to $290 a ton, of which farmers received $133. Nkrumah was brought down by the army in February the following year. Cocoa prices then rose, only to fall again in 1971-72, and in January 1972 there was a second coup. At present there is a dramatic increase in price of over $5,000 a ton, although who benefits from the increased income—laborers, farmers, middlemen, or soldier-administrators—is hardly in doubt. Over the past two decades since independence, the largest share has always been retained by those farthest from the trees which bear the crop.

It would be absurd to suppose that the manufacturers of Hershey bars or Nestlé chocolate sit in their boardrooms and say, "We don't like the government and its leader in Ghana [or the Ivory Coast, or Trinidad, or some other part of the tropical world]—let's drop the price and destabilize the fellow." That is implausibly malevolent. Ghana is not Chile. And it is hardly credible that both Nkrumah, on the left, and Busia, who was very much on the right, were the targets of an international and capitalist conspiracy. There is more to fear from the indifference of the developed world and its markets. One must also note the importance of the size of the cocoa crop, which is determined not only by previous price levels but by the incidence of disease, the age of the trees and the farming population, and a number of local factors which are as important as (and related in a complicated way to) the actual price per ton. Nor was it true that the military turned out the politicians in 1966 and 1972 simply because the economy was badly hit, although they certainly gave that as one of their reasons for intervention. But when all these qualifications are made, the Ghana economy may very accurately be called a dependent economy and, in a sense which is not always as clear as is sometimes argued, we can say that the politics of Ghana are critically dependent on the shifting fortunes of the country's cocoa economy.

It is not, to be sure, a tale of total woe. Ghana grew rich, comparatively, on cocoa. Until the middle 1960's it was probably the wealthiest nationally and by per capita income, of the tropical African states. Cocoa built the roads, harbors, railways, schools, hospitals, and universities; it capitalized domestic trade and its local markets; it gave impetus to the nationalist movement as well as to the main opposition party to Nkrumah. It has continued to finance the state and its military rulers. The cocoa industry (for that it certainly is) was the creation of local farmers and their families who responded very successfully to the world demand for a new cash crop. There were no plantations, no foreign capital. It was the Ghanaian cocoa farmer who was the rural entrepreneur throughout the southern and central forest country and who made the economy what it was and is. But although the growth of the industry was, until recently, a success story of an impressive kind, the economy as a whole is fastened to an erratic world, and the effect has been to bring about a dependence on the operation of distant markets which has not altered substantially since the 1920's.

Even so, Ghana might be said to be more fortunate than many of its West African neighbors. Although it has to face competition from the tropical areas of the world, including its western neighbor the Ivory Coast, which began to grow cocoa when the market looked promising, it does not have to compete with the rich. Its problems are largely those of an aging industry (and an aging farming population) which it is by no means impossible to revive since there is ample land for new farms and latent farming skills which can be used. Consider, however, the more intractable problems of the ground-nut farmer in Senegal or the Gambia or northern Nigeria, whose local economies are bound quite as tightly to the price of peanuts as that of Ghana to cocoa. How splendid it would be if a sudden demand arose in the richest market of all, through the cessation of production in, for example, President Carter's Georgia. It does not seem likely to occur. However fervently a Carter Administration may wish to help the poor of the world, it will certainly draw the line at plowing in the new President's own domestic product. Earlier kings in England were more generous (or more ruthless) in the suppression of home-grown tobacco in favor of colonial tobacco from Virginia. But that was long before the age of democracy.

Attempts have been made to escape from this economic dependence. Ideologies of self-reliance through industrialization and state-controlled agriculture have jostled with those of a belief in growth through imported capital and skills. Ghana under Nkrumah, Guinea, and Mali might stand uncertainly for a dominant strain of "socialist self-reliance" in the hope of restructuring society; the Ivory Coast and Liberia might stand for a quite different policy. Some states, like Ghana, have tried to move from one to another under different regimes. The difference may be expressed somewhat inelegantly by two quotations from a study of Ghana under Nkrumah and the Ivory Coast under Houphouët-Boigny:

Structural transformation emphasizes industrial development more than agriculture. With agriculture transformationists emphasize capital-intensive, often large-scale schemes aimed at fundamentally changing the technology and organization of peasant life. They see little hope in the export sector as an engine of growth and emphasize reduction of dependence on the outside world. Distrust of the market mechanism, a large role for the state in mobilizing and managing resources, and a low tolerance for inequalities in income distribution tend to be typical of their world view.

The gradualists tend towards the opposite position in all these respects. They emphasize outward looking growth and the potentials of the export sector, focus on peasant agriculture, the importance of individual incentives and the use of the market.

They are more kindly disposed toward private capital, both foreign and domestic, and give a smaller role to the state in the development process. They are rather more concerned with efficiency and growth than with equity in income distribution. [3]

Of the two countries, the Ivory Coast must be reckoned easily the more successful today, and it is an interesting exception to the general pattern, although in a sense it is going through the economic expansion which Ghana experienced (in a different setting) a generation earlier. But the figures of growth—setting aside the vexed question of equity in income distribution within the Ivory Coast as a whole—are impressive. Per capita income stands at $460, compared with Ghana's $430, although a decade ago when Houphouët-Boigny and Nkrumah met in Abidjan as representatives of very different views about what policy to follow, Ghana was certainly ahead.[4] The gross national product in the Ivory Coast is said to have quintupled between 1960 and 1976, an increase of between 7 and 8 percent per annum after allowing for inflation. The 1973-74 recession which followed the rise in cost of oil imports was quickly met, until today the country can claim a reasonable measure of success not only in agriculture and industry but in agro-industry—the processing of food crops and timber for export. The Ivory Coast is the second largest producer in the world of cocoa and is beginning to outgrow its neighbor, Ghana; it is the third biggest coffee producer after Brazil and Columbia; and it is likely to become the world's largest exporter of palm oil by 1980. Its industrial production, too, increased by nearly a quarter between 1970 and 1974, not only by import substitution, but also by the direct export of manufactures, including textiles on an almost Asian scale. If that is a doctrine of gradualism, it is of an extreme kind. And if it rests on a belief in capitalist dependence, it is a very confident belief.

These strong indices of growth have been achieved through the instrument of a single party (the *Parti Democratique du Côte d'Ivoire*), which at first sight is much like a standard communist apparatus of rule except that it is devoted to the development of a planned capitalist economy. Nor has there been any reliance on mining, as by Liberia, Zaire, and Zambia, or on oil, as in Gabon and Nigeria: only on imported capital and skills plus local enterprise. The number of French advisers, administrators, and settlers grew conspicuously after 1960, a remarkable paradox in black Africa, to reach a total of nearly 50,000; but the French connection is beginning to lose a little of its importance. French capital is declining as a proportion of total foreign investment: the present ratios are, roughly, French capital 41 percent, non-French-foreign investment 22 percent, investment locally 37 percent. There is a Stock Exchange and a growing Ivoirian middle class at managerial as well as rentier levels.

The image shines bright—on one side. But turn the coin of growth and the picture is less attractive. It is right to take full account of the caveat generally entered in relation to its success. Patrick Gilkes has noted "the dangers slowly becoming apparent in the Ivoirian system." They are "the overall neglect of social problems and of health in particular, income discrepancies between urban and rural workers, and between the elite and the mass of the people, the growing and unfulfilled aspirations of school and university graduates and the future of the role of France ... and the pool of a million or more cheap labour from Upper Volta, Mali and Guinea."[5] Politically, too, the Ivory Coast is likely to have to face a difficult period. While the economy roared along after independence, the state itself was "arrested"—immobilized by the heavy weight of presidential power. Houphouët-Boigny is now (since 1975) in his fourth five-year term of office, a watchful 72-year-old. The party leaders, tightly controlled by close associates of the president, like Philip Yacé as president of the National Assembly, have stifled political life. Nor is it simply a question of who will take Houphouët-Boigny's place one day, but whether the structure of political control is strong enough to continue both the direction and the pace set since 1960. There have been uneasy rumblings of discontent, including trade union and student strikes in 1968 and 1969. They were quickly brought to an end, but the pot of discontent must be bubbling away under the heavy lid imposed by an ailing leadership.

It is easy enough to jump up with cries of "neocolonialism" and "growth without development," and to frame the caricature of an "ice-skating rink economy of a tropical dependency."[6] But the growth and development are undoubtedly there on a scale that has eluded other African states. If such figures could be produced by less conservative-minded regimes, there would be applause from many who now cast doubt on their achievement. Houphouët-Boigny has also given the state a quarter of a century of political control, and it is possible to argue that the Ivory Coast has reached a plateau of growth and national wealth on which future governments can indigenize the economy, open some safety valves of political life, and fund its social needs. The balance is equivocal between failure and success in such a context.

Those at ease in Abidjan, if indeed that is the case, are very much therefore the exception. But I do not think that ideological categories divide the good and the bad, the successful and unsuccessful. There are no clear opposites. Socialism and capitalism are simply abstracts in the dependent life of most West African states. It is, for example, a nice question whether Nkrumah's socialism in Ghana in the early 1960's accumulated more debts and dependency than Busia's indigenous capitalism after 1969. But can anything be done collectively to mitigate the effect? Whenever the West African governments have tried to act together on a regional basis in relation to coffee and cocoa and iron, either with the somewhat distant example of the European Economic Community (EEC) in mind or on the hardly less distant model of OPEC, they have found immense difficulties in the way. There are too many competitive producers and too immediate a dependence by governments on revenue from exports. There are no cocoa-based Kuwaits, nor can one easily stockpile palm kernels or slow down the rate of production of cash crops. It is true that commodity prices have risen in an extraordinary fashion over the past few years, but they have returned in the form of manufactures multiplied by the inflationary costs of production in the developed states. The current rate of inflation in Ghana is beginning to run at Latin American levels, jumping from a consumer price base index of 100 in 1963 to 383 by 1975 and over 1,000 by 1977.[7] The indebtedness of almost every government, except those of Gabon and Nigeria, which have oil, is endemic, and borrowing continues (when creditors can be found) in order to pay the interest on accumulated debts.

It is not a total helplessness—not yet at least. The twenty or more governments of the region have put together a new

Economic Commission for West Africa (ECOWAS), and they have joined forces with similarly placed states in other parts of Africa, the Caribbean, and the Pacific in relation to the nine member governments of the enlarged European Community. A Treaty of Association was signed in 1975 in Lomé, the Togolese capital, in a joint effort to help investment through a European Development Bank and to facilitate trade by preferential tariffs.[8] In recent years, for example, to go back to cocoa, there was a marginal duty of between 4½ percent and 9 percent on the general import into EEC of new cocoa beans and a high 18 percent duty on imports of semiprocessed cocoa butter, which is the first stage in making chocolate. But all cocoa products (raw beans and cocoa butter) from the Associated States were zero rated. A similar preferential arrangement was negotiated for other imports, including refined palm oil, sawn timber, plywood, and manufactures. There have been joint negotiations more recently over the possibility of controlled or stabilized commodity prices and the rescheduling of debts. The result has not been spectacular. The African countries remain competitively at odds with each other and comparatively poor, and the nine European states have not lost very much. There has also been an African uneasiness about the inventiveness of the developed world which may find synthetic substitutes for primary products, or which may take fright at the import of cheaply produced manufactures. But at least there is the attempt by a number of poorer countries to bargain with the richer societies of the developed states within an agreed framework of consultation. It is probably also true today that the European governments are no longer so vulnerable to the charge, despite their history, of neocolonialism or superpower imperialism, as is the United States (despite *its* antecedents) vis-à-vis Latin America, or the USSR (despite its ideological pretense) vis-à-vis Eastern Europe.

One last comment on dependence. When Prospero left to regain his dukedom in Milan, Ariel was free to wander, but how did Caliban spend his newly won independence? Did he not try to lose some of the attributes of his former serfdom? In a sense that is true of West Africa. It has tried to find local roots, and to grow from them—a search for autochthony. Constitutions have been drawn up in an effort to give expression to an African personality. Socialism has been given an African title. In some states there has been a clumsy attempt to reach African solutions on Marxist premises, in others to base Marxist/Socialist solutions on African experience. Foreign policies of nonalignment have been announced, Pan-African ideals proclaimed, and an African or national curriculum substituted for the earlier European-based teaching at various educational levels.⁹ In brief, an attempt has been made to give an African expression to as wide a spectrum of national life as possible. How successful that has been must be conjecture, and it is probably too early as yet to pronounce any overall verdict. If we single out any one aspect, failure is usually more evident than success. The special constitutions have collapsed. There is no adequate substitute for the French or English language, and the indigenization of education has to struggle with local fears and technical needs. Even the process of bringing the domestic sector of the economy under local control (whether by the state itself or by its encouragement of local capital) has been patchy. Yet the pattern of adaptation is everywhere apparent, particularly in the coastal states, since it was there that western civilization and African culture were most closely interwoven. Despite the history of the slave trade, despite (or because of?) the longer history of colonialism in West Africa, and despite the high level of economic dependence and the failure of a number of civilian governments, there is a more confident basis to local society. There is less xenophobia than in other parts of Africa. And there is a more relaxed acceptance of the need to live with the colonial past, although the region also has its brutal, repressive regimes, most notably in Guinea under Sekou Touré.

Second, disparity—the difference between the large and small, powerful and weak, richer and poorer states in West Africa and the relationship between them. It is not to deny a previous assumption that there is unlikely to be any change in the ex-colonial map of states. The former colonial state stands guard, so to speak, over its nationalist successor by virtue of its defined frontiers and established structures of power. And yet if West Africa is Balkanized, and if historical parallels were to be drawn, the map might begin to be worried at by revisionists, irredentists, and ambitious politicians. There is even a sense in which there are alternative colonial maps waiting to be given expression. Nigeria lost the southern Cameroons to its eastern neighbor in 1960.

The Ewe in Togo, and many of those in the former British Mandated Territory of Togoland who were formally incorporated as part of Ghana in 1957, have tried to reconstitute a Greater Togoland, of which the boundaries were to be those of the old German colony before 1914. The Ivory Coast at one time included Upper Volta—the last change in favor of separation was as late as 1947. Even "Senegambia" once existed. One of the very few examples of the extinction of a colonial state occurred at the extreme western end of the region when Morocco and Mauritania (but not Algeria) agreed to put an end to the Spanish colony of the Sahara: and it is possible that other very small states may be gobbled up.[10] The oil-rich Cabinda enclave north of the Congo river looked at one time during the fighting in Angola in 1976 as if it might be a candidate for partition between Zaire and the Congo (Brazzaville). By a quirk of colonial history it had been part of Portuguese Angola, and it is still a northern extension of an independent Angola. The Gambia, too, must always be at some risk from its larger neighbor.

A great variety of states, therefore—poor and oil-rich, coastal and inland, large and small, radical and conservative, Christian and Muslim, ex-French, ex-British, ex-Portuguese or ex-Spanish—divide the region in a senseless mosaic. Will it not be reshaped into a different pattern? Some of the poorest are quite defenseless. The Sahel countries of the savannah areas, from Senegal to Niger, have suffered drought and famine as national afflictions much more serious than the political instability of soldiers and politicians. But the sheer unattractiveness of their plight is some sort of safeguard against external predators. And that is probably true of the greater part of West Africa. It is tucked away out of the world's alarms if considered alongside Latin America and the United States, or eastern Europe and the USSR, or Southeast Asia and China, and it is much less strategically important than eastern and southern Africa. Since the classic Balkan conflict is usually an extension or reflection of great power rivalry, West Africa is fortunate at least in that respect. It has so far escaped such pressures. It is true that Nigeria had to turn first to Britain, then to the Soviet Union, for military supplies during its civil war; Biafra turned to France; and there are United States as well as Soviet interests along the coast. But West Africa is still marginal, not central, to Washington and Moscow. Left to themselves, therefore, the pervasive weakness of most West African states seems likely to preserve the mosaic.

Except for Nigeria? It is a singular fact that there are probably as many people in Nigeria as in the whole of West Africa from Mauritania to the Nigerian border ("probably" since the census figures are either inaccurate or politically inexpedient to publish.)[11] The most plausible figure is seventy million plus—twice that of the next most populous state in the continent, Egypt. Moreover, Nigeria has money. Its gross national product was estimated for 1975 at nearly $25 billion, more than twice that of the Ivory Coast, Ghana, and Senegal combined.[12] I do not think that any government in Lagos is likely to become directly aggressive, despite its army of well over 200,000 troops, if only because the federation has more than enough to absorb its political energies in the sheer effort to keep together as one country.[13] But Nigeria does raise the interesting question of indirect power as influence. The notion of nonpolitical maps, which have their own moving frontiers and lines of force, will be used later in connection with central Africa. But they also exist on the West Coast. Both the Ivory Coast and Ghana are centers of attraction for large numbers of migrant workers moving south to seek employment in the mines or coffee and cocoa farms, or as traders and domestic servants. In most sizable West African towns there are settlements of "strangers" who exemplify the intricacy of local market forces and the extent to which traders, laborers, and cattle drovers move from one country to another in search of profit and employment. Governments do not much like them. They occasionally turn them out, as Busia did in Ghana in 1971, when there was a mass expulsion of illegal immigrants many of whom seeped back in again. But in many ways the movement of local traders is a greater tribute to Pan-African sentiment than the flying journeys of high dignitaries from one airport capital to another. And the Nigerian economy is eminently such an economy, huge, ebullient, oil-rich, varied, chaotic, attracting money and trading interests from all over West Africa in addition to American, European, Russian, and Japanese businessmen.

Is economic strength of that kind likely to be translated into political and diplomatic power? It might one day. There was undoubtedly some uneasiness about Nigeria among the French-speaking states in the 1960's, an anxiety (encouraged by Paris?) reflected in the recognition of Biafra by the Ivory Coast and Gabon during the civil war. But such fears seem to have diminished, or were overborne by the market opportunities presented by an oil-rich Nigeria, and evidence is beginning to appear of Nigerian leadership and skill backed by money throughout the region. In 1976 special grants in aid of over one million naira* were made by General Gowon's government to the former Portuguese colonies of Guinea Bissau, Cape Verde Islands, Angola, and Mozambique, and about five million naira to a wide assortment of countries, including eight governments in West Africa. Investment holdings have been taken in iron ore companies (in Guinea) and in manufacturing industry (in Benin and Togo), in addition to direct grants to Commonwealth Development funds and the African Development Bank. The federal government played a dominant, often a commanding, role in fostering relations between a number of West African governments, as between Chad, Cameroun, Niger, and Nigeria through the Lake Chad Basin Commission, and in the negotiations leading to the May 1975 Economic Community of the West African states; and it acted as spokesman for the ACP group of fifty-two Associated States during their bargaining sessions with the EEC. Nigeria was also host to the grand Festival of African Culture in Lagos in December 1976. For the present, it is true, the Federation is held down by its own weight and diversity. Moreover, a return to civilian rule is planned for 1979, and a complicated transfer of power from military commanders to politicians is under way which is bound to be complicated and dangerous. Almost anything could go wrong. It would be premature, therefore, to see Nigeria as exercising military or political power, whether vis-à-vis Rhodesia or in relation to states closer at hand. But speculations of that kind are interesting, since they may well belong to the future, provided of course the future includes a stable and productive Nigeria under a confident government.

That being said, the differences among the West African states seem as likely to increase as to diminish. They are islands of political control over which a local regime attempts to impose its authority until it is removed by a contrary government.

*1 Naira = $1.65 (end of 1976).

Ex-French, ex-British, ex-Portuguese, Muslim and Christian, Marxist and capitalist, brutal and mild regimes are no less divided one from another, and hardly more competent at managing their domestic affairs, than the early national governments of the first European states. Perhaps the sole advantage the African governments have is, in a sense, their very dependency. They are not autonomous in their diversity and have somehow, however minimally, to work together if they are not to continue forever to suffer individually.

Is there no single answer, then, to our third area of inquiry, domestic disunity? Can one not say where power lies in these very diverse states, or what the common basis is of their fear? Crowned with such a wealth of laurel at independence, why should the West African leaders be no longer at ease? Well, there *is* a simple answer:

> *The strongest poison ever known*
> *Came from Caesar's laurel crown.*

Yet it is perhaps not power which poisons or corrupts in West Africa but the haunting fear of its loss. Nor is it difficult to explain why there are such fears, since the penalties attached to defeat have been severe. But why that should be so, why successive governments have turned so savagely on their predecessors or on their opponents, is not easy to understand. I turn finally, therefore, to the unsettled pattern, nationally, of power and authority.

It is difficult to know where either power (to enforce command) or authority (to command obedience) lies. The basic problem of all the West African states is how to bring power in line with authority on the basis of something more than a precarious and conditional assent. In theory there should have been no major difficulty. Nationalism was to be a bridge between the ordinary citizen and his new rulers, modernity the process whereby each state would be brought under the control of a new elite of national outlook. Tribalism would be eroded or would dissolve into nationalism. Colonial authority would vanish and be replaced by a new African Personality. The politician, civil servant, soldier, and entrepreneur would recognize their mutual interests as a new social class whose exploitative instincts would be checked by national institutions—parliaments, constitutions, parties, elections. Thus the state would be representative both territorially and socially. Its authority would be recognized on that basis, and political life would be steady.

In practice, conflict developed at both elite and local level. The former were divided, the latter never brought fully into national politics. Almost without exception there has been a double problem among West African states, a territorial problem in relation to community interests which it would be naive to see as tribal, and a social question, relative to wealth and power, which it would be simplistic to misread as class. The effect has been to intensify competition for control of the central machinery of government between numerous contenders (politicians, civil servants, trade unionists, soldiers) who see themselves not as a single stratum of class interests but as rivals for control of the state. There are several explanations why that should be so. The educated elites are divided (it is said) because they cannot as yet see themselves fully as Nigerians, or Malians, or Togolese, and they turn therefore to social groups of a local kind with which they can identify. Or it is because they are not sufficiently numerous or autonomous to become a distinct economic class, or because the scarcity of local resources intensifies competition for jobs and position, or—quite simply—because the leaders see politics as a game in which the winner takes all: the price of repression is thought worth the cost of disunity. Very likely each explanation is partly true. But given the fact that the elite are divided, it is hardly surprising that the soldier is often the winner. The particular circumstances of the military coups which are so conspicuous a feature of West African politics vary considerably, but there are common elements. Armies have guns, soldiers have ambitions, the circumstances are often propitious, external interests press hard to advance their own interests (if only by proxy), and the success of one coup draws on the others. There are military reasons why some soldiers want to enter politics in order to put an end to a civilian government which (they say) is interfering with the army, as under Nkrumah in 1966; and there are political-civilian weaknesses which may predispose the army to intervene, as in Sierra Leone in 1967. Robin Luckham was able to put together many varieties of the armed coup, based on the premise that the boundary between the military and civilian society is often blurred, permitting an easy passage of power from one to the other, although of course it is easier for control to move from politicians to soldiers than vice versa.[14]

Yet army as well as civilian leaders have been uneasy in office, since the conditions that provoke a major shift in the location in power from party to military control do not cease to exist when soldiers rule by decree. In the Congo (Brazzaville) for example, Major Marien Ngouabi ousted President Alphone Massamba Débat in 1968 but was assassinated in March 1977, whereupon the military junta that succeeded him promptly executed Massamba Débat. In the Chad, Félix Malloum came to power after a coup in 1975 when President Tombalbaye was assassinated; but in both 1976 and 1977 there were further attempts at a coup directed at *him*. It is significant, too, that both civil and military governments have looked with great suspicion at universities as institutions of privilege from which the next generation of leaders is likely to be drawn. It is symptomatic of a divided elite that it does not trust its educated young. Nor is it now possible to believe, as it used to be argued, that the military are instruments of modernization. They are undoubtedly instruments of change, but soldiers march clumsily onto the political stage and appear awkward or brutal, and often both. Admittedly, there may be short-term benefits. It is difficult to believe that Nigeria could have moved forward from the tight federation of three or four regions to the more open structure of nineteen states without the direct command of the army. But military government also brings its own uncertainties, including the extreme danger of armed division. The military coups in Sierra Leone, for example, were a remarkable illustration of the ineptitude of army rule. In March 1967 Albert Margai lost the election he had somewhat imprudently held and turned to the army for help. More accurately, he turned to Brigadier Lansana, who, like Margai, was from the Mende-speaking chiefdoms. Lansana agreed to support him in office. Two days later both Margai and Lansana were overthrown by a group of junior officers who formed a National Reformation Council under Lt. Col. Juxon Smith. In April the following year there was a further upset. The NRC was forcibly dissolved by a number of noncommissioned officers and privates who brought together an Anti-

Corruption Council, arresting eighty-four of their army and police officers but recalling to active service Col. Bangura and Col. Genda. Eventually, after a great deal of confusion, the Council handed control of the country to a National Government under Siaka Stevens, the former Opposition leader whose party (All People's Congress) had won the 1969 elections. Stevens then set about consolidating his rule by declaring a state of emergency and detaining his opponents. The whole affair was a charade of military maneuver, party conflict and tribal rivalry, ending in tragedy in July 1975 when Lansana and two former party leaders were executed after a court martial found them guilty of attempting a further coup in the summer of 1974.

The Nigerian story of military intervention is still more somber: coups within the coup by assassination and the massacre of one political/ethnic group by those of another in a terrible slaughter of soldiers and civilians alike. Luckham has described each military uprising in masterly fashion. The first coup, in January 1966, was against not only the civilian government of Alhaji Abubakar but the army command under Major General Ironsi. There had been "blatantly rigged elections"[15] in the Western Region in 1965 followed by widespread violence. The army was brought in to restore control, and thus began its own record of death. Luckham tells "how the killings depleted the upper military ranks of the [army] hierarchy and the more senior age groups."[16] Two of the four brigadier/major generals were killed, another imprisoned, and over a third of the lieutenant colonels and colonels murdered or imprisoned. The attack on the officers, one needs to add, was in addition to the murder of many of the federal and regional government leaders. The effect on the army was very bad. "The gap in experience and in ascriptive qualities such as age and seniority between the upper and lower ranks of the officer corps, between commanders and subordinates, was made still narrower than it had been before. Talking of this time, young officers say it was one in which they felt quite distinctly that the social distance between themselves and their superiors had decreased; that both familiarity and hostility between high- and lower-ranking officers were greater; and that particularistic relations of friendship and clientage, tribe and region tended to develop at the expense of organisational ties."[17] But there was a more sinister aspect still, for the January coup altered substantially the ethnic composition of the officer corps. "It is striking that almost all of the conspirators came from the same ethnic group, the Ibos."[18] Since most of those killed were northerners or Yorubas. "the Ibos moved automatically from a position of numerical inferiority among the most senior twenty or thirty officers to a position of numerical superiority.... During the first month after the 15th January coup, Ibo officers held every post of any importance in the army except Chief of Staff (Army) ... and commander of the 1st Brigade.... All the five Battalions, one of the two Recce Squadrons, the artillery field battery and all three training units were under the command of Ibo officers."[19] Little wonder, therefore, that belief in an Ibo conspiracy was widespread; and in April 1966 the tables were turned with a vengeance. A second coup saw the massacre of Ibo soldiers and civilians by northerners. "In general, being an Ibo was sufficient grounds for slaughter during the seizure of power in army units at the early stages, though there was more selectivity later on in preparing lists of 'suspects' for killing. It appears that non-Ibos whether from the East, Mid-West or West were only killed if they got in the way during the seizure of power, if they were suspected of sympathy with the January coup, or if particular Northern troops by whom they were confronted made the false assumption that they were Ibo. ... The officers who carried out the coup were entirely Northern...."[20]

If the Nigerian experience is taken as an extreme example of a general case, we must conclude from these grisly accounts that army rule is no more a guarantee of peaceful change than party rule. Since the end of the civil war General Gowon has been forced out of office and his successor, General Murtala Mohammed, assassinated. One can easily understand why the present Head of State General Obasanjo is eager to restart the machinery of demilitarization in an effort to take the army out of politics before the end of 1979. African armies can hold the state together for a time, but they, too, reflect society as a whole—divided hierarchically by rival elites and open to all the communal disputes that plagued their civilian predecessors.

There is a pervasive fear, therefore, of group loyalties which run counter to national identities. "Tribalism" is too clumsy a description—after all, the Nigerian federal army kept together on a multi-ethnic base throughout the civil war—but the element of local patriotism is everywhere very strong. I use the pleasant-sounding phrase "local patriotism," since it is common enough to condemn tribalism as irritating or dangerous and reactionary. So of course it can be. But it may also be argued that what is condemned as tribalism is often a basic unit of loyalty from which nation states, if they are to cohere, must be painfully constructed. If countries are a mosaic, as most West African states are, the local pieces are the essential constituents. The irony of the search for unity lies not in the assertion by party or military governments of the paramountcy of national interests over strong local sentiments—that is understandable—but in the claim that only the former has validity. In practice, the central government frequently lacks the authority to exact obedience, though it claims to be all-powerful, whereas the local loyalties of a clan or chiefdom or region or language group, recast in modern form, must find expression by dissent. The effect is an uneasy trade-off between the center and locality, each suspicious of the other yet needing its support. National politics then become "tribal" either because the center splits into factions which seek mass support from ethnic solidarities, or because an aggrieved local community seeks to oppose the government by appealing to its own national leaders.

The image I often have in mind, rather uncertainly, is that of a stepped pyramid. At the top, on a narrow area, there stands nervously and uncomfortably the ruling elite of military or civilian leaders, advised by senior civil servants and open to persuasion by the growing number of local and foreign entrepreneurs. The lower slopes are crowded with contractors, traders, skilled artisans, teachers, clerks, and wealthy farmers, and the urban poor, down to the broad base of peasant farmers and their laborers. Marx and Engels would very easily have classified them into embryonic classes.[21] But the several slopes of the pyramid are ethnic solidarities, now politically alert, of which West African society is composed. A cross section through the pyramid at a particular echelon can be defined by wealth and occupation and their usual concomitant, education; but it is also necessary (if one is talking politics) to remember that the police officer who has risen through the professional ranks of the force, or a barrister who is a member of the Bar Association, or a teacher, or engine driver, or house servant, may still retain a good deal of affection (including political sympathies) for his place of birth as a member of a particular language group or region or tribe. The analogy is not perhaps very satisfactory, since the slopes of the pyramid are often more numerous than the model allows and may vary in shape and composition at one particular time or another. Still, it is right to argue that any interpretation of political behavior must take into account not only a person's modern status, but his community of origin. To put the assertion in reverse order: political authority at a national level is likely to be splintered by communal divisions, whereas the politics of ethnic solidarity at a local level have to contend with new loyalties attached to occupation or wealth or class.

Nigeria, to which we return as the great exemplar of these difficulties, has known such divisions to excess. The focus of national loyalty is terribly blurred, and successive governments on all sides, from the colonial administration to nationalist leaders and military commanders, have tried to devise a framework of control to mediate both social and territorial antagonisms. It is easy to dismiss such a search as old-fashioned or not in keeping with the reality of political behavior. Perhaps Alexander Pope had the answer:

> *For forms of government let fools contest.*
> *Whate'er is best administered is best.*

But some apparatus of control has to be devised to adjust the many and the one, since the only rulers who might have endorsed Pope's lines are the now departed British. Quite apart from the difficulty, still to be met, of reconciling military and and civilian interests and of deciding what form of executive should be established and how it should relate to the legislature, there is the extreme problem of number. How many constitutional divisions should Nigeria contain? It is a domestic question most West African states have to face in relation to their own regional or local authorities. Over the past three decades, Nigeria has experienced division into three, four, one, twelve and nineteen. A month after the January 1966 coup, for example, General Ironsi denounced the former colonial pattern of federation (of first three, then four, regions) and forced through by

Decree No. 34 of 24 May 1966 the decision that Nigeria should be a unitary state: "All Nigerians want an end to regionalism."[22] Ironsi was killed during the second coup in July, and General Gowon reversed the decision, saying: "The basis of trust and confidence in a unitary system of government has not been able to stand the test of time"[23]—even though it was the murderous use of the gun rather than the passage of time which had compelled the change. Decree 59 of 31 August 1966 brought Nigeria back to its former federal structure, but the question of the future number of units and their relationship *inter se* was left open, and it was not until the eve of the civil war a little over a year after Gowon had taken office that a number was decided upon—twelve—and given constitutional form. It might be thought that military rule would be nonfederal by nature, since it has (at least in theory) a centralized structure or control and a unitary chain of command. But in May 1967, by military decree, Gowon produced what Ojukwu (who was shortly to lead the Eastern Region into armed secession) called a one-man coup d'état. The decrees established a twelve-state administrative structure for Nigeria. Then civil war intervened and Ojukwu was defeated, Gowon announced his intention to return Nigeria to civilian rule but went back on his promise and was removed. Mohammed took his place only to be assassinated, and his successor, Olusegun Obasanjo, has kept steadfastly to the timetable of transfer by a date not later than October 1979. The number of states, however, is now to be nineteen. The draft constitution published by Chief Rotimi Williams' Committee is based on the assumption of that number; and one may hope very much that the aggregation of nineteen state loyalties may be a secure arithmetical formula for a peaceful as well as a federal Nigeria.

So much for this brief account of West African politics. The decade and a half since the great year of independence in 1960 has been full of interest, but crowded, too, with misfortune. The anguish of the civil war in Nigeria has been known to one degree or other in almost every West African state. Only the Ivory Coast can point to steady economic growth. Only the little Gambia, quixotic almost in its cheerful persistence with democratic forms, has escaped the torment of plots, assassinations, imprisonment, treason trials, armed intervention, and gross disorder. If there are saviors in West Africa, they are the African civil servants who have kept the former colonial state together, often enough on a care-and-maintenance basis. But West Africa has also shown that politics keeps breaking through whatever formula of control is adopted in the attempt to reduce their effect. Elites are divided, communities are divided. Taking any West African country at random and reading about its politics, one quickly becomes aware of that distinctive pyramid of conflict whose protagonists are quarreling elites in uneasy alliance with communal dissatisfaction. We may open at random Irving Markowitz's book on Senegal, quoting Leopold Senghor himself: "There are no classes at war today only social groups struggling for influence. Tomorrow they *will* be at war with one another ... if we allow intellectuals to form a class." Then a comment by Markowitz himself: "In a country with a population estimated at 3-4 million, Senegal contains Wolof, Serer, Peulh, Toucouleur, Mandingue, Bambara, Diola, Sankole, Mandjaque, Balante, Bassari, Coniqui and Lebou peoples.... The Diola of Casamance—a district separated from Dakar by climate, vegetation, distance, poor communications and transport—constituted the major element in the main organised opposition."[24] The picture is one of antagonistic social groups seeking support from rival ethnic communities. Yet Senghor's earlier vision had been that of a harmonious society of leaders and local interests in *une nation des patries*—a nation of fatherlands, each of the latter being "a culture rooted in a native soil," whereas "the Nation gathers such Fatherlands together in order to transcend them."[25] The image was splendid. But how difficult it is to realize may be seen from the politics of ethnicity even in a number of developed industrial societies—in, for example, Canada or Belgium or the United Kingdom. Nor is Senegal very different from its West African neighbors. Its dependence on external markets, and the regional imbalance of the country, are, as we have seen, common enough. But they are not, unfortunately, the main problem. The root cause of discontent and the prime difficulty of political control is that shared by all the West African countries, the weakness of their identity as states. The consequence is that governments lack a moral base of authority, and the ordinary citizen, at every level of the social and political pyramid, has to suffer the exercise of power by men who cannot command and must therefore try to exact obedience. How fortunate, then, is passivity of the peasant base of the pyramid!

3. E Pluribus Plures

Out of the many has come not one, but many. We return to our general theme, that the colonial state has persisted as a national unit of control despite attempts at secession and, in the three or four countries with which we shall be principally concerned, despite efforts to construct some larger entity. Within each state, however, there have been substantial shifts in the central location of power as rival groups have fought each other, often murderously, to obtain control. We shall also have to note the effect of outside interests which have begun to gather in the area of the Indian Ocean. It is hardly to be wondered at, therefore, that the politics of Uganda, Kenya, Tanzania, and Zanzibar have been troubled. Since the end of World War II, there have been peasant revolts, racial conflict, mutinies, famine, murderous leaders, the falling out of nationalist heroes, local wars, foreign entanglements, and a shift of power from one section of the community to another—a host of plagues. Pharaoh himself knew no worse. And the picture is no better if one goes back farther into the past. East Africa was always an area of scattered communities, immensely varied in language, race, structure of rule, economic life, and religious ceremonies. There are Bantu, Nilotic, and Nilo-Hamitic peoples, many still living in extended agricultural settlements, like the Kikuyu and Sukuma, or moving from one encampment to another as pastoral nomads, like the Masai and the Boran. In precolonial times there were segmentary clan groups—tribes without rulers—and little more than the beginnings of small-scale chiefdoms. Only in the Bantu-speaking area of what became Uganda were there politically developed centralized kingdoms like Bunyoro and Buganda. Many of the smaller communities were also cruelly harassed in the nineteenth century by the Arab slave trade, which extended its caravans westward from Zanzibar to the Great Lakes, although for those who like to believe that there is good

E Pluribus Plures

in every evil, it is possible to note the consequential spread of Islam as a unifying religion and of a shared regional language, Swahili.[1] With imperial control came the additional shock not only of colonial rule but of European settlement. Whereas the mosquito and mephitic swamps of West Africa had kept out the European farmer, the cool and fertile highlands of East Africa attracted settlers in growing numbers from Britain in the years immediately following the two world wars. Indians, too, arrived at the turn of the century to work on the construction of the Kenya-Uganda railway. Many of them stayed, and others followed, as clerks, shopkeepers, and traders.

Even colonial rule was sometimes uncertain of itself. The boundaries of all the countries in the region have been ragged. Kenya was enlarged in 1902 by the addition of the former eastern province of Uganda (to the present annoyance of Field Marshal Amin) and of northern Turkana (to recent protests by Somalia): it lost Jubaland in 1925 to Italian Somalia.[2] Tanganyika was transferred from German rule to the League of Nations in 1919 and administered under mandate by Britain, which did little more than keep order and encourage (quite successfully) the growing of coffee under a benign form of indirect rule. After World War II it became a trust territory of the United Nations, still under British rule, until independence was peacefully achieved in 1961. Three years later Nyerere agreed to a union with the clove islands of Zanzibar and Pemba. They had become independent in December 1963 only to undergo an armed revolt early the following year under the Uganda-born fanatic "Field Marshal" John Okello, by which power was bloodily transferred from Arab to African control. (It is commonly said that some 5,000 Arabs were killed, a similar number driven into exile, and the remainder dispossessed of property.) Somalia, too, was born of a union, peacefully consummated in December 1960, between the former Italian trust territory of Somalia in the south and British Somaliland in the north on the basis of common clan affiliations and a single Somali language. In Uganda, British rule was always uneasy, since it rested on a formal treaty, drawn in 1900 between the young King or "Kabaka" of Buganda and the British commissioners, on the basis of which colonial rule was extended, often enough through Ganda agents, over the rest of Uganda.[3] Still greater uncertainty existed in Kenya, where a relatively small number of settlers (about fifty thousand) dominated the local legislature and its finance committee; and although there was an early declaration in 1923 by the British government that "Kenya was primarily an African territory,"[4] the possibility of minority settler self-government was never really removed until the 1950's.

Despite these internal problems, colonial rule took root and an uncertain African nationalism attached itself as best it could to the last stock of colonial growth, accepting the frontiers of each state as they were at independence. The movement toward self-government came almost a decade later than on the West Coast and owed a great deal to the example, if not the precept, of that earlier loss of colonial rule; but each of the East African territories moved forward separately by different routes.

Tanganyika, for which the United Nations envisaged a timetable of independence stretching to 1981, was seen by the colonial government at one time as a multiracial society of Africans, Asians, and Europeans (despite the overwhelming preponderance of the former) and hardly less plausibly as the location of a vast mechanized experiment in farming, for which the United Kingdom government spent over $70 million in an effort to produce ground-nut oil and fats for the war-stricken British economy. Neither hope was realized. The ground-nut scheme collapsed, and the political scene was substantially altered in July 1954 by the conversion of a Tanganyika African Association, formed as early as 1929 by mission-educated African civil servants, into a national political party—the Tanganyika Africa National Union—under Julius Nyerere. TANU won a decisive victory in the first elections in 1958 and 1959, whereupon independence in this poor and empty land was hustled through by the end of 1961.[5]

Uganda's independence came only after a quarrel between the Kabaka, Frederick Mutesa II, and the colonial Governor, Andrew Cohen. The Baganda said they wanted self-rule not for Uganda but for their own kingdom, and the Kabaka was exiled in 1953. He was brought back in 1955; there were political arguments, elections and parties, and religious disputes between the Catholic majority and Protestant minorities, as well as territorial differences between the kingdoms—all the familiar accompaniment, that is, to self-government but without any strong single nationalist movement. In December 1960 Buganda declared itself

E Pluribus Plures

unilaterally independent. The British took no notice, and in September 1962 the whole country moved forward into independence, Buganda on a federal basis, the other kingdoms in a semifederal relationship, under the Lango (Nilotic) leader Milton Obote as prime minister and the Kabaka as President.

The route to Kenya's independence was full of pain. It lay through the murderous Mau Mau rebellion among the land-hungry and urban-poor Kikuyu. More than 50,000 British troops had to be flown to the colony in 1952 to contain the uprising, which was atavistically brutal and rigorously suppressed. It was as much a civil war among the Kikuyu as between Africans and Europeans—by the end of the emergency in 1955 over 80,000 Africans had been detained and 13,000 killed, whereas European civilian deaths numbered 32—but the effect was almost certainly to convince the British government that African self-rule was essential. So many troops had been used under direct British control, and so much money spent to mend the destruction, that settler rule was now out of the question. The familiar search for acceptable African successors began quite early.[5] But since the Kikuyu were very divided, and Jomo Kenyatta, their most prominent leader, was under detention until August 1961, other communities began to claim their share of what was clearly not far off, namely political independence and a controlled distribution of land in the former White Highlands. Political debate began to take shape under the stress of elections around the two Luo leaders, Tom Mboya and Oginga Odinga, and a loose gathering of pastoral and coastal peoples under Ronald Ngala, primarily in the form of a Kenya African National Union (KANU) versus a Kenya African Democratic Union (KADU). Both parties were divided by fractional groups, but were persuaded eventually to coalesce under Kenyatta, and on this basis the Colony became independent at the end of 1963. European settler influence, peacefully mediated by moderate leaders like Michael Blundell, had by now diminished to a small share in Kenyatta's government. The Asian minority watched and wondered, and the Mau Mau guerrillas came out of hiding but were kept conspicuously out of favor.[6]

By the end of 1963, Tanganyika, Uganda, Kenya, and Zanzibar were all fully independent. But these East African countries were also part of the continent where there was more than a flicker of Pan-African sentiment, if only because the British had sketched an alternative colonial map of interterritorial union in an effort to draw the region together. Prior to independence there were Governors' conferences, an East African High Commission, a network of common services under joint boards in control of railways, harbors, ports, telegraphs, and airways; there was an army, and the beginnings of a common market in goods and currencies. Of considerable antiquity were the hopes of many who foresaw a larger East African state. The Kenya-Uganda railway of 1902 was followed by an East African Currency Board of 1905, a postal union of 1911, a customs union six years later. The High Commission came into being in 1948 to be replaced in 1960 by the East African Common Services Organisation and in 1967 by the East African Community. Other institutions began to reflect the possibility of union: an East African Court of Appeal, a Parliament, and a Ministerial Council, a University at Makerere in Uganda, local research centers, a publishing house in Nairobi. Today, however, almost the whole of this interwoven pattern of colonial legacies, economic interests, and Pan-African hopes has gone. The three excolonial states have moved away from each other in suspicion and hostility.

One last point of introduction. It was said that traditional precolonial society over a large part of East Africa was splintered, then put together in a wider colonial setting, though remaining uncertain of its new loyalties. But the present governments are divided from each other in quite another sense: ideology. Very likely that, too, is the outcome of the lack of a common index of identity. Since, as Nyerere once observed, the East African nations are "exotic," ideology was brought in as an additional brace of national support. When the old and primitive strength of a village community is sapped and the new ties of nationality are weak, it is then perhaps that an explicit ideology is given expression.[7] Ideologies in many of these recently independent states are often the expression of a political rather than a philosophical will: hence the contrasts in East Africa between programs of belief issued from Dar es Salaam and less formal pronouncements by the Kenya or Uganda governments. Kenya's Socialism is not at all like Nyerere's *Ujamaa* or the now forgotten

"Common People's Charter" of Amin's predecessor, Obote, although each in its own way had behind it the "impulsions . . . of economic development and national power."[8]

Here is a wealth of themes to explore, linked to the colonial past: a struggle to seize and adapt to local purposes a central machinery of control, the crumbling of a pan-East-Africanism, the divergent growth of ideologies, and the probing interests of external powers. They are taken one by one.

Colonial governments once held the belief, elaborated by academic writers of the time, that colonial rule ought properly to be only a scaffolding within which a new African state could be built by local effort. The builders would be the chiefs and elders, modified later into chief, elders, and educated young men. As a belief it was no more naive than current dogma about the efficacy of mass participation under guidance of a single party or a corrective army. In effect, however, the colonial scaffolding of administration became the most substantial part of the postcolonial state, and the rather timid attempts at social engineering by well-intentioned colonial officials in their local districts have their parallel today in the bid by zealous nationalists to restructure local society—an ambition that does not envisage any serious disturbance of the incumbent party or military government. (In that respect they are much like the colonial officials who were wholly in favor of reform, including political reform, providing it did not encompass their own demise.) In practice, the primary obstacles in East Africa to such attempts to change a fundamentally peasant society remain much the same today as they were earlier: the vagaries of rain, wind, soil, disease; the balance between food and cash crops; recalcitrant farmers; blockheaded administrators; and the lack of bargaining power on the part of the local government in relation to distant markets. Yet there is the double dilemma today to which there were no exact parallels in the colonial period, namely the pretense of nationalist governments that they are able to administer more than they can manage, and the damage of political dissension at a national level. The first half of the problem can be easily stated. It is that the administrative incapacity of the East African governments may be among the chief impediments to their wish to plan.[9] The second dilemma—that there is no fixed and certain location of political power at the center—is still more critical. It is not that East African leaders have been unaware of the problem. They could hardly be so. The major difficulty has been to choose a satisfactory structure of government which could at the very least continue the excolonial administration by other means. The precariousness of their rule was presented in startling fashion in January 1964 when sections of the now national armies, formed out of the East African King's African Rifles, mutinied. A British task force was in the Indian Ocean and obligingly put down the rebellions, whereupon the independence of the new states was restarted, so to speak, by outside help. But each of the three governments has had the task of coping, by their own efforts, with the general question of political security.

During the immediate postindependence years, for example, Milton Obote feared the consequence of excessive competition between rival communities in Uganda. How could a government in Kampala be formed and survive which did not offend powerful local interests by appearing closer to one community than to another?

If the pull of the tribal force is allowed to develop, the unity of the country will be endangered. To reduce it to its crudest form, the pull of that tribal force does not accept Uganda as one country, does not accept the people of Uganda as belonging to one country, does not accept the National Assembly as a national institution but as an assembly of peace conference delegates and tribal diplomatic and legislative functionaries and looks at the Government of Uganda as a body of umpires or referees in some curious game of "Tribal Development Monopoly."[10]

Sensible comments. But the remedies adopted by Obote were an extraordinary case of a cure being worse than the disease. He did not try to balance out his opponents, or to moderate conflict, but attempted rather to destroy his critics and bolster his own position with a mixture of armed force and socialist rhetoric. He may possibly have believed that tribalism on the scale presented in Uganda was an exaggerated colonial-based phenomenon: but he was to discover, at the cost almost of his life, that such seemingly contrived groups, once formed, have a

E Pluribus Plures

disturbing ability to take on a life of their own; tribal kingdoms claim to be states, chiefdoms turn into parties, segmentary clan groups join together for political ends.

Obote began in fine style. A referendum in 1964 on the question of the lost counties brought their transfer from Buganda (by his own prime-ministerial order against the president) to Bunyoro. Thereafter, however, troubles multiplied. Southern Sudanese rebels, Tutsi refugees, Congolese guerrillas began to cross the borders north, south, and west. The smuggling of arms and gold gave credence to rumors of government corruption, and in February 1964 Obote abandoned all attempts to play any game but force. He arrested his own Cabinet Ministers, suspended the constitution, abolished the federal status of the kingdoms, and established a General Service Department of surveillance under Akeno Adoko, his cousin and fellow Lango tribesman. When the Buganda Lukiko (Assembly) tried to exclude his government from its territory, Obote turned to the army, which took the Kabaka's palace by direct assault, inflicting severe casualties. In that storming of the hill, the soldier Idi Amin distinguished himself. The Kabaka escaped into exile and died there.[11] His kingdom was divided under a second constitution promulgated in 1969 which forbade all opposition parties. Obote's Uganda People's Congress (UPC) had been elected to office in 1962 prior to independence on a narrow majority vote.[12] Now it attempted to monopolize power on its own authority, on the basis of a Common Man's Charter which offered African Socialism and a complicated electoral system.[13] Elections were promised for 1971 but an assassination attempt (by a Muganda) wounded Obote. He recovered, went to the Singapore Commonwealth Conference to inveigh against British arms sales to South Africa, and (it is said) left orders for the dismissal of Amin, whose growing power in the army he very much feared. But, like the bear who was given a pill, Amin blew first. A coup d'état got rid of the UPC and the new constitution, shifting the basis of power not only from civilian to military rule, but away from the Langi and Acholi groups around Obote and away from Buganda. Very likely it was fortunate for Obote that he *was* out of the country, since he is still alive, in exile in Dar es Salaam, unlike the 100,000 or more whom Amin is said to have put to death.

E Pluribus Plures

Amin, one might say, is a black Leviathan without Hobbes' assurance of the ruler as protector. Power rides naked through Uganda under the muzzle of a gun. An enlisted rifleman in the King's African Rifles in 1946, Amin was a corporal in 1948 and Uganda heavyweight boxing champion in 1953. He was commissioned on the eve of independence, despite the fact that the colonial government in Kenya wanted to try him for murder after the discovery of the mutilated bodies of a number of Turkana tribesmen in the area formerly patrolled by Amin's platoon. (Obote refused to hand him over to the authorities in Nairobi.) When Sir Walter Coutts was Governor of Uganda, he warned against Amin: Obote did not take the advice. By 1970 the small army which had numbered 1,200 men at independence had grown to 20,000. A year later, Brigadier Okoya had been murdered, Brigadier Opolot had been moved out of direct command, and Amin was in full control, defensively protected by Nubian soldiers and those of the Kwakwa and related tribes of his own West Nile district, acclaimed at first by those who looked to the army to suppress the banditry of Obote's last year in office.[14] Those around Amin are no better, though perhaps no worse, than he. They are Moslem peasant soldiers, promoted rapidly from the ranks, cruelly opposed to any rival community, bloody enough to murder anyone who confronts their rule, whether it is the chief justice or the vice-chancellor of the university or the ordinary citizen, and clever enough to balance one tribal community against another or Catholic against Protestant, with the full brunt of the attack falling on the Langi and Acholi. The shade of Mutesa must look with special irony on the quarrels and blood feuds of his supplanters. Asians, too, have felt Amin's power, being summarily robbed and evicted from Uganda in 1972 and having to wander the developed world for asylum.[15] But Amin himself is not free from threats and plots against him within his own armed forces. For all its outward show, it must be a life of brutal fear bolstered by quick revenge.

Neither Kenya nor Tanzania has suffered as cruelly, although the Revolutionary Council in Zanzibar under Abeid Karume, who was also First Vice-President of the United Republic of Tanzania, ran Uganda a close second in the ferocity of its control prior to his assassination. In Kenya, Kikuyu dominance under the huge paternal shadow of Kenyatta has helped to bring

E Pluribus Plures

power and authority together within the central quadrant that is the heart of the country. Like the Ivory Coast on the other side of the continent, Kenya is very much the colonial administrative state nationalized under elite control on a widening industrial base. The move toward single-party rule after independence by the elision of KANU and KADU and the suppression of the regional councils in December 1964 was paralleled by the Africanization of the administrative structure of colonial times, and both brought sharp criticism from those who disliked the concentration of power in that particular form. The non-Kikuyu were suspicious; the politically left among the educated elite raised cries of neocolonialism.

The road to unity was rough for those who objected to its direction. Within a few years of independence, divisions reappeared. Odinga was forced out of the vice-presidency in 1966 and joined forces with the Kikuyu Bildad Kaggia and others to form a more radical movement, the Kenya People's Union. He was later replaced as vice-president by Arap Moi, the non-Kikuyu, Kalenjin-supported leader.* Accused of obtaining financial help from communist China, Odinga charged the government with elitism: whatever independence for Kenya might mean for the few, he said, it was *Not Yet Uhuru* for the many.[16] Then in July 1969 Mboya was assassinated by a Kikuyu. Bildad Kaggia moved back to KANU; Odinga (though he had been opposed to his fellow Luo tribesman, Mboya) retained a personal hold within his own Nyanza province, but he was pushed into the political wilderness. "It was fairly clear," writes Colin Leys, "that after three years of almost complete political frustration even the KPU leaders found the ideology of tribalism hard to resist."[17] Nevertheless, when, in the ugly dissension between Kikuyu and

---

*The pattern of tribalism in Kenya is broadly as follows: Kikuyu, 2.2 million; Luo, 1.5 million; Luhya, 1.5 million; Kamba, 1.2 million; Kalenjin, 1.2 million; other, 2.4 million (of whom no group exceeds 3/4 million). These tribal communities have many of the characteristics of party groups, which, based on traditional allegiances and drawn together by colonial rule, are now rivals for control of the postcolonial state. Kenya is likely always to be centered on the Kikuyu, who have nonetheless to act in association with one or another of their tribally opposed neighbors in order to retain their dominant position. Tribal politics are very far from the traditional patterns of life, but they are no less real for that.

Luo which followed Mboya's death, there were demonstrations against Kenyatta in the local Luo capital of Kisumu, the KPU was banned and Odinga was detained. The Asian community, too, came under attack. A Trade Licensing Act confined areas of domestic business to citizens, the effect being to squeeze out the many thousand Asians, some 60 percent of the total, who had not adopted Kenya nationality.

Perhaps one should add that Kenya has always had a heady flavor, attractive to many, repugnant to others. Perhaps it is the altitude. Excitement has had to live with extremism, beauty with violence. The early settlers under men like Lord Delamere were often eccentric. (There is a pithy saying that Kenya was "a place in the sun for shady people," and the very representative view, in respect to British exservicemen—that "Kenya was for officers, Rhodesia for NCOs.") It is easy to see Kenyatta, Oginga Odinga, and many of the younger politicians as being in a line of political descent in that vein: Odinga, the Luo aristocrat in support of ex-Mau Mau (Kikuyu) detainees; Kenyatta, the former detainee and social anthropologist, whose book *Facing Mount Kenya*, based on his London Ph.D. thesis, is still very readable,[18] defender of female circumcision, an uncrowned King at Court in modern Kenya, and an old-fashioned socialist in charge of a full-blooded capitalist economy—there is something very British in *that*. But there is also a violent, corrupt side to Kenya's political life and its parliament, press, and high-quality administration. In the early months of 1975, for example, there were murderous bomb explosions in Nairobi and Mombassa; and in March that year there was the *cause célèbre* of the murder of J. M. Kariuki, a junior minister, former Mau Mau detainee and Kikuyu of the Fort Hall–Nyeri group. Critical from time to time of the government, he had tried to champion the poor and pull down the proud. When he died, public anger ran wide. The report of the Select Committee of Parliament, which inquired into his death, appeared in June, and it not only accused the police of trying to cover up the crime, but charged the Administration with complicity. The previous month the government had established a committee to look into corruption and nepotism (including tribalism), but when it became clear that its findings would be of a very general nature only, the majority in parliament would have none of it; they wanted their own committee and detailed individual investigations. (It was, one may remember, the year of Watergate.) They were warned off by Kenyatta, and by October the following year the revolt was suppressed. Jean Marie Seroney, the deputy speaker, and Martin Shikuku, a former Minister, were held in detention and so, later, were three other MPs; the press was disciplined by the dismissal of the European editor of the *Standard*; strikes were forbidden; and the university was put under restraint. In such times, men have to be very bold to act. Yet there are such critics still within the party and parliament.[19] The broad grounds of their accusations are always corruption in high places and land hunger among the destitute: there is too much private wealth conspicuously displayed, and too few safety valves for dissent. Kenya is, after all, very much a capitalist country of the *nouveau riches*. The 1950's were ugly, the 1960's were a time of great expansion under favorable circumstances as land became available and Africans displaced Europeans throughout the country and in the public service; but the 1970's have been a decade full of uncertainty, not least because a great taboo is rigorously imposed on debate over Kenyatta's successor.[20] The "land of sunshine" is very much therefore a country of shadows. And who can say whether the control and authority wielded by Kenyatta can be peacefully transmitted to others?[21]

Still, Kenya is not Amin's Uganda: far from it. Despite the imbalance in wealth locally, and the corruption, the economy has continued to grow. There is also a collective strength in KANU's base of Kikuyu-plus-alliances, which does not look as if it will be easily lost. Politics, too, are far from dead. As early as 1971 Odinga was out of detention and had rejoined KANU, although still banned from standing for election to parliament or for the vice-presidency again. When elections were held in October 1974, there were 737 KANU candidates for the 158 contested seats and 88 of the sitting MPs were defeated, among them four cabinet ministers (including Dr. Njoroge Mungai, the foreign minister) and thirteen junior ministers. (Kenyatta was returned unopposed as an MP, and uncontested as the presidential candidate, to begin his third five-year term in November 1974.) Moreover, throughout the disputes that followed the election, the Kikuyu center has held in relation to parliament, party, and the administration, while Kenyatta, hero of the war and fortune's son, still marches indefatigably on (although march perhaps may be too vigorous a description for a leader now well into his eighties).

There has been a similar continuity in Tanzania, although there was a brief period immediately after independence when Nyerere abruptly resigned as prime minister to make way for his deputy, Rashid Kawawa, until the introduction of the republican constitution in December 1962, when he was elected president. Was the sudden resignation early in 1962 a result of moral dissatisfaction with the ruling TANU party or a loss of nerve, or was it a calculated maneuver to balance left and right within the trade unions and party? Skepticism and admiration have fought a running battle over Tanzania's experience of single-party rule, flanked by extremes of opposition on one side and adulation on the other. A net of obfuscation, too, has been thrown over the past decade by western observers, cast by devotees of American political science and woven with Marxist rope. Whereas a skillful argument has been mounted over Kenya with respect to theories of development, it is often the facts that are subject to debate in Tanzania. There is a parliament, but is it really an assembly of any worth? There are elections, but do they serve any purpose? There is a party, but what shape, function, and substance does it possess?

The stated purpose is clearer than its practice. Tanzania is a very poor, very rural, African country—among the poorest in the world. It is often unable to feed itself or to pay for the minimum level of imports needed to maintain the state. Colonial rule and settler enterprise in a fertile country gave Kenya a considerable economic base, reinforced by an energetic spate of social engineering as the result of the emergency: but nothing at all comparable took place in Tanzania. What could not be continued, therefore, since there was so little to carry forward, brought the search for innovation. Tanzania's main advantage is its relative freedom from ethnic conflict, not because there is any strong sense of national identity but because its local communities are many and dispersed. There is also a lingua franca in Swahili. Nevertheless, above the broad plain of rural poverty, there is the familiar hierarchy of privilege—urban workers, traders, teachers, clerks, party members, party officials, party leaders, parliamentary party members, presidential party executives. For

Tanzania is preeminently a party state, and therein lies the argument. Perhaps the best way to show the width of its debate is through contrasted quotations, although one may also note in passing Cranford Pratt's observation that "the most prosperous farmers in Rungwe District would be unlikely to earn a net income as high as the wages of the lowest paid functionary in the civil service."[22]

Nyerere has been, above all, a teacher, a mwalimu. *He is a teacher of a special sort. He is a teacher of morality.*[23]

The degree to which academic writers have succeeded in mystifying themselves about Tanzania is breathtaking. To give but a few examples: education for self-reliance, which bears more than a passing resemblance to Bantu education in South Africa, has been described as a "revolution by education"; resettlement of offenders, a device for eliminating "undesirables" by incarcerating them permanently after their prison sentences have been completed, is a "socialist innovation in penology"; corruption and mismanagement in the state sector are caused by "imperialist agents"; discussion of a burgeoning archipelago of detention centres, and of the appalling and brutal conditions in these centres, is the work of "spies and saboteurs."[24]

Ujamaa, then, or "familyhood" describes our socialism. It is opposed to capitalism, which seeks to build a happy society on the basis of the exploitation of man by man; and it is equally opposed to doctrinaire socialism which seeks to build its happy society on a philosophy of inevitable conflict between man and man. We, in Africa, have no more need of being "converted" to socialism than we have of being taught democracy. Both are rooted in our past.[25]

Here in this Union conditions may arise in which it is better that ninety-nine innocent people should suffer temporary detention than that one possible traitor should wreck the nation . . . Development must be considered first . . . Our question with regard to any matter—even the issue of fundamental freedom—must be, "How does this affect the progress of the Development Plan?"

The last quotation is from Nyerere's "extraordinarily honest address,"[26] given at the opening in 1964 of the University College in Dar es Salaam when he was seeking to justify "the introduction of a law which gives the government the power to detain people without trial. I have myself signed detention orders."[27] In respect to the priority given by the party to the Development Plan, one is always reminded a little of the story told of Lenin:

Once when hunting in the woods near Moscow, he was approached by an old man who was picking mushrooms. "How are things, Grandpa?," asked Lenin. "Have you found enough mushrooms?" "To the devil with the Bolsheviks!" answered the old man. "Under their rule even mushrooms don't grow." "What's the matter? Don't you like the new government?" "Why should I? They've stolen and destroyed everything." "Wait, wait, old man," replied Lenin, "when we build our factories we will have enough."[28]

Such are the promises of the revolution of expectations in the face of peasant fears, and the story (suitably adapted and without the terror as yet of Stalin's collectivization) might easily have come from Tanzania.

The conflict of views, as in the contradictions of Nyerere himself, may well baffle the more distant observer. Cranford Pratt, who was once principal of the University College in Dar es Salaam, believes that Nyerere has a vision "of the transition to a socialist strategy" whereby "participation must mean active and direct popular involvement in politics including the regular, recurrent choice of political leaders through democratic elections."[29] John Hatch writes that the publication of "additional guidelines" to Nyerere's advocacy of African Socialism "immediately aroused workers, students and some peasants to attack authoritarian and unnecessarily bureaucratic attitudes amongst party or government officials."[30] But the local publication (by Pratt's former university) on the 1970 elections is at best ambivalent, at worst painfully labored, in respect to such virtues.[31] For example: "The Party failed to make campaign meetings a political classroom [since] at most meetings the people lost the sense of participation because they were not allowed to question the candidate." Similarly we are told very ambiguously that "the pattern of centralised control over the political process seeks deliberately to avoid open discussions of divisive issues while at the same time seeking public support for such issues." Pratt, too, argues that where there is coercion it is "primarily nationalist not socialist . . . an expression of an impatient nationalism not a coercive socialism."[32] But the distinction cannot be very comforting to those being coerced, whether it is the peasant who is forced into a socialist village settlement (*ujamaa vijilini*) or a trade unionist restricted to a remote area of the country because of his opposition to the party.

The source for much of this curious mixture of qualified admiration and exasperated criticism lies not only in the sympathetic magic of the words employed as incantations—socialism, participation, mobilization—but in the unusual features of the single-party institutions that are used to govern the country. The party has encroached on other organs of the state to the point where its senior members are given official precedence over both the administration and parliament. So far so good, as a Marxist-socialist system of control, but there are also elections, held in two stages, the first being a party primary to select the two candidates (neither more nor less) who may stand in each constituency; and the effect has been rather non-Marxist. Balloting has actually led to the defeat of members of the government as well as back-benchers in parliament in the three elections of 1965, 1970, and 1975.[33] There are also presidential elections, but they are largely ritualistic, committed to the reelection of Nyerere. In the last contest in 1975 he was returned with more than 90 percent of the vote.

The origins of this strange mode of control date from 1962, when a republican constitution was introduced, and from a time when debate in the national executive of the party was more lively than in the assembly, which, designed in theory for a two-party system, was dominated in practice by TANU. A legalized one-party state on the basis of a close identity between parliament and party might, it was hoped, breathe life into politics. Whereas Nkrumah, in Ghana, was content to let the single party stifle the electoral system by having all its candidates elected unopposed, Nyerere appointed a commission of inquiry into how best a single-party state might be made to work. It was late in reporting, and when its findings appeared other ideas were also being debated. In 1967 the Arusha Declaration was published, proclaiming the need for socialism, self-reliance, and equality and for TANU as its main instrument of control. Within these general formulations there were specific aims, including *ujamaa vijilini*, or village self-help on a community basis.

Considerable care, therefore, has gone into the handling of political affairs by Nyerere and TANU, more perhaps by the former than the latter. There are strong tendencies in a contrary direction, understandably enough in a poor country where material possessions are highly prized if only because they are hard to come by. There is a subdued capitalist ethic among party and nonparty members alike which struggles to embody itself in individual practice, just as there is a full-blooded socialist program seeking to find a lodgment in local society. Who knows how long the present experiment will last? It is dependent on one man, structurally, philosophically, politically, and, very likely, morally; and what Tanzania may become after Nyerere is anyone's guess. There is also the danger that TANU will settle into an ossified bureaucracy, reducing its elective base and maximizing its powers of control. A party that genuinely attempts to serve the national interest may easily end by being the chief interest served. There has already been a shift toward authoritarianism, whether as the result of attempts at "villagization"—the regrouping of homesteads in communal villages—or by bringing the economy under a much greater degree of state control.[34] There have also been internal party disputes, including the hurried departure into exile in October 1969 of the former general secretary, Oscar Kambona, and the detention of trade-unionists, university students, and army officers.[35] To these local tribulations has to be added an uneasiness about the country's neighbors, whether it is in relation to Kenya over the East African Community or to Uganda over border quarrels.

Still, there are elections, there is a constitution, and there is a parliament. Nyerere, too, is still very much in control. Of course, the National Assembly is not representative in a literal sense, and it is a matter of concern to many observers that its members are *élitiste*—"rather unrepresentative of the typical Tanzanian peasant and ... set apart from him. ... There is a vast difference in socioeconomic terms between the educated M.P.s and the adult population."[36] But it would be very surprising if that were not so. It is not easy to imagine a parliament of peasants, or to see what use such a gathering would be. It is also said that the Assembly is the party's lap dog: no bite and little growl.[37] But that there are—for the present at least—elections, however limited, and a parliament, however docile, is surely better than the alternative. Being an old-fashioned libertarian I believe with Edmund Burke that "as long as the solid and well-disposed forms of this constitution remain, there ever is within Parliament itself a power of renovating its principles and effecting a self-reformation, which no other plan of Government has ever contained."[38] Whether the Tanzanian elite will see it that way, and whether the form of the constitution is solid and well-disposed, are difficult questions. The chances of some kind of representative, parliamentary system continuing in Tanzania may not be good, but, they are not, perhaps, nil.

During these years the East African Community began to crumble. The degree of disintegration is now very advanced. The triumvirate of the three presidents has not met since 1971, an eloquent comment on the collapse of an association to which the British gave a good deal of attention and for which Nyerere was at one time ready to consider the delay of his country's independence in the hope of being able to move forward on a joint basis. Kenya, too, was originally pledged to the aim of "political union with the neighbouring countries of Tanganyika, Uganda and Zanzibar."[39] Yet the present Community is itself the diminished outcome, under a new treaty of association in 1967, of the earlier Common Services Organization. Because of disputes between the three capitals over the advantages of union, there was a dispersal of the organization away from its Nairobi base. The headquarters were established at Arusha in Tanzania, the Harbours Corporation went to Dar es Salaam, Posts and Telegraphs to Kampala, and so on. But a formal devolution of institutions could not solve the underlying problem of the disparity of wealth between the three states. In the past, it had been distrust of white settlers in Kenya that kept Uganda and Tanganyika at a distance. Now it was the fact that Kenya was much the strongest of the three economically, and it was feared that to him that hath, still more would be given.[40] Kenya manufacturers, for example, were capturing the common market at the expense of Tanzanian and Ugandan industry, and quarrels developed over tariffs, freight charges, and the issue of industrial location. Kenya had an expanding mixed economy which continued the pattern of the 1950's and '60's, and Tanzania was increasingly—if not very successfully—committed to a "Socialism in one country" policy of self-reliance and nationalization under party control. Uganda was a still more difficult case, being an inland state dependent on the line of rail to Mombassa. Amin threatened war against both neighbors, not least because he owed Kenya a great deal of money and because irregular forces, nationally loyal to Obote in exile in Dar es Salaam, began to cross his border in August 1972. The end of the Community, which is now well in sight, is likely to be precipitated by a lack of funds for its institutions, since without the transfer of payments to its offices salaries cannot be paid nor services provided. The dissolution of almost every form of interterritorial unity has been clearly demonstrated over the past decade. Each government has gone its own way in trade, banking, and communications. The University of East Africa has been reduced to its three former constituent colleges, East African Airways has been grounded in an argument over payments, debts have accumulated with the International Monetary Fund, nonconvertible currencies have been maintained, and the citizens of one country are harried by the governments of the other two. The unit state, therefore, has triumphed over an idealism of colonial origins and pan-African sentiment.

These difficult economic conflicts would almost certainly have bedeviled whatever arrangements had been decided between the extremes of a full federal structure and total separation; but politics, and in particular the politics of ideology, have been critically decisive. Each of the governments has been absorbed in its own local apparatus of control like a captive who makes his prison cell his world. But the prison is not in this respect the colonial past, which could have carried the three states either toward federation or, as has happened, toward separation. No doubt the latter route was easier—breaking down is always simpler than putting together—but the former was never impossible. Unfortunately, however, the practical obstacles to the coordination of services and institutions were made more difficult by contrasted ideologies of which the philosophy, if one may besmirch the term, of military government in Uganda has been only the most glaring point of difference. Contrary to those who once saw socialism as an international brotherhood of equality, it is capitalism (no doubt with an attendant market force of control) which has spread its nets of trade and finance across frontiers. Socialist policies have resulted in autarchy. Kenya reaches out to its neighbors. Tanzania turns in on itself in self-reliance, unless one makes an exception of the union of Zanzibar and Tanzania, and even there the lack of cooperation has been more striking than the unity. Nominally, of course, both Kenya and Tanzania are socialist countries, the latter by Nyerere's program of *Ujamaa*, the former by its declaration of principles in the government white paper on Socialism. In practice, Tanzania uses the party-state to direct its urban and rural economy, whereas Kenya, though it has a single-party government, is an administratively controlled state with a well-developed export sector of the economy to which the indigenization of farming and trade has been energetically devoted. If the unpleasant image of one is the party *apparatchik*, that of the other is the get-rich *bourgeois gentilhomme*. Tanzania is the captive of itself, Kenya of an international economy, but at least the prison of Kenya's dependency has international dimensions. *Cui bono?* That is a complicated matter of interpretation which cannot yet be answered.[41]

There is, finally, the intrusion of interests external to East Africa, including the Horn of Africa, where Somalia and Ethiopia, and more distantly the Sudan, have turned for help to outside powers. Who is to blame—the USSR, the United States, Libya, and Israel, who come bearing gifts? Or the governments of the African states that invite such offers? One has simply to ask the questions to know the answer: both. If it were not for the claims of the Somali government to incorporate within a larger state the Somali-speaking peoples of Djibouti, the Ogaden province of Ethiopia, and the Northern Frontier District of Kenya,[42] or if it were not for the recent civil war in the Sudan, or quarrels between Kampala and Nairobi or Dar es Salaam and Kampala, the need for arms and money would be less pressing. But also if it were not for Soviet interests in the Indian Ocean, or American interests in oil and a fear of Soviet policies, or Arab hostility to Israel, and Israel's determination to weaken the ring of encircling countries, there would be less suspense.

E Pluribus Plures

The most dangerous point of future conflict may be the area of greatest poverty and vulnerability: Djibouti. Although quite arid, and empty of resources, this new republic controls the seaport and the terminus of the line of rail from Addis Ababa to the coast. The French abandoned their sovereignty in June 1977 but offered protection for a further two years. And help will surely be needed. The port is critically important to Ethiopia now that its other outlets at Assab and Massawa on the Red Sea are threatened by the Eritrean Liberation Front. But if Ethiopia's interests are primarily economic, those of Somalia are political and irredentist, a claim symbolized by the five stars of the Somali flag denoting the former Italian and former British Somaliland, the Ogaden area of southern Ethiopia, the northern district of Kenya—and Djibouti.[43] The USSR began to consolidate its hold on Somalia but then extended its help to Ethiopia, to the annoyance of President Siad Barre in Mogadishu, who saw his former ally arming his worst enemy. The Arab world has for centuries been interested in a Muslim "Horn of Africa." The United States is uncertain what to do, now that it has lost its influence in Ethiopia. The East African coast and its islands have been quickly drawn therefore into potential conflict abroad, linked always to more distant threats. During the 1960's and '70's the East Germans arrived in Zanzibar, the Chinese built the railway from Dar es Salaam to Lusaka and the North-South highway in Somalia, the Russians moved heavily into Aden, and the Americans increased their hold on the Indian Ocean base at Diego Garcia. The Ethopian government took arms first from Washington and then from Moscow; Fidel Castro appeared on the scene; the Libyans replaced the Israelis as suppliers of arms to Amin; there was Arab help for the Eritreans; and Israeli commandos landed at Entebbe—an extraordinary array of interests, quite apart from the busy daily concerns throughout East Africa of European, American, and Japanese businessmen.

No future line of events can be traced from these shifting patterns of conflict, nor is there any clear way ahead for any of the African governments involved. East African unity is too bold a concept, the precolonial units too precarious a venture, for those who are struggling to retain what they have inherited. In the face of such doubts one can readily understand why the present leaders of Kenya, Uganda, and Tanzania cling so fearfully, amid so much that is unsure, to the colonial state as a focus of national interest while trying to build within its administrative framework their own structure of party or army power. The currents of contemporary history are all awry. Better, it must seem, to hold fast to what exists at a national level—particularly if it still offers, however uncertainly, a mode of control to those who are endeavoring to seize hold of their colonial past.

4. The Middle Zone

From Zaire and Angola on the Atlantic Coast, across the inland states of Zambia, Rhodesia, and Malawi to Mozambique on the Indian Ocean, lies the vast area of central Africa, linked not by a shared colonial past, as in East Africa, but by a residual colonialism of a rather different sort. We can employ the notion of alternative maps of finance, trade, and communication—maps which place restraints on governments, of whatever political complexion they may be. Less precise, but hardly less real, are those shifting frontiers of belief which confine men's minds, bounded by race or ideology; and they too need to be considered. But within the middle zone there is also a failed British map—a double failure, of a more familiar kind. The original intention of adventurers like Cecil Rhodes at the turn of the century had been to bring as large a part as they could of the whole of southern and central Africa under the one flag, reaching north from the Cape of Good Hope. But as early as 1910 the vision began to fade. The Union of South Africa stopped at the Limpopo River, although it was to be enlarged in practice by the addition of South West Africa in 1919, while to the north there remained separate colonies under Portuguese control in Angola and Mozambique, a Belgian administration in the Congo and Rwanda and Burundi, the self-governing Colony of Southern Rhodesia under settler control, and the two northern British protectorates Nyasaland and Northern Rhodesia. The British also refused to transfer control of the three High Commission Territories of Bechuanaland (now Botswana), Basutoland (now Lesotho), and Swaziland to the South African Government.[1] A generation of time elapsed. Then in 1953 the conservative government in London gave approval to a Central African Federation of the two Rhodesias and Nyasaland. That, too, collapsed a decade later. Northern Rhodesia and Nyasaland became the independent states of Zambia and Malawi,

The Middle Zone

and Rhodesia (now often called Zimbabwe) moved toward its unilateral declaration of independence in November 1965. Belgium had already abandoned its rule, while to the west and east guerrilla forces were beginning to take the long march to Marxist rule under the MPLA in Angola and the Frelimo in Mozambique.[2] A huge jigsaw puzzle of broken pieces.

Throughout these central regions, history has pulled in opposite directions: history as economics toward collaboration, history as politics toward separation. Such is the general theme of the argument which follows. The Central African Federation was (among many other things) a limited attempt at congruence, to join the two together, but the scheme broke down on the conflict of race. And even had that fundamental divide not been there, it is open to doubt whether there were any regional structures of control—any political or constitutional map, that is—capable of preventing the 1953 Federation from dissolving into individual states with distinct ideologies and different standards of living. If to that triple variety of a half-socialist Zambia, an authoritarian Malawi, and a white-minority-controlled Rhodesia we add the Marxist areas of former Portuguese rule and the troubled area of Zaire, it seems probable that, however unified the imperialism of trade would like to be, it will be out of joint for many years to come with the inherited politics of colonialism. In the kingdom of political control, economic determinants are usually subordinate. But the balance in central Africa is much more even, tilting first this way and then that, so strong are the economic pressures for collaboration. In a sense, the problem has become one of dissociation and reengagement: dispensing with the colonial maps and drawing new directions of a nationalist kind. But the first is difficult and the second at best uncertain. For those who like theory with their argument, these central African countries have also tested the problem of dependency in the context of "trying to do something about it." The result is not quite perhaps as ineffective as the theorists sometimes suggest. There have been changes of direction, in politics as well as in trade and communications, although none of the countries—unless it be the two former Portuguese territories under what must be a very primitive version of Marxism—has produced that structural transformation of the political economy which alone is said to herald an authentic revolution when everyone will be much happier. In general, the examples to be looked at bear out the not very startling truth of the argument that in a world of divided labor political change is easier than economic transformation.[3]

Look first at the economic map and at the contours of finance and trade which run across it. There is a central heartland of copper, diamonds, coal, and chrome (plus much else besides) for which the arteries of rail and road reach out to the ports and overseas markets. The surrounding countryside tries to feed the urban population that clusters along the line of rail and contributes its own exports in the form of meat and tobacco, coffee, tea, and maize. Power lines also cross the frontiers, as from the Kariba Dam across the Zambesi between Rhodesia and Zambia, or from the damming of the Cunene river in Angola to supply not only local industries but power and water to neighboring Namibia. There is also the huge Cabora Bassa Dam in Mozambique, the largest hydroelectric generating station in Africa—double the size of Kariba, 70 percent bigger than Aswan—which sells its power to South Africa; a capitalist transaction, one might add, profitably conducted today by President Machel's government in place of the Portuguese Administration, whose decision to carry out the project was once the target of a good deal of anticolonial opposition. Now presumably there are grounds for gratitude.[4]

These economic charts of trade flows, migration patterns, power grids, and road and rail networks cannot be ignored by the governments that come within their range. Mines may be nationalized, but socialist copper and Marxist gold still have to be dug out and transported, just as the power grid has to be operated and irrigation channels kept open if people are to be fed, factories maintained, the shops supplied with goods, and services provided. Frontiers have to be crossed, since the main areas of mineral wealth in this immensely rich heartland are scattered through four or five countries: around Kolwezi and Lumbumbashi (the former Elizabethville) in the Katanga/Shaba province of Zaire; at Broken Hill, Kitwe, Ndola, and Luanshya along the Copper Belt of Zambia; in the high-quality coal and chrome of Rhodesia; within Botswana, whose mineral wealth is only now beginning to be measured fully; throughout Namibia, on which Providence has bestowed (or inflicted?) a plurality of people and

The Middle Zone

an extraordinary range of mineral deposits; and, preeminently, in the industrial/mining complex of the Rand in the South African Republic.

If such goods are to be exploited and shipped to where they are wanted, labor must be recruited and the road and rail links kept open to the coast. Until a decade or so ago there was an intricate network of labor migration throughout the area, financed and controlled by the South African, Rhodesian, and colonial-administered governments. Malawi, Mozambique, Lesotho in particular, and the rural areas of Zaire, Zambia, and Rhodesia drew much of their local wealth from earnings and remittances by those who journeyed into the urban centers to work as miners or clerks or skilled artisans of one kind or another. They also drew revenue—Botswana and Mozambique especially—as transit areas through which the chrome, iron, diamonds, and copper traveled by truck and wagon to the exit ports at Lobito in Angola, at Durban, East London, and Cape Town in South Africa, and at Maputo (formerly Lourenço Marques) and Beira in Mozambique. How marvellous were the ways of capitalist enterprise and how tortuous! Between Maputo and Beira in Mozambique, for example, the railway still runs for part of its way outside the country through Rhodesia. But the major line of rail in southern and central Africa ran from Durban through Natal and the Transvaal northward, under Rhodesian management through Botswana into Rhodesia, then up over the great railway bridge (high above the Victoria Falls) across the Zambesi river into Zambia; out again from Lusaka through the Copper Towns into Zaire, when it became the *Chemin de Fer du Bas Congo et Katanga* until it entered Portuguese territory, where wood-burning locomotives carried the freight through central Angola as the Benguela railway, owned by a British company, to the Atlantic coast at Lobito. Between Rhodesia and Zambia, European engine drivers would hand over the controls to Africans; but the lines of rail and the goods they carried belonged to the great world of capitalist production and consumption far beyond the continent, a world which sent its own products, including petroleum, into southern and central Africa back along the same route, a world dominated by familiar names—the British South Africa Company, de Beers, Anglo-American, Union Minière, Metal Climax, Rio Tinto-Zinc.

The Middle Zone

There were other links in this marvelously clumsy chain of profit and control. For example, a road-rail-lake route ran north by rail from the Zambian Copper Belt to the landing stage of Mapulungu at the southern end of Lake Tanganyika, then by steamer either to Kigoma on the east bank and by rail across Tanganyika to Dar es Salaam, or to Albertville on the western shore of the lake and along a rail spur to the main Congolese railway. The most powerful of the lake steamers was the Liembe, which had been assembled piece by piece in good German fashion prior to 1914, then sunk (in good British tradition) during World War I, salvaged in the palmy days of peace, and put to work again over the next half century: an appropriate symbol, one might think, of the makeshift yet persistent European force that had to grapple not only with the problems of distance but with its own rivalries. There were roads, too: the Great North Road (a dirt track of a thousand miles or so) from Lusaka to Dar es Salaam, and a similarly misnamed Great East Road to the rail head at Salima on Lake Nyasa, where a single railway track ran due south through what is now Dr. Banda's country to join the line from Rhodesia at Biera in Mozambique.[5] The trunk roads were as unlike the Massachusetts Turnpike as the steamers and locomotives were unlike the freight liners of the St. Lawrence Seaway or British Rail or even Amtrak. Yet they kept the copper, gold, diamonds, and chrome moving out and the oil and manufactures moving in, the whole driving force of this early characteristic "imperialism without empire" being as Joseph Conrad described it at the beginning—"to tear treasure out of the bowels of the land was their desire, with no more moral purpose at the back of it than there is in burglars breaking into a safe"—until it was controlled and managed, with some mitigation of the brutality of the exploitation, by the assertion of colonial rule.

We have had to use the past tense because from the time of the breakup of the Central African Federation at the end of 1963 the problem facing its former member states and their more distant neighbors has been either that of wrenching the old pattern of communication into a new framework of trade or of denying its services to particular governments in order to exert political pressure by economic means. How difficult the latter exercise can be may be seen from the history of British

The Middle Zone

attempts at sanctions against Rhodesia after Ian Smith's declaration of independence in 1965, when a program conceived in terms of weeks is still being painfully implemented more than a decade later. But first we need to turn to the political map.

How strange it is! Zaire seems periodically to collapse—almost—yet is able neither to divide nor to unite its vast regions, like a huge encampment from which a sizable number of inhabitants try from time to time to distance themselves in order to rearrange their lives in a different setting. Repression lives close to anarchy, while the road to excess seems only to lead to greater excess. It is of course Conrad's *Heart of Darkness*. "Going up that river was like travelling back to the earliest beginnings of the world when vegetation rioted on the earth.... The reaches opened before us and closed behind, as if the forest had stepped leisurely across the water to bar our return. We penetrated deeper and deeper into the heart of darkness. It was very quiet there." Conrad made the thousand-mile journey upriver in 1890 from Matadi to what were then the Stanley Falls and back in "a little begrimed steamboat, like a sluggish beetle." "The subdued thundering mutter of the Stanley Falls hung in the heavy air of the last navigable reach of the Upper Congo." There was no haunting memory of achievement, "only the unholy recollection of a prosaic newspaper 'stunt' and the distasteful knowledge of the vilest scramble for loot that ever disfigured the history of human conscience."[6]

The vast region was precipitated into independence in June 1960 to avert a French Algeria or Dutch Indonesia. Slow at first, the Belgians then moved desperately fast. As late as 1955 in the Catholic journal *Conscience Africaine*, Van Bilson daringly put forward a proposal for self-government within thirty years, and was thought extreme. In December 1958, however, Nkrumah's Convention People's Party held the first All African People's Conference in Accra, at which Patrice Lumumba, a former railway clerk, represented his own *Mouvement National Congolais*; and in September the related Kongo people across the river in the French Congo voted in the referendum held by de Gaulle. The following year, in the main towns of the Belgian Congo, local elections were held from which a new spokesman appeared —Kasavubu. He was then the leader of the *Alliance des Bakongo* (Abako), which sought at first to reunite the ancient Kongo

Kingdom that had once extended its rule across both banks of the river: "Leopoldville, Brazzaville, Kwango, Angola and Pointe Noire formed in times past, for centuries, the united state of the Ancient Kingdom of the Congo ... divided in 1885 between France, Belgium and Portugal."[7] The ferment of an anticolonialism was beginning to work—it could hardly be seen as nationalsim in relation to the colonial empire of the whole country—and there were three days of fierce rioting by the military *Force Publique* in January 1960 in the capital. Embryonic parties came to birth and grew quickly with the help of rival leaders regionally based: Lumumba and Antoine Gizenga in Stanleyville (now Kisangani), Kasavubu in Leopoldville (now Kinshasa), Albert Kalonji in the diamond-rich south Kasai province, and Moise Tshombe in the copper area of Katanga around Elizabethville (now Lumbumbashi) as leader of the *Conféderation des associations tribales du Katanga* (CONAKAT). Regionalism had fed on tribalism, which turned to these local heroes for expression. A patched constitution for six regions brought an uneasy independence under a government that had Kasavubu as president and Lumumba as prime minister; it was formed a week before the final instruments transferring power were signed. Like a good bourgeois nation, the Belgians, almost as divided in Europe as those they had ruled overseas, prudently escaped the worst. The fighting came later, first by the *Force Publique*, which mutinied a month after independence, and then when Tshombe in Katanga and Kalonji in south Kasai proclaimed their own independence. Within twelve months the new republic had four governments—two outright secessionist movements and a disputed central government between rival claimants in Kisangani (Stanleyville) and Kinshasa (Leopoldville)—until the United Nations, brought in at the invitation of the Kinshasa government, restored a kind of order. Colonel Mobutu staged his first coup in 1961; Lumumba was murdered, and the whole territory was divided into a Federation of twenty-one states. Civilian leaders continued to rule uneasily in Mobutu's shadow, but there was civil war in the east under self-styled revolutionary leaders (helped for a time by the Chinese) and local rebellions in the provinces. Hammarsjkold died in an air crash, and United Nations forces eventually left the country in June 1964. By a strange sequence of events Tshombe then became prime minister

The Middle Zone

under Kasavubu in Kinshasa and invited back a number of Belgian and other expatriate administrators; Kasavubu dismissed Tshombe; and Major-General Mobutu deposed Kasavubu. Thereafter, from 1965, the country settled down to a decade of harsh and corrupt peace under the civilian/military leadership of President Mobutu Sese Seko.

The economy flourished, since Zaire has great resources; and Mobutu, despite his "revolution of authenticity" in the renaming of names, began to open the country to outside interests. At the end of 1975, the earlier nationalization measures were rescinded and the larger enterprises handed back to their former expatriate owners on a 40 percent ownership basis.[8] And feeling, no doubt, more secure at home, Mobutu ventured into foreign affairs, moving troops and irregular forces into Angola—encouraged, it is said, by the CIA—in support of the National Front for the Liberation of Angola (FNLA), whose leaders he had harbored against the MPLA. By early 1977, however, it was as if time had not simply stopped but turned back. Katanga, or "Shaba," was again a battlefield, its local forces in rebellion against Mobutu but assisted this time by Angola, and large tracts of Zaire were once more a

> *darkling plain*
> *Swept with confused alarms of struggle and fight*
> *Where ignorant armies clash by night.*

Further south and east of Zaire lie the three Central African states Zambia, Malawi, and Rhodesia. They are heirs of the 1953–63 attempt to unite economic advantage with political control. In effect, however, the former was as much open to doubt as the latter: dependence did not mean equal advantage, and there is some evidence to show that most of the anticipated benefits of federal unity were predicated on a profederal growth rate which actually declined after 1953.[9] The politics of partnership within the European-dominated structure turned out much as was expected: as critics said at the time, it was the partnership of the rider and the horse. But the worst problems in the tug and pull of politics and economics came not with the breakup of the Federation but after the declaration of independence by the Rhodesian Front government in 1965 and the

The Middle Zone

imposition of sanctions. The politics of race now began to destroy the economics of cooperation. And neither Zambia nor Malawi was well placed to take the strain. In many ways they were more vulnerable than Rhodesia itself, the actual target of the weapons used.

After a brief civil disobedience campaign of protest against the Federation, Zambia struggled into independence in October 1964, singularly ill-equipped to deal even with the problems of internal control. As uncertain in its way as Zaire, though on a much reduced scale, the difficulty facing its government in Lusaka has remained one of balance, both between the wealthy Copper Belt towns and the poorer rural areas, and between rival communities which use the regional structure of the country to press for a larger share of resources. Bemba, Lozi, Illa-Tonga, and Nyanja often see the central government as a kind of prize to be distributed among their own communities at the expense of others, as during the famous Central Committee elections for the ruling United National Independence Party at Mulungushi in August 1967 when an uneasy alliance of Bemba and Tonga clashed with an equally uncertain Nyanja-Lozi opposition.[10] The flag of secession was even raised at one point by the western Barotse province. In 1964 all the indices of political development were unfavorable—a nervous ruling party, a barely existent administrative cadre, and a pleasant, modest leader, Kenneth Kaunda, almost too nice for the job he thought he had to do.[11] "At independence," observed the Local Manpower Report a decade later, "the scarcity of educated manpower was extreme."[12] There were just over a hundred African graduates and scarcely more than a thousand certificated secondary school leavers. There was as heavy a reliance on senior expatriate administrators as there was on skilled expatriate miners. Moreover, road, rail, power, and labor patterns all led south across rebel Rhodesian territory into South Africa, or what was then still Portuguese Angola and Mozambique. No wonder the UNIP leaders were nervous. And there were domestic causes too: the African National Congress—the parent body from which Kaunda and others had broken away in 1959—was still strongly entrenched under the veteran leader Harry Nkumbula both in the south and in areas of the central province. After the Mulungushi election, for example, the Bemba temporarily had their way, whereupon not only the southern Ila-Tonga but the western Lozi area began to swing toward the ANC. Then Simon Kapwepwe, vice-president from 1967 to 1970 and a former foreign minister, broke with Kaunda to form a Bemba-dominated United Progressive Party.

To the east lies Malawi, so poor that it received direct British subsidies until 1973. It is very much "Dr. Banda's country," for it is he who dominates the political scene and, it is fair to say, it was he who was the chief agent in breaking up the Central African Federation. Malawi's enforced membership in 1953 was particularly resented, since the territory (as Nyasaland) had been kept free of Cecil Rhodes's British South Africa Company by the good offices of the Scottish Missions at the end of the nineteenth century and, despite a small community of settlers in the Shire Highlands, it had successfully resisted being drawn into closer association with the two Rhodesias. There was also a lingering tradition of militancy kept alive by memories of the brief rebellion against colonial rule staged by John Chilembwe in 1915. Federation was strongly opposed, therefore, and when the rather dormant Nyasaland African Congress, which had been drawn together in 1944, began to grow in membership, its local leader looked round for a national hero. Neither Henry Chipembere nor Kanyama Chiume quite fitted the bill. But Dr. Hastings Kumuzu Banda did, eminently so, notwithstanding an absence from the country as a medical practitioner in the United States, Britain, and Ghana for over forty years. He returned to Malawi and was immediately acclaimed as leader by the Congress. Locked up by the British after countrywide riots and a declaration of emergency in March 1959, his party banned, and a Royal Commission of Inquiry on its way to the capital, Banda was a national hero almost overnight. The Report of the Devlin Commission appeared later that year and was severely critical of the colonial administration. It noted that the local security forces had made unnecessary arrests and had used illegal force, that stories of an impending massacre were untrue, that there was almost universal opposition to the Federation, and that the effect of the emergency measures had produced—"no doubt only temporarily—a police state." In brief, it reached the conclusion that the existing position was thoroughly bad and probably untenable.[13]

The Middle Zone

The findings of the commission affected both local attitudes and Colonial Office policy. It was one of a number of reports (those on the deaths of Mau Mau prisoners at the Hola Camp detention center in Kenya also appeared in May and July 1959) which are commonly said to have moved the conservative government in London under Macmillan as prime minister, Iain Macleod at the Colonial Office, and (after 1962) R. A. Butler at the New Central African Office, to consider not only the possible dismantling of the Federation but the pace of decolonization as a whole.[14] Certainly the effect on the Central African Federation was dramatic. In April 1960 Banda was released from detention. In October the (Monckton) Report of the Royal Commission, which had been appointed to review the federal constitution, proposed a loosening of the ties between the three territories, a widening of the franchise, and "the right of secession under certain conditions."[15] Elections were held in 1961 and Banda's Malawi Congress Party swept the polls. Ministerial responsibility was granted in January 1963, the Federation was formally disbanded at the end of that year, and Dr. Banda's Malawi received its independence on 6 July 1964—six years to the day after his return to the country. A hero of his time indeed!

But although Dr. Banda could move Malawi constitutionally out of the Federation, he could not move his country geographically out of its landlocked and dependent position. In the eyes of his opponents, the nationalist hero now developed horns and a tail. It was the old story of the Sorcerer's Apprentice. The radicals had created a force they could not control and which turned against them. Within eighteen months of independence, six of Banda's ministers had resigned or had been forced out. Chipembere took to the rugged hill country east of Lake Nyasa and launched an armed attack on Fort Johnston in February 1965; after a running battle with local army forces (under British officers), he and his supporters fled north to Tanzania, while Banda was installed in Zomba as president of the republic in July. The following year a small band of exiles led by the former Minister of Home Affairs, Yatuta Chisiza, invaded the country, but they too were driven back, and Chisiza was killed. Banda was alone and in full control, his country once again close to being a police state. And who can tell whether that will be only temporary?

The Middle Zone

For all Banda's reliance on expatriate help, Malawi is very much an African country. Rhodesia, on the other hand, is still politically a world apart from Africa north of the Zambesi. It is perhaps an anachronism, for whereas white minority governments were once the rule, they are now the exception; and the *proportion* of white to black in Rhodesia is quite unlike that of South Africa, although that does not diminish the immediate power and force of the Rhodesia Front government in Salisbury.[16] The country is also unusual in having never been administered as a dependent territory: there was no period of colonial control, only rule by the British South Africa Company, until 1923, and then an elected European-settler government. Thereafter for over half a century, Southern Rhodesia was treated as something more than a self-governing colony and something less than a full dominion within the Commonwealth. It was restricted by London only in its external affairs and by constitutional limitations on its policy toward the African population which were rendered wholly nugatory by virtue of their disuse. By 1965, after the breakup of the Central African Federation, the Rhodesia Front government under Smith could not imagine a world in which politics did not remain in the grasp of men, preferably European, who held a controlling interest in the country—or, if they could imagine it, they were not prepared to advance its prospects. Enactments such as the 1930 Land Apportionment Act and the 1951 Land Husbandry Act ensured protection of the very uneven distribution of resources between the races.[17] Other legislation guaranteed the interests of the white labor force, while constitutional arrangements preserved European minority rule under a complicated system of voting, both at the federal level between 1953 and 1963 and within Rhodesia itself. After World War II the European minority, many of whom by now saw themselves as Rhodesians of long standing, were given a still larger assurance of their position by the influx of new immigrants from Britain and Europe: well under 100,000 in 1945, they numbered over 225,000 by 1965. But the African population, too, slowly began to assert itself. Broken in earlier defeats as tribal kingdoms by European force, they began the painful search for new forms of association through trade unions (at first illegal, then allowed in 1959 following widespread unofficial strikes after World War II) and

The Middle Zone

proto-political associations like the African National Congress, which had been founded in 1934. African separatist churches, too, were formed, and there was a growing urban population in the townships around Salisbury and Bulawayo.

By the early 1960's, therefore, even within the structures which were intended to bring African and European interests together at federal and territorial level, it was possible to discern an ominous trend: the Europeans began to move to the right, away from the mild reforms of the 1950's, while the Africans moved more militantly to the left. The change can be seen in the succession of white Rhodesian leaders: Godfrey Huggins (1933) to Edgar Whitehead (1953), to Winston Field (1962), to Ian Smith (1964), the sharp break occurring in 1962-64. Similarly, the African politicians moved from the African National Congress to the National Democratic Party (1960), to the Zimbabwe African People's Union (ZAPU), 1961, and its breakaway Zimbabwe African National Union (ZANU), 1963, to the present Patriotic Front, the turning point coming again in 1962-64 with the banning of both ZAPU and ZANU and, a decade later, the beginning of armed incursions into Rhodesia from across its borders. At the national level the difference between Smith and Garfield Todd, and between the Rhodesian Front and the former United Federal Party, represented a substantial shift in attitudes. Of course, the structure of control in the 1950's was as it is now; but where there was once the expression of liberality and the hope of maneuver, there is now guerrilla warfare on a scale and intention unthinkable to the former (black) ANC and (white) UFP.

Where will it end? There is little point in divination when all the auguries are uncertain. Prior to 1965, the British tried to adhere to six general principles of consent before they would agree to any final bestowal of independence.[18] They were argued out in London between the Labor and Conservative parties and at successive Commonwealth conferences, and they might have become the basis for peaceful change. Then on 11 November 1965 Smith aped the American Declaration of Independence and raised the flag of freedom for the white minority. The previous May, his Rhodesian Front party had secured all fifty European seats of the total of sixty-five in parliament, while the African opposition was divided between the "collaborators" (including the fifteen African MPs) and those who, like Joshua Nkomo, had refused in 1962 to take part in the elections and were now in detention or exile.[19] In face of the unilateral declaration of independence the Conservative opposition in London would not, and Wilson's Labor government declared it could not, use force at such a distance and in such a setting. Moreover, Harold Wilson seems genuinely to have believed that, against so vulnerable a state and its tobacco economy, economic sanctions would quickly take effect. Smith, on the other hand, assumed that his large southern neighbor (who could easily strangle the Rhodesian economy) would recognize an identity of interest between South Africa and Rhodesia in proving that sanctions will not work. Smith was more knowledgeable than Wilson. The lines of communication were kept open, the Rhodesian currency was sustained, oil was moved north, and normal trade allowed to continue across Beit Bridge between Rhodesia and South Africa. Indeed, South African businessmen did rather well out of Rhodesia's difficulties by acting as middlemen, picking up the trade with Zambia that Kaunda tried to deny to Smith.

Still, it is true that sanctions have had the effect of bringing Smith to the point of negotiations. South Africa, too, would no doubt like to see a settlement it could approve of, if only to buy time for its own policies. Parallel with the consolidation of white control in Rhodesia, including the proclamation of a Republic in March 1970, went the episodic series of talks between Smith and a long series of protagonists: Harold Wilson, Lord Alport, George Thomson, Lord Goodman, Sir Alec Douglas Home, Henry Kissinger, Ivor Richard, David Owen.[20] The list grows longer and the uncertainties multiply. Throughout it all, the white Rhodesians so far have "left it to Smithy," who has been a good deal more shrewdly stubborn than his would-be mentors—and tormentors—have been able to admit. As Good observed, "he had in him a stubborn combative streak, the gift of political cunning, and the commanding virtue of being Rhodesian-born—the first Southern Rhodesian Prime Minister of that distinction"[21]—qualities which were to carry the Rhodesian Front to a decisive victory once again in the August 1977 election, the last to be held on a narrow franchise among the predominantly European electorate.

It is possible of course that Anglo-American pressure and

The Middle Zone

African guerrilla action will succeed in transferring power under British auspices. It will have to be pressure on Vorster as much as on Smith, unless the combination of African resistance, Russian weapons, Cuban help, and other unknown factors will succeed militarily where argument has failed. At the end of 1977 there was still no clear prospect in view. The South African government was enigmatic and Smith remained evasive despite an enforced commitment to majority rule by 1978. There was considerable unease within his own party, and the African leaders were as widely divided from one another as before. White Rhodesia had always relied on black nationalist disunity. "The split between ZANU and ZAPU in 1963, and the resulting violence gave the new Rhodesian government a ready excuse to ban them."[22] Those in exile were in no better accord. "In March-April 1970, Chikerema of ZAPU approached Herbert Chitepo of ZANU in Lusaka with a view to unifying their two movements. The ZANU executive agreed to meet him but found the tribal and ideological splits within ZAPU too great to bridge. . . . There were reports of an agreement between Nkomo and Sithole in their Rhodesian prisons to step down in the interests of unity and call upon Robert Mugabe to head a new party," but that, too, came to nothing.[23] A new movement did emerge—the Front for the Liberation of Zimbabwe (FROLIZI)—under ZANU and ZAPU commanders and with the backing of the OAU Liberation Committee; but it soon collapsed. Later again, a Patriotic Front was formed by Nkomo and Mugabe, who were supported by rival guerrilla units operating within Rhodesia. At the same time, Bishop Abel Muzorewa (who had formed the African National Council in December 1971 to protest to the Pearce Commission against a tentative Smith-Douglas Home agreement) and the Rev. Ndabaningi Sithole appeared to have wide support within Zimbabwe itself though rivals against one another.[24] Between such groups there were shifting alliances, woven from the often uneasy relationships between the Ndebele (minority) and Shona (majority) communities, as well as between radical and reformist leaders. The European minority also took alarm. There was now an annual net emigration, usually to South Africa, of those who feared the widening theaters of war on the frontier and along the main trunk roads that linked the country to the south. Terrorism walked the land on both sides of the conflict, reminiscent of the mid-fifties in Kenya, and the ferocity of revolution was matched by the brutality of suppression.

Who can tell along what tortuous paths the opposed fears of the African and European communities will be resolved, or in what sense they may respond to external pressures? Only one melancholy certainty is clear. The liberal hopes of an earlier generation, never very strong, are gone—hopes of a Rhodesia that might be different from South Africa, or of a Central African Federation that would be multiracial, or of an independent Malawi and Zambia that would reflect the democracy of nationalism. Repression is on the increase in all three territories. The despotism of Banda and the authoritarianism of the ruling party in Zambia may lack the racialism of the mass detentions in Rhodesia, but to those locked up, the color of the jailer may be a good deal less important than the brutal fact of imprisonment. One of the dispiriting features of the controversies over Zimbabwe has been the clear understanding, by delegates brought together to try to reach agreement on independence, of the importance of not being second in any final settlement. It is assumed that only those who come to power first will survive: hence the history of conflict between the African leaders whose "efforts unfortunately were directed neither at foreign opinion nor at the destruction of settler power, but rather at securing hegemony over the nationalist movement by one group through the destruction of the other."[25]

Whatever the politics of nationalism may produce, it seems likely that economic compulsions will continue to have their effect. They are probabilities rather than certainties, since it is always possible that a large part of the economy of central Africa will suffer collapse or be forced to take on new patterns. We are back to our main theme of economic and political maps. But before looking at them again, we need to say something briefly of the end of Portuguese rule in Angola and Mozambique.

Both countries are large. Angola is very large indeed, second in size only to Zaire in Africa south of the Sahara. Neither is heavily populated. Angola may have about six million and Mozambique something under ten million, comparable to the population of greater London distributed through western Europe as a whole. That may account for the extraordinarily slow

The Middle Zone

success of the nationalist movements, even when they turned to armed revolt in 1961 in Angola and 1964 in Mozambique. The insurgents were always able to escape defeat; the Portuguese could win battles but never the war. Eventually, however, a familiar counterpoint was noticed. Armed conflict abroad, of a wounding and extravagant nature, was being answered by unrest in the metropolitan country, as had happened between Indonesia and Holland, Indo-China/Algeria and France, the Congo and Belgium, Vietnam and the United States. In Portugal the effect came as an unexpected response to the music of time when early in 1974 there was a coup in Lisbon. On 22 February of that year General Antónia de Spínola published a book, *Portugal and the Future*, which argued that there was now no possibility of a lasting victory in Angola, Guinea-Bissau, or Mozambique. The verdict was confirmed by General de Costa Gomes, Chief of Staff of the army, but opposed forcibly by Salazar's successor, Marcelino Caetano. Then on 25 April a number of young officers, battle-weary abroad, Marxist-inclined at home, produced the Movement which overnight swept away the fifty-year-old dictatorship. Although no one was clear what to put in its place, the act of demolition did include ending the war in Africa. Thus the African rebellions had helped to bring about the seizure of power in Lisbon by a military junta which, in turn, put a final end to nearly half a millennium of Portuguese colonial ambitions, including all the cloudy dreams of a trans-Atlantic Lusitanian Empire.

The earlier refusal of the Portuguese to quit Guinea-Bissau—a torrid and unprofitable enclave—was hardly credible, except on the ground of the most general principle of no surrender. Mozambique, too, was largely unrewarding, particularly after Frelimo began to make headway among the African population. But Angola was a prize hard for Portugal to forfeit, especially if one counted the oil-rich outpost of Cabinda, north of Zaire. Angola has cotton, coffee, hardwoods, minerals, rich fishing grounds, fertile land, and a divided population. After 1964 there was an economic boom—more growth than development—as Portugal admitted the outside world to share its plunder in order to pay for its retention. The relative cohesion of Mozambique can be seen today in President Samora Machel's rule, compared with the air of permanent crisis in Angola, although one can also see its continued reliance on the transit and labor market in South Africa with which it maintains a formal and correct relationship of dependency. In 1975 the Mine Labour Organisation of South Africa still recruited a third of its labor (poorly paid at that) from Mozambique, numbering some 115,000 out of the total wage-earning population of 850,000 in what was still a country divided by guerrilla fighting. A proportion of migrant labor earnings is still retained under contract and remitted in gold by the South African authorities to the Mozambique government, and still the South African government honors its undertaking to keep a minimum freight tonnage moving along the railway to Maputo.[26] The disunity of Angola, and the inability of any one nationalist movement to encompass the whole country, were reflected in the struggle among rival parties—the National Front for the Liberation of Angola, the Popular Front for the Liberation of Angola, and the National Front for the Total Liberation of Angola. It needed Cuban and Russian help to establish Agostinho Neto and the MPLA in office. That was an unforeseen joker in the pack—several thousand Cubans airlifted by the Russians across the Atlantic after an appeal by Neto to Moscow by way of Havana, or conceivably direct to Moscow, where Brezhnev turned to Castro. Cuban troops ferried by the USSR, the FNLA upheld for a time by the United States, UNITA helped by South Africa, Moroccan troops conveyed by France to Zaire: the ghosts of the Berlin conference must surely have awakened from their imperial death to watch the reenactment of their play.

Throughout the early '70's Mozambique moved steadily, though by no means uninterruptedly, toward independence. Frelimo suffered the loss of its attractive Portuguese-educated leader, Eduardo Mondlane, who was assassinated in 1969. It also went through something of an internal purge in 1970-71—common enough no doubt in revolutionary parties trying to establish their identity—when the more radical elements under Marcellino dos Santos and Samora Machel ousted their rivals. They succeeded throughout substantial areas of the country in establishing an administration parallel to that of the Portuguese army; but it was the change of government in Portugal that enabled negotiations to be opened between Machel and Lisbon, and independence was formally proclaimed, in the presence of the new Portuguese prime minister, on 25 June 1975. President

The Middle Zone

Machel gave his party the promise of "permanent struggle for revolutionary socialism," and there was a general tidying up of what was left of the local private sector. Opponents of a European dictatorship, the Frelimo government may nonetheless succeed, with outside help, in establishing their own form of *uno stato totalitario*; but although the party remains the dominant force, it has not been unopposed. In March 1975 (before independence) there were stories of an attempted coup, and in December (after independence) Machel had to suppress unrest in the army. It is still open to question whether he will follow earlier heroes like Ben Bella into disgrace and imprisonment or whether, like Sekou Touré, he can continue to struggle on. But in Angola, no one in 1974-75 could tell who would be there in Luanda even to run up a flag of independence. There were at least three main actors in a moving theater of war, in which each was dependent on external prompters, managers, and suppliers of money, weapons, and men.

The tragedy of the conflict reached the high point of misery and absurdity in November 1975 in the declaration of Angolan independence by the Portuguese High Commissioner, after the last Portuguese troops had left, without any formal transfer of power, since there was no single inheritor to receive the instruments of succession. In the North, Holden Roberto of the FNLA inaugurated a "Popular and Democratic Republic."[27] At Luanda in the central provinces, Agostinho Neto of the MPLA announced the birth of a People's Republic, while at the other end of the huge country Dr. Jonas Savimbi (who had once been a close colleague of Holden Roberto) formed a third government at Huambo, the former Nova Lisboa, under the auspices of his grandly named UNITA. Moscow recognized Neto; Zaire and the Americans put money and weapons behind the FNLA; Zambia gave encouragement to Savimbi, who turned for help to South Africa. The Chinese supported first UNITA, then the FNLA, presumably not on any merits of the case but as part of their tireless campaign against "big-power hegemony" and "Soviet social imperialism." The greater part of 1975, prior to November, was spent in abortive meetings of one kind and another. Portugal had tried quite early in the year to reach a compromise settlement—the Alvos Agreement—which actually envisaged elections and a coalition government of all three would-be successors.

The Middle Zone

There were attempts at reconciliation under the OAU in Kenya, Uganda, Zambia, and Tanzania: all to no avail. By July tribal, regional, and racial riots had spread from the main towns to the countryside and there was a mass exodus of Portuguese across the border with Namibia. Then the proxy wars began. The South Africans, who had moved north ostensibly to protect the hydroelectric installations on the Cunene river, joined Savimbi's UNITA forces to advance rapidly into Benguela and Lobito. The FNLA moved south. The Portuguese gave up. The Cubans began to arrive. The Americans withdrew their support. The FNLA collapsed. The South Africans retreated. And the OAU, led by Nigeria, began one by one to recognize the MPLA as the lawful government of Angola.

Of course it is wrong that such divisions should exist, or if not wrong it is certainly a pity. Basil Davidson, the most knowledgeable of those who foresaw the eventual end of Portuguese rule (though certainly not its manner of passing), tried to warn against tribalism. "The logical extension of reformist nationalism being micro-nationalism, what justification would remain for a country called Angola? Why in that case should not the leaders of the Kongo, or at least those who were their leaders in the 1960's, be given their original demand, and allowed to secede as a separate state? What logic should prevent the Mbunda of Angola from joining the Mbunda of Zambia? Why not reunite the Lunda with their brethren in Zaire?"[28] The rhetoric is persuasive, and a case for the retention of the colonial territories as new states is very strong. But the basis for survival of any government of Angola remains elusive. Neto himself was very nearly dislodged by an armed group of conspirators within his own ruling MPLA at the end of April 1977. No doubt whoever rules in Luanda will in time succeed to their colonial (or Cuban) legacy of control, as other African leaders have done elsewhere. It is the best that can practically be expected, since to hope for more would be as utopian as earlier colonial fallacies. One may easily agree that what "independent Africa needs [is] an entirely new framework in which micro-nationalism gives way to nationalism, and nationalism to supra-national organs of cooperation and continental development."[29] But who has any proper hope of its attainment? There was, however, in the wide area of central Africa that transnational unity of trade and communications

The Middle Zone

which once tried to assert itself against the political nationalism of the colonial state. What has happened to the tug and pull of those opposed maps of economic and political power?

They are still there, though in rather different form. Each of the countries in this middle zone has tried either to strengthen its politics by altering its economics or to moderate its political life in order to preserve its economy. In 1974, for example, Rhodesia hurriedly constructed a direct rail link of one hundred miles between Rutenga and the border with South Africa at Beit Bridge. Malawi began to scale down its heavy recruitment of mineworkers (120,000 in 1975) into South Africa, and in good Banda fashion relations were put on a new footing with Frelimo on the ground that whoever controlled the exit ports at Beira and Nacala, whether they were Portuguese colonialists or national Marxists, had his approbation. At the same time, however, Banda tightened control at home, expanding the army by the addition of a third battalion and curbing the slightest sign of dissent from Jehovah's Witnesses, disgruntled northerners, and whoever else gave cause for suspicion. Both Mozambique and Zambia closed their borders with Rhodesia but increased their trade with South Africa, thus appeasing the lion while hunting the jackal—or, expressed more abstractly, combining principle with expediency.[30] The Botswana government under Sir Seretse Khama has not dared to close its main economic life line, the Rhodesia-South African railway; the spreading guerrilla war has also meant that it is impossible to police, as well as impolitic to try to close, the long border with Rhodesia. During the past decade, the economics of survival have had to adjust to the politics of belief, but none of the African governments in central or Southern Africa has been able to choose either to the exclusion of the other: to pay the full price of principles and risk economic collapse, or to give full rein to the economy regardless of the politics of nationalism and race.

Nowhere has the dilemma been more acute than in Zambia. Try as it can the government has been unable to twist itself wholly around and turn its back on the white south. It has gone as far as it dares, and the consequences have been very unpleasant—not only the economic consequences, but the political price exacted of the party leaders in Lusaka. The most spectacular shift in the map was the building by the Chinese, under an

The Middle Zone

interest-free loan of $350 million, of the Tanzam, or "Tazara," railway from Zambia to Dar es Salaam. But the damage inflicted by guerrilla campaigns across Zambia's main lines of communication has been considerable. "Following the closure of the Benguela railway in the face of Angolan hostilities . . . copper exports were cut . . . by 30% and 40% for Roan Consolidated Mines (RCM) and Mohanga Consolidated Copper Mines (NCCM) respectively. Thus what had appeared to be a realistic balance of payments forecast in the January 1975 budget turned into a gross underestimate. The overall payments deficit for 1975 [was] double the original forecast, while inflation continued to advance toward 20% levels and real GDP declined by 3%."[31] There were several problems, too, in switching export-import patterns northward. The harbor at Dar es Salaam has a limited capacity, the Tazara railway could until recently handle only some 20,000 tons a month. Gradually conditions improved, until the northern route is now taking almost 60 percent of the country's foreign trade. But other measures have been needed in an attempt to reduce the dependence on Rhodesia, including rapid exploitation of new coal reserves, expansion of the power station on the Kafue river as an alternative to Kariba, and encouragement of local manufacturers and purchase of goods from the north instead of the south, although the latter in itself raises the problem of cheap Kenyan imports competing with local manufactures.[32] The overriding compulsion has been simple enough: politics plus copper. Zambia lives by copper. It is a railway/copper state at the heart of the great industrial heartland of central Africa. Copper provides its export earnings, half its gross national product, a sixth of all its direct wages, and very much more than that through the overspill of mining wages into the rural areas. Once again, however, it is an externally related dependency. Copper prices, like those of cocoa, fluctuate widely: at £1,400 per ton in April 1974, copper dropped to £500 in 1976, causing a 20-percent devaluation of the local currency.

It is right to add Zambia is a comparatively rich country, thanks to copper. Many of its citizens eat better and live longer because of copper. But such advantages also make it more necessary for the government to put its political and economic maps into some degree of congruence. By the middle of 1974, for example, Kaunda was willing to move toward some kind of accommodation, however tentative, with South Africa, if only to ease his own economic position, and to bring pressure to bear on Rhodesia. As Ralph Young noted of the meetings between Kaunda and Vorster, the intention was well understood on both sides: "the striking cooperation achieved between President Kaunda and Mr. Vorster did not obscure their underlying differences: détente meant re-ordered priorities while preserving long term aims."[33] Nonetheless, Kaunda was able to speak approvingly of South Africa's willingness to help. He also looked kindly on Savimbi and Unita in Angola, not least because they appeared to be in control of the Benguela railway and the port of Lobito, which still carried some 40 percent of Zambia's copper abroad. Kaunda wanted compromise, not conflict, over Rhodesia, Angola, and South Africa. In 1969 he had tried to write such optimism into the Lusaka Manifesto.[34] He also disliked foreign intervention and talked of Soviet and Cuban forces in Angola as "a plundering tiger and her deadly cubs coming in through the back door." But he could get neither the politics nor the economics right. Neither map would fit the other, or, indeed, tell him which way to go. Smith turned sour, and at the end of May 1976 Kaunda agreed to allow guerrilla action across the Zambian border, only to have the main Post Office and the High Court building in his own capital blown up. The previous year Herbert Chitepo had been assassinated in Lusaka, and Kaunda ordered the arrest of Chitepo's fellow ZANU members. Then insurgents under Adamson Mushala, a former UNIP politician, crossed into Zambia's northwestern province, and Kaunda accused South Africa of aiding them.[35]

Détente was over, and compromise was over. But still the politics went sour. A single-party state had been enforced in 1973, not to protect but to curb dissent, although in the elections of that year there was still open competition and a number of senior party MPs had been defeated. But by 1976 there was much less freedom. Cabinet ministers were detained, the governor and deputy governor of the Bank of Zambia dismissed, the university closed for three months, lecturers and students locked up, and the country as a whole placed under a full state of emergency. Kaunda was also obliged to expel Unita representatives from Lusaka, to recognize the MPLA government in Luanda, and to join the "front line presidents" of Tanzania,

The Middle Zone

Mozambique, Botswana, and Angola in their support of the Patriotic Front's commitment to military action in Rhodesia. Yet still the Benguela railway remained closed because of anti-MPLA guerrillas in Angola, and still Ian Smith was there in Salisbury, armed and succored by Vorster. Zambia was tormented by the impossibility of aligning its economic needs and political interests.

How long will such conflicts last in this enormous middle zone? New patterns of trade and communications, extending northward by a doubling of the Tazara railway and the deepening of the harbor at Dar es Salaam could begin to reshape the export map at least of Zambia and possibly of the eastern area of Zaire. But that of course suggests the continuing existence of a political and military battle line across the continent, and that may be realistic. But suppose Rhodesia, as well as Zambia, were under African control. And suppose (peering into the mists of time) the whole of central and southern Africa were one day to be free from white minority rule. Would the countries of this vast region be united by the strife that had once divided them? Perhaps we might be back, in an utterly different setting, to those early dreams of trade and politics, or at least to the *modus vivendi* which came to exist between the colonial powers and South Africa. On the other hand, new ideological and political maps may begin to take shape to affect once again the alignment of economic interests. Relations between Zaire and Angola, for example, are very bad. They are much worse than they were between Portuguese Angola and the Belgian Congo. Can it be that colonial capitalism was good and independent nationalism is bad? It is not pleasant to think so. But there are related puzzles to worry over. For example, the smaller states of the area—Lesotho, Swaziland, Namibia, Malawi, Botswana—have arrived at a precarious security in the balance between black and white nationalism. They have been protected not only by their separate colonial existence but by a kind of political geography, like those strange islands of quiet one has heard of in the battle area of no-man's land, or the miniature states that perch across the frontier between larger powers. Who knows, however, what forces might be released by a free and black and militant South Africa, supposing such a transfer of power comes about in Pretoria? If the OAU rules of the game continued to be observed,

The Middle Zone

and if the main theme of this book were upheld—namely, that the colonial state has a certificate of respectability in respect of its sovereign identity—then the mosaic of central and southern Africa would be preserved. But still the disparities of power would be there. The force of the South African economy (if that, too, were maintained) would be powerfully at work still, pulling labor into the mines and farms and urban employment from its poorer and weaker neighbors, and the political map of sovereign states would still need to record the transnational contours of trade and communications, finance, labor migration, and power supplies. Perhaps one should add, hesitantly, that it might be prudent for the Namibian leaders, assuming they wish to retain some kind of separate identity, to achieve an independent international existence before the revolution arrives in Pretoria. It would indeed be ironic if a black South Africa were to succeed in rearranging the political map to fit the economic maps, as King Chaka and Cecil Rhodes, Field Marshal Smuts and General Hertzog, and a whole generation of Afrikaner leaders once hoped to do with respect to South West Africa and the incorporation of the three High Commission Territories. But I am trespassing on borrowed time, and would much prefer, no less prudently, to leave such problems for the future.

5. White Power: Cohesion without Consensus

An earlier chapter looked at the mystery of a revolution that comes to an end or lies fallow, but we must now consider more familiar territory: the possible gestation, birth, and life of the revolution-to-be. For that South Africa has within its state and society the potential for revolution is rarely doubted. It is a strange and wicked country—anachronistic and atavistic, as if left over from the past to trouble the present. Africans are not treated worse today in South Africa than black men and women were in the United States 150 years ago. They are not bought and sold as property. Their survival, too, is assured, by contrast with, say, the American Indians or the Aborigines of Australia at the turn of the century. They are more free, or less unfree, than the serfs in Russia before emancipation. But the extraordinary feature of South Africa is that it is still bound to a rigidly divided society which, if it is not slavery, is certainly close to serfdom. To behave in the twentieth century in a modern industrial state as if it were still the nineteenth or eighteenth century is very unusual —so unusual, in fact, that many people simply refuse to believe that it can be done. The whites deny that the parallel is just, the nonwhites refuse to believe it can last. It is this conflict of belief, as well as the opposition of interests, which seem to presage tragedy; for if revolution comes, it will certainly be tragic, not only for those who fear its consequences but for many who now want to hasten its arrival. In such terrible situations there is also very often an element of fatalism. It comes to be believed that what must be will be, although whether that point has yet been reached in South Africa I do not know.

The usual run of argument is more confident than that. It takes as its frame of reference the assumption that, sooner or later, revolution *will* come. And since it may be quick and sudden, it is also said that we ought to be prepared for it. But what signs are there in South Africa of imminent or inescapable revolution? That is the main theme of what follows, although no doubt we shall have to pursue subsidiary arguments as well if we are to arrive at any kind of conclusion. It is no easy task. The South African revolution has been predicted more or less annually since the 1950's, prompting as early as 1958 Julius Lewin's exasperated article "No Revolution Round the Corner," which pointed out that although the ingredients of revolt may very well be present, they have by no means reached the critical point of fusion, and that there are very powerful constraints on those who have tried to cause the explosion.[1]

We might turn first, therefore, to the ingredients. What is the explosive mixture which many believe is making for revolution? They may be listed quite simply.

First, nationalist conflict. Leaving aside for the moment the question of race, and looking back over the past fifty or so years of South African history, it is easy to be impressed by the tenacity not of an exported European nationalism but of a solid, dour, assertive Afrikaner *volk*. It was always impossible to see the Kenya settlers as a nation, and running up a white Rhodesian flag of independence in 1965 still conveyed a good deal of the bravado of settler rule under a new Union Jack. But that is hardly the case in South Africa. There is a very distinct identity to the Afrikaner majority among the white minority. The common indices of nationality are there: a language (Afrikaans), a religion expressed through the Afrikaner churches which have been very much the Afrikaner National Party at prayer, a fabled history isolated from Europe, and a stratified society (extending through that history) which is now locally rooted, as New Zealanders or Australians or Americans are locally rooted. Of course there is a difference of number from other colonized areas of the world, since the white population—Afrikaners and English-speaking alike—now appears to be crowded out by others of different racial stock.[2] Still, it would be wrong not to recognize the force of an Afrikaner nationalism, which is different in kind from, say, the now vanished French Algerians. It is a nationalism shaped by a self-aware history within a state fully expressive of its interests, in defiance originally of an imperialism of which the disadvantaged Afrikaner was once thought to be the victim—the rifle-carrying Boer farmer on his horse gallantly opposed to the armed might of a capitalist empire until forced into temporary submission by the Peace of Vareeniging in 1902.

Afrikanerdom is a rare achievement to the extent that it not only brought under nationalist control the union of the four British colonies of the Transvaal, Orange Free State, Natal, and the Cape but infused its politics, laws, and administration with a decidedly non-British life. Since its earliest years Afrikaner society has been divided internally between those like Smuts and Botha, who began by fighting and ended by admiring the English, and those like General Hertzog in the 1930's, who grudgingly accepted the need to cooperate locally and internationally with the British, or like Oswald Pirow (a former minister of defense) and Hendrik Verwoerd (later prime minister), who were not simply anti-English, anti-British and anti-Commonwealth but by the time of World War II were pro-German, anti-Semitic, and pro-Nazi. Through a long history, however, the Afrikaner community held fast to church and state. They could give lessons in this respect to others who seek to indigenize a would-be nationalist society and its institutions—not least by their determination to purify the dialect of the tribe, since they succeeded remarkably in elevating a kitchen language (as Afrikaans was once held to be in relation to Dutch and English) into the dominant language of the state.[3] The political parties, too, were divided between the former South Africa Party, led by Smuts—who tried in a sense to combine the legacies of Rhodes and the Cape liberal-Afrikaner Hofmeyr—and the National Party under Hertzog. The two coalesced, then divided and refashioned themselves to become the United Party versus the "Purified" National Party. But Afrikanerdom was also watched over by the leaders of half-secret associations like the Broderbond, a hooded enclave, and the more extreme Ossewa Brandwag. Such societies kept alive the early republican sentiment of the Great Trek in opposition to more liberal Afrikaners many of whom served courageously with their English-speaking compatriots when South Africa voted by a narrow margin to join the United Kingdom in 1939.[4]

By the 1950's, the Afrikaner was growing very self-assured. The poverty of the poor whites of the Depression, who were hardly able to scratch a living on the farms or who were unemployed in the towns to which they drifted from the *platteland*, was now no more than a bitter memory. The National Party had come to power in 1948, only narrowly, with a minority of the votes; but it was to stay in office as the dominant party, attracting both English-speaking and Afrikaner voters, until the present day. A whole generation of South Africans has known no other government.[5] In 1960 Verwoerd carried the country into a republic, then out of the Commonwealth. The Great Trek, it might be thought, was over at last. The Transvaal and Orange Free State Afrikaner had won the Boer War. Writing shortly after the 1948 election, Keppel-Jones noted that the Nationalists had been "steadily absorbing nationally-conscious people till . . . in the Western Province and elsewhere people whose ancestors were of a different political persuasion now feel as if they themselves had lived through the experiences of the Trek, thrashed the Rooinek at Majuba and suffered in a concentration camp."[6] Through the Afrikaner universities, through the movement for Christian National Education, through the Reddingdaudsbond, and later through economic agencies of the state, the Afrikaner has come fully into his own.[7] He is certain therefore not to surrender lightly what he has come to possess. It is of course also true that South Africans as a whole—English-speaking, Afrikaans-speaking, Africans, Colored, Indians—have been drawn more and more into the world of international trade and finance. Gold ensured it, and other riches confirmed the growing dependence of the economy on the external world. The Afrikaner is no longer the Boer farmer on his horse but often enough the businessman in city clothes. But what arguments can be deduced from that? The governments of Malan, Strydom, Verwoerd, and Vorster can hardly be seen as puppets on an internationalist capitalist string. The story might be simpler if they were so, although that too may be doubted, since the world at large—capitalist, communist, and nationalist alike—is as perplexed to know what to do about South Africa as is the government of the republic itself.

If the society built harshly and repressively in the Afrikaner image were not so wicked, it might also be easier to feel sympathy for its future. For no sooner had the Afrikaner displaced the once dominant Anglicized element than he found that others were claiming his inheritance. African as well as Afrikaner nationalism had been growing. The Afrikaner had triumphed over the humiliation of being an outcast in an Anglicized society, but the much larger number of nonwhites were becoming aware of being outcasts in a racially dominant state. There were laws to tell them so, police and magistrates to enforce the fact. Two ominous and contradictory forces were at work. Africans were becoming an indispensable part of a labor-intensive economy, not only in the sense of their long-imposed role as hewers of wood and drawers of water but as skilled artisans and consumers. Yet they were also cut down politically. Even the very limited franchise rights once exercised by the "Native" and Colored voter in the Cape were taken away despite solemn undertakings and legal safeguards, while outside South Africa, throughout the continent, African nationalism was transforming colonial states into independent republics under African control. As the 1950's and '60's gave place to the present decade, the withdrawal of European rule was virtually complete. There were sovereign black states not only from the Zambesi to the Sahara but within and bordering South Africa itself: Lesotho, Botswana, Swaziland by 1968, Mozambique and Angola by 1975-76. Yet Africans within South Africa had one of the oldest political parties in the continent, the African National Congress (ANC), founded in 1912, a year earlier than the National Party had emerged as a breakaway movement from the South Africa Party. Only the True Whig Party in Liberia—a *black* settler society—has had a longer continuous history and its leaders have had the advantage of power and office.

The history of the ANC represents the terrible difficulties in the way of organized nonwhite protest. It began by singing "God Save the King" in the hope of betterment, and ended by throwing bombs despairing of reform. Until well after World War II, almost into the 1950's, the principal nationalist movement (and the ANC was certainly that) tried to avoid violence. The limited success of Gandhi's passive resistance movement encouraged its commitment to nonviolence, since it was in South Africa that Gandhi, as a young lawyer arriving from India, developed his philosophy of *satyaghra* when confronted with the disabilities imposed on the Indian community in Natal. As late as 1953, Dr. Njongwe, then acting president of the ANC in the Cape, was reported as saying: "with the historical example of Gandhi before us we turned to Passive Resistance largely because it secured results without creating bitterness between the contenders."[8] And despite an early failure to prevent the passing of the discriminatory Natives Land Act of 1913, the ANC continued to protest peacefully against the internal passport system of "pass laws," by which the movement of Africans from the impoverished Reserves to the towns and white farming areas is largely regulated. As in later years, the Congress was challenged by more radical organizations, notably by Clements Kadalie's Industrial and Commercial Union, but the South African government, then as now, was quite up to matching any level of protest by an equal or superior degree of suppression, whether against the violence of white miners during the great Rand strike of 1922, the burning of passes by Africans, or civil disobedience campaigns among the Indian population. It was during the interwar years, first under Smuts and then under Hertzog, that the South African government began to formulate its own doctrines of belief, of which the most elaborately articulated was separateness, or apartheid. The persistence of the ANC is all the more remarkable, therefore, since it is certainly not true—at least in other parts of the world—that the greater the oppression, the greater the resistance. State power, if it does not collapse from external pressure, is all too often the victor.

Yet by the 1950's the tide of revolution in South Africa looked as if it was rising very fast. The ANC was being pushed in the direction of forcible protest against tightening the pass laws and extending them to women. In 1949 the ANC Youth League had been formed by a group of younger members whose names were to become familiar across the international world: Oliver Tambo, Walter Sislu, Nelson Mandela, and Anton Lembede. Against the older generation of leaders—Albert Luthuli, Dr. Xuma, and Professor Z. K. Mathews—they drew up a program of action markedly different in tone from earlier declarations of intent, as explained by Nelson Mandela:

My Lord, up to 1949 the leaders of the ANC had always acted in the hope that by merely pleading their cause, placing it before the authorities they . . . would change their hearts. . . . But the forms of political action which are set out in the Programme of Action meant that the ANC was not going to rely on a change of heart. It was going to exert pressure to compel the authorities to grant its demands. [9]

White Power: Cohesion without Consensus

A widening area of agitation brought together a number of allied grievances. Often enough they arose from what might seem trivial matters—the price of potatoes or a penny increase in bus fares—unless one was living at a bare subsistence level in the huge townships of the Transvaal or Natal or the Cape on the restricted edge of the cities of white power and wealth. When the bus fare was raised in the Alexandra Township, people refused to pay and walked instead until the increase was canceled. Resistance also took shape more distantly in the Native Reserves, as in the hut burnings and trade boycotts of East Pondoland in 1960. But it was in the white urban areas that a Campaign of Defiance of Unjust Laws looked most dangerous.[10] In 1955 the ANC, the Indian Congress, the Coloured People's Political Organisation, and the White Congress of Democrats met at Kliptown in Johannesburg and drew up a Freedom Charter. There were mass riots against the pass laws in Johannesburg by October 1958, in Pretoria in January 1959, and later in Cato Manor, Durban, and Paarl. Policemen were killed, rioters shot dead, police stations attacked, houses burned. When bombs were exploded the government brought in armored cars and mobilized commandos. Weakened by these pressures, the unity of the ANC was broken. An Africanist group was formed within the Congress in 1958, dissatisfied with the "multi-racialism of the ANC, its domination by Communists in the Congress of Democrats, and its lack of militancy in implementing the Programme of Action of 1949."[11] The following year a Pan-Africanist Congress (PAC) was called by Robert Sobukwe and Potlaka Leballo, directed at achieving a "government of the African by the African and rejecting the idea of a multi-racial society."[12] A point of crisis—one of very many thereafter—came on 21 March 1960, when the PAC mounted a national anti-pass campaign, and a large unarmed crowd of supporters gathered around the police station at Sharpeville. The police opened fire, and over two hundred Africans were killed. The government ordered Sobukwe's arrest, declared a state of emergency, banned both the ANC and the PAC, detained many hundreds of their supporters, and confirmed its authority to do so by enacting a succession of punitive laws under which suspects could be held in solitary confinement for first 90 and then 180 days, and torture was added to coercion to break or weaken those brave enough to resist.

White Power: Cohesion without Consensus

African nationalism had tried to assert itself, and it had been crushed. Secret organizations of a more violent disposition then attempted to take their place: a National Liberation Committee, which became the African Resistance Movement; the *Umkonto we Sizwe*, or "Spear of the Nation," linked to the ANC; and *Poqo* ("Alone" or "Pure") in a similar relationship to the PAC. Sabotage and bombs were now the weapons. "We felt that without violence there would be no way open to the African people to succeed in their struggle against the principle of White supremacy."[13] Albert Luthuli, the aging leader of the ANC and a Nobel Prize winner, continued to plead the early aims of the Congress. But multiracialism and nonviolence now seem unlikely virtues in a republic which has grown increasingly repressive and divided since 1961. Using the immense power of the state, Afrikaner rule has beaten down African nationalism, confining it to sporadic violence of the kind seen recently in the township of Soweto in Johannesburg. African anger is persistent, pervasive but, for the present, contained.

Second, however, and of course reinforcingly, racial conflict. Although there are other victims of white power—including sizable Indian and Colored communities and the very earliest of all settlers, the Hottentots and Bushmen—the repressive nature of a white-dominated regime has not brought all its opponents into one opposed force. The prospect of a single South African nationality uniting Africans, Indians, Colored, and the more prudent or brave among the white population is still distant. Indeed, it seems unlikely that there is as yet one indivisible African nationalism, although there is certainly a unifying African detestation and (so far as it dares) defiance of white control. Even within the townships, which draw their shifting populations from across the republic and beyond its borders, the South African authorities have been able to make use of tribal or national differences between Zulu and non-Zulu, Xhosa and non-Xhosa.[14] The unifying bond of African resistance has been not the recovery of a historic nationalism, since that would assume opposed identities, but race: not the Indians, not the Coloreds, not the Progressive or Marxist elements among white South Africans, but African black versus European white. Broadly speaking, this was true of the 1950's and '60's, when "organised opposition ... by and large followed the pattern of racial stratification of the country. The Congress Alliance was compartmentalized into the South African National Congress, Coloured People's Congress, and SACTU (the South African Congress of Trade Unions); the pan-Africanist Congress drew an almost exclusively black membership, the Non-European Unity Movement largely relied on Coloured members, the Liberal Party on White."[15] There have been many courageous links between individuals across the racial/color boundaries. Helen Suzman continues to fight constitutionally, politically, democratically, for a Progressive Party policy of tolerance. But looked at *en masse*, racial conflict must be seen as a very powerful element of revolution among those which are said to foretell disaster. Indulgent and mild-mannered Marxists have tried to substitute class for race, but it is not a very convincing attempt.[16] The peculiar distinction suffered by South Africa is that racial conflict has been reinforced by economic differentiation. Stanley Trapido, perhaps the ablest among current expositors of South African politics, noted some years ago that "the explanation of South Africa's singularity is political as well as economic. Alone among industrial societies which generate and attract sufficient capital for those economic enterprises upon which they wish to embark, South Africa has not incorporated the major part of its working class into its social and political institutions."[17] That is the basic dilemma. Race as a factor of conflict is common enough, as is religion or class. After all, the Malay and Chinese live uneasily together in Indonesia and Malaysia, as do Tamils and Sinhalese in Sri Lanka, or as Greeks and Turks once did in Cyprus. Usually, however, the two communities are in close numerical balance, enabling a seesaw to be maintained between cooperation and coercion, or there is a workable division of political and economic power, or (less agreeably) the dominant majority sits as heavily as it can on the minority—as in the United States. South Africa is unique in having a racial minority, and a white minority at that, which uses the power of the state to keep subjected to it more numerous communities of a different racial makeup. That the European minority is a wealthy ruling class and the majority a black proletariat-cum-petit-bourgeoisie sharpens the racial antagonism, but it is the racial, not the class, divisions which have prevented the black working class from being incorporated into the industrial society of South Africa and which leaves it exposed—so it is argued—to revolution.

There is a third cluster of argument, however, which still looks for an economic base on which revolution might be mounted. After all, South Africa is a very large state of considerable industrial wealth built by the growth of manufacturing out of mining. It is also dominant in relation to its neighbors, and within the vast areas of Southern Africa "practically every mineral is to be found within its confines, particularly gold, diamonds, uranium, vast reserves of coal and iron ore . . . as well as copper, platinum, chrome and asbestos in enormous quantities."[18] If the economic map of South Africa and its neighbors is looked at as a whole—counting Swaziland, Lesotho, Botswana, Namibia, Malawi, Mozambique, Rhodesia, and Angola, some two million square miles—the mineral wealth, industrial power, manufacturing output, communication network, and power supplies are very great indeed.[19] But the economy is also absolutely dependent on African and Colored labor, and it is not difficult to believe that economic forces, now pent up but struggling to find expression, will burst wide the restrictive framework of apartheid and its two concomitants, job reservation in the white areas and mass unemployment in the homelands. For apartheid or separateness, is nonsense. The white areas of urban South Africa and the European farming sector are full of Africans either in permanent employment or in search of a job, despite all the legislation designed to encourage only the temporary sojourn of those holding jobs and the enforced removal of the unemployed. Christopher Hill records the misery of the African worker in the white city:

To be an urban African means to be a tree without roots because of the many laws and regulations that dog you all your conscious life. The only time you are allowed to forget your humble and insecure role in the white man's area is when you are asleep, or engrossed in your work if you are fortunate enough to be in a type of work which can command your full attention without a constant reminder that you do not belong.[20]

Yet African labor is the foundation of the economy. That is the basis of the argument that a growing industrial and consumer power, combined with the desperation of the jobless, will break the South African state by revolutionary action of the kind that begins with strikes and boycotts and ends in political violence. Then, say the simple Marxists, down will come the whole structure of white privilege, a collapse brought about by what is essentially a veiled civil war within existing society that finally breaks into open revolt. Thus the development of an industrial society will have cut the foundation of white privilege from under its feet. The European minority will then have proved to be their own gravediggers; their fall, and the victory of the African/Colored proletariat, are equally inevitable. So runs the gospel. And there is surely some truth to it. As long ago as 1955 the Tomlinson Commission[21] added up the arithmetic of separate development to reach the conclusion that it made no sense economically, territorially, or morally within the existing pattern of land allocation between white and black. It makes far less sense now, after two further decades of growth.

Unfortunately, as in most economic debates there is a quite contrary argument drawn from the same premise, namely that economic forces will open a road to accommodation through growth whereby prosperity is recognized as being dependent on a rising standard of living among Africans and Coloreds who are already being slowly but surely incorporated into a single South African society. Again, what begins as economics ends in politics, but of an ameliorative nature. Revolution is not so much bought off as grown away from and made irrelevant. It is, it seems, a hope nourished by Andrew Young and endorsed by President Carter. South Africa will be led marching through Georgia to the land of reconciliation. It is perhaps the Oppenheimer (Anglo-American) belief, too, that economics will make not only nonsense of apartheid but sense of politics.

Either way, therefore, economic pressures are seen as making for radical change, as the result of bloody insurrection through mass industrial action or as the beneficial outcome of a rational policy of growth. The former theme, we might note, can be supported by arguments in favor of economic sanctions to force the process; the latter policy can be advanced by its direct opposite—controlled but increased investment. There is, however, a third possibility, arising from the growth of economic factors, but it comes under a very different head, under which it is discussed later.[22]

Fourth, there are international pressures. It is wrong (people argue) to see South Africa in isolation. A revolution, like history itself, needs a good shove in the right direction to get it going. The Russians needed 1917, the Chinese World War II, to achieve their success. Black South Africans will also need help, and gradually it begins to look as if it will be provided. Cautiously but confidently one can say that South Africa is now seen not only by Moscow but by Washington as ripe for change within a period for which it is prudent to make some provision. Each of the superpowers will push for change, although each, of course, will hope for different results. Black American pressure, joined by a fear that any government in Washington will have of being on the losing (white) side, will see American pressure for precisely the kind of reforms that will give events in South Africa a shove forward. The quick and violent response in 1976 by Africans in Soweto to Kissinger's visits to South Africa was a harbinger of future reactions to come. Slowly, too, but with something almost inexorable about its advance, black Africa has drawn near. Of course during the brief time that we live, the pace seems very slow. But that is because we do not, as we should, think historically. In fact, the rate of African success has been remarkably quick. West Africa in the early 1950's, East Africa in the late '50's, the Central African Federation broken in 1963, Portuguese rule overthrown in 1974: can South Africa really last beyond 1984 or 1994? African opposition to European rule persists despite all the rivalries between the OAU members: in a sense the appetite has grown with eating, and that kind of opposition is not to be measured in guns or money or diplomacy but as a shifting quantum of aversion and enmity, however much it may seem to be masked from time to time by opportunity or necessity.

The brief history of dialogue is illustrative in that respect. The phrase was used to describe the willingness of some African leaders to engage in debate with the South African government. In Pretoria it was seen by Vorster as part of an outward movement that would establish South Africa as a state having normal diplomatic ties and solid material links with the rest of the continent. The apparent success of the policy began to be seen about the time of Lesotho's independence in 1966 under Chief Lebua Jonathan as prime minister. State visits were arranged, diplomatic relations were opened with Malawi and the Malagasy Republic, and Pretoria was drawn into negotiations with Lusaka over Rhodesia; Houphouët Boigny in the Ivory Coast, Dr. Busia in Ghana, and the governments of Gabon and of Zaire began to talk of the need for dialogue rather than force as a lever of change. The moves were sufficiently alarming to upset a minority within the National Party and to start a debate between the *verligtes* (enlightened outward-looking) and the *verkramptes* (stubborn inward-looking).[23] But by the early 1970's the movement was forced back. All but a captive minority of African governments returned to hostility and to direct support of guerrilla action in Rhodesia. And who can doubt that Rhodesia has always been seen as the prelude to South Africa even when South Africa's help was sought to bring about the prior stage? Internal convulsions with the republic will keep external pressure alive, and that in turn will play the midwife to local demonstrations. Either by erosion under such pressures or by some dramatic chain of events not foreseeable but certainly predictable, the end will come. The combination of Super-Power rivalry, black African concern, and domestic violence will ensure it. And when the end does come, it will seem absolutely explicable and inevitable. Men often confuse what happens with necessity as if all that takes place is ordained: with respect to South Africa, however, they will be right to interpret the event as carrying the stamp of an inevitable process.

So the full sweep of argument runs, and there is one further phenomenon which those who believe that revolution is at last around the corner now say is taking shape: namely, that white South Africa is beginning—only beginning, but the start is there—to lose confidence in itself. There is more talk of the inevitable. Indeed the South African government itself is busily trying to meet such an end by a policy of internal decolonization or devolution. Homelands, Bantustans, provincial councils, Transkei independence, and talk of a South African Commonwealth of associated states—what is all that but a whistling in the dark to comfort men and women who are beginning to know in the depths of their being that white rule cannot now be maintained?

Joined together, therefore, the destructive force of opposed nationalisms, racial conflict, economic contradictions, and international pressures will bring about the explosion of revolt. So it is often argued. But when all the prophecies are recorded, and all the ingredients of revolution fully assayed, can one really be certain that the whole unlovely system will not go on working within its own structure for as far ahead as one can see? Max Gluckman, a pre-eminently thoughtful scholar, was always unsure. Gluckman lived among the Zulu and observed "the hostility of the colour groups" between chiefs and African people on one side and South African government officials on the other.

I did not send this first analysis, written in terms of a series of hatreds and oppositions, for after reading it through, I asked myself: "How is it that people, Black and White, go about their business so easily, relatively peacefully, and accommodatingly, despite these hatreds and hostilities?" And I remembered that they had done so in Johannesburg, despite clashes and oppression. Therefore I sought for, and found, bases of "cohesion." The South African social system was then, and has become increasingly, a horrible one, morally. But it worked and works, in total and in its parts.

Cohesion, as distinct from consensus. Men may not agree with the structure of society within which they live, but they have to go on living and they find innumerable ways of doing so. To look into the distant future or to examine a society at its highest levels of hatreds and opposition may distract attention from the immediate. It might well be, as Gluckman argued, that "at some time in the future the differential incorporation of the ethnic groups must produce . . . violent disturbance and radical change. In the immediate present my duty as a scientist was to try to understand how the system worked, and was likely to continue working in at least the short run. Thirty years later it still works."[24] That was at the end of the 1960's and we are nearly a decade on again. In a sense the observation is of the workability of a complicated society as industrial South Africa has become, in which "social relationships extend across racial barriers weaving complex and varied patterns of inter-racial contact and creating common interests transcending those of race."[25] As Gluckman commented, convergent interests might be thought more appropriate, but "I feel that one must speak of 'common interests' because this emphasizes the high degree of fairly long-term collaboration that establishes systematic inter-dependence in the economic sphere."[26]

What are these common or convergent interests? As Gluckman noted, it was Engels who stressed that slaves had an interest in the system of slavery, but what are black South African interests in apartheid? We need to turn the question a little, or widen it perhaps, and ask: what are the forces—and that may be the appropriate word—working in the opposite direction from those looked at earlier, restricting or delaying or even forestalling revolution? I want not merely to reexamine our previous list of ingredients but to look at the circumstances as they now are in respect to continuity and change.

In relation to the economy and its effects, it was noted earlier that there was a third interpretation quite different from those which pointed either in the direction of the violence of revolution or to peaceful accommodation by way of radical change. It is that the economy will continue to expand and adapt but without any fundamental disturbance of its racial/class structure. Everyone may become better off or worse off, but there will be no major shift in the proportionate allocation of wealth and status. The whites become richer or poorer, and the African and Colored and Asian populations prosper or suffer accordingly within the hierarchy of opportunities available. Something of that kind has been taking place. Over the past decade or so Europeans have moved up from skilled-manual to technological jobs. Africans have moved up below them to fill the vacancies. The change can be seen in precise as well as general form, varying from one sector of the economy to another, leading to "job dilution" (i.e., Africans doing "white man's work") and the slackening of regulations about job reservation.[27] Such changes mirror in a short span of time much more fundamental shifts over the past one hundred years "from commercial agriculture to diamond and gold mining to manufacturing industry in the English-speaking sector and, most recently, Afrikaner financial and industrial capitalism. Each has merged into the others, but each has also seen the emergence of a new group of beneficiaries from the surplus accumulated."[28] But as Trapido (from whom the quotation is taken) has noted, "it is argued that as Africans come to do more skilled and semi-skilled work their bargaining power will increase, which will affect not only wages but political relationships also [but] the experience of the various phases of South Africa's economic growth suggests that the economic and political systems combine to maintain existing relationships."[29]

To this one might add the argument that if the dominant Afrikaner element in European society continues (contrary to what was asserted earlier) to believe that white power can be sustained, it may actually move toward its relaxation. Perpetually imposed, Afrikaner rule may risk changes that it might otherwise fear and forbid. For such a state of affairs to exist, some degree of external pressure would actually be helpful. So at least the record of the past decade and a half might be thought to indicate. Using the argument of the republic under siege, the leaders of the National Party have moved Afrikanerdom much further than they might otherwise have been able to do in the direction of that peculiar form of enlightenment which places Vorster among the *verligtes*.[30] It is significant perhaps that the most serious outburst of hard-line *Verkrampte* protest under Hertzog and the Herstigte Nationale Party (HNP: Reconstituted National Party) came as this external pressure slackened during the brief period of dialogue, when presumably the plea of the need to close ranks under attack was less cogent.

One must also reckon with the efficiency of repression. The oppressive power of the state runs as a dark thread through any assessment of the strength of the regime. The 1950's—the seedbed of many present hopes—when revolt was active, was also a time of weak security. But it is now commonly assumed that the government is much more efficiently equipped. It learned to be so, to a greater degree than its opponents could, during the period of mass action, until today there is no evidence of any organised threat to its rule. Riots lead to armed police action but they are quickly contained, and the leaders of the 1950's are either under house arrest, as Sobukwe was or, as Mandela is, still on Robben Island, or with Oliver Tambo (Acting President of the ANC) in exile. The last decades of the twentieth century are not necessarily tilted in favor of the survival of oppression when its power rests on a single dictator (as under Franco or Salazar or Peron) whose death brings the end of the system. But there is great collective power in a minority regime that can mediate its authority through a wide range of beneficiaries, as in South Africa through its white electorate. The assassination of Verwoerd in September 1966 (by a mad white South African) scarcely ruffled the surface of party politics. Nor was there (contrary to earlier assertions) any conspicuous sign of faltering among the white electorate. It is true the Progressive Party has marginally increased its support and the HNP has been put down; but the structure of white power remains intact, amply fortified by the police, army, civil service, judiciary, and the ruling party.[31]

There is at least the possibility, too, that even if—a very large if—power began to be contested violently in South Africa, the opposed sides might not be simply white and nonwhite. There are substantial communities between the European minority and the African majority. There are over two million people of mixed descent in the western Cape whose language is Afrikaans or English. There are nearly three-quarters of a million Asians. And neither the Colored nor Indian communities can be placed automatically on the side of revolution. Just as the absurd dividing line of color is blurred, so may the political sympathies of what is a very mixed racial society be blurred. Despite every effort of the South African government over the past sixty years since union to draw a sharp and offensive line of privilege between white and nonwhite, and despite a common front of protest from time to time among the African, Colored, and Indian communities, there has been both tension and distinction between Africans and Indians, Africans and Coloreds. Hilda Kuper described the relationship in 1971: "in the racial hierarchy of South Africa, Asians were placed by the Whites in positions inferior to themselves, superior to Africans, and more or less equal to but separate from Coloureds."[32] Rigid controls have confirmed the pluralism of race and culture. "Non-whites are increasingly governed by state departments of African, Coloured and Indian affairs which insulate them. . . . They are separated by this system of separate incorporation which relates them in different ways to the total society."[33] Africans are particularly disadvantaged, since they are divided "into ethnic sub-groups under Bantu authorities or in Bantustans and by a differential incorporation into urban areas, white rural and African ethnic areas."[34] The effect of common oppression is not necessarily joint resistance. Of the Indian population Hilda Kuper notes that "the fact that Indians are still politically more privileged, and that proportionately more Asiatics than Africans are educated and wealthy, may alienate Africans further from Indians and hence intensify the dependence of the Indian minority on Europeans. The negative stereotype of Indians held by many Africans is perpetuated by the contrast between their own low subject status and the Indians' 'pariah citizenship,' [and] Indians fear that there may be a further deterioration of their position if Africans seize control"[35] —a fear that must have increased since the expulsion of Asians from Uganda and their precarious position in both Kenya and Tanzania. The Colored community, although radicalized in ways not known before, may have similar anxieties, since they too are relatively privileged. They have also been seen from time to time by a minority of liberal Afrikaners (an ambiguous category in itself) as potential allies to whom the franchise should be restored and full citizenship accorded eventually, although it is a nice question whether it will not be too late for negotiation by the time any major concessions are offered. But however skeptical one may be of such overtures, the plurality of South Africa might still complicate the arithmetical factor of conflict in ways not easily calculable. White to nonwhite is 1 to 4.5, but non-African to African is 1 to 2.5, and the communities on both sides of the equation are very sizable.[36]

There is one last factor of uncertainty in relation to those exile voices prophesying war, although, in common with all arguments about South Africa, it needs to be hedged about with qualifications. Successive governments in Pretoria in recent years have attempted very hesitatingly to reduce their direct area of control. Their vortrekker ancestors once constructed a laager of wagons against the enemy, and their successors attempted to protect themselves by "a new laager made up of laws and restraints."[37] To many Afrikaners now there is yet another possibility: that of an inner citadel of white power ringed by a barrier of nonwhite communities, including dependently sovereign states. It is of course the apartheid of separate development carried a stage further, in the sense of a greater readiness among Afrikaner politicians to make a virtue of necessity.

White Power: Cohesion without Consensus

What that need is becomes clearer when we look at the policy. It is to do something, or be seen to be doing something, if only to buy time. After all, buying time is a familiar political hope. It is perhaps the only policy that all politicians instinctively recognize as basic to their trade. Very possibly, white South Africa has been encouraged by Smith's purchase of more than a decade of time by combining stubbornness with a willingness to talk reform. Vorster could certainly buy more time than that, given the lack of African power (domestically and externally) to enforce change and the pervasive hope of the United States for amelioration. But time can also be made available—so it seems to be argued in Pretoria—by a form of withdrawal from what is seen today as inessential to an inner position of control. We might, therefore, by way of conclusion, look at this aspect of white power.

The change in policy is fairly clear. Nor is it quite as novel as might be thought. It dates from the South African government's acceptance—a necessary acceptance—of the independence of Lesotho, Botswana, and Swaziland at the end of the 1960's and from what seems to have been a realization of the advantages of control without responsibility. There was a time when South Africa wanted very much to incorporate the former British High Commission Territories within its own boundaries. Now the intention is quite plainly to devolve rather than to absorb. Hence the change-around of policy toward Namibia, the formal declaration of independence of Transkei, and the promise of future sovereign enclaves to come. In such shifts of attitude one might also include the present ambivalence in Pretoria toward Rhodesia, wavering between reluctance to abandon so brave a white stand against sanctions and a half-belief that a black-ruled, or black-white ruled, Rhodesia might protect South Africa's interests better than a rebel white regime if only one can get the right kind of Africans in office in Salisbury—or, for that matter, in Windhoek or Luanda and Maputo.

The Transkei is an interesting case in point. It is the most geographically self-contained of all the projected homelands, with a long pedigree of local autonomy. It was declared to be independent among as much festive ceremony as could be evoked on 26 October 1976. No one outside South Africa believed it. The United Nations, like the OAU, refused to recognize Matanzima's government in Umtata. The OAU insisted on the territorial integrity of South Africa. The rest of the world withheld its assent, not primarily, as one might suppose, because of misgivings concerning the fitness of the territory to receive independence but because of suspicion about the donor country. The South African authorities like to point out that the Transkei is "larger than twelve other African states, bigger than Switzerland and twice the size of Wales,"[38] although the comparison I rather like is with New England: it is "larger than . . . the American states of Connecticut, Rhode Island and Massachusetts combined."[39] Its per capita income, however, is very unlike that of Switzerland, Massachusetts, or Rhode Island: it is under $100 a year from local resources, though roughly double that if remittances are taken into account, since—like Lesotho and large areas of Malawi and Mozambique—the Transkei is preeminently a labor-exporting country. Of its two million population, some 350,000 are migrant workers in the republic and the proportion is annually increasing. More remarkably, there are an additional one million Xhosa-speaking Africans, originally from the Transkei but living permanently and inescapably resident in the white areas of the Republic.[40] The Transkei government also requires South African help for something like $40 million, or three-quarters of its budget—a helpless dependency, although that has not prevented Matanzima from opposing the republic on local issues.

Namibia is different. It is huge, larger than Pakistan in area but with under a million inhabitants. It is also mineral-rich almost beyond the dreams of international avarice. That places Namibia, too, in a capitalist-dependent category, for how else could its 700,000 people manage their affairs? In this respect, it is by no means unique. There are a number of similarly rich-poor states—Papua New Guinea, for example, except of course that Namibia has South Africa and not Australia as its protective power. The territory is also divided between Germans, Afrikaners, Ovambo, Okavango, Damara, Rehebothers, Herero, Nama, Coloreds, and (in the great desert areas) Bushmen. As if that were not complicated enough, the principal port, Walvis Bay, is legally South African territory. Armed bases cover the Caprivi Strip, south of Angola, and a guerrilla war of fluctuating fortunes is still being fought in the border areas—a greater threat, one suspects, to President Neto's regime in Luanda than to the South African government in Pretoria. Toward the end of 1976 an interracial conference met in the old Turnhalle building in Windhoek and drew up proposals for independence. Once again the international world refused to accept South Africa's seal of approval, since the South West African People's Organization (SWAPO), a principal though by no means the only claimant to control of an independent government, had declined to take part. SWAPO's present leader is Sam Nujoma, but others are in prison or detention or exile. Resolution 385 of the United Nations called for free elections, removal of the South African army, release of prisoners, and administration of the territory by a United Nations council. Meanwhile, the mining companies prosper and South Africa remains in control.[41]

One may note, in parentheses, that there is a marked arbitrariness in the refusal of the rest of the world to accept South African policy towards the Transkei. If Lesotho or the Seychelles or Equatorial Guinea or Costa Rica can be independent, why should the Transkei be denied? Unlike Lesotho or Botswana it has at least a coastline. Why should colonial rule be the determinant of sovereignty? Nor is it easy to see that SWAPO or any other government in Namibia would make very much difference to the country's dependence. Neither territory would be thought remotely capable of separate existence in any century but our own strangely divided world of pygmy states and Super Powers, but if the community of nations can find a place for Djibouti, there ought to be room for the Transkei. There is no need to bestow full approval of a policy which seeks to extend a pattern of a sovereign dependency to domestic areas of South Africa itself, but to the extent that independence for the Transkei (as for Namibia) increases—however marginally—their political distance from the Republic, it seems right to applaud (if not very enthusiastically).

If South Africa does give up Namibia, and if it bestows some degree of autonomy on a number of scattered homelands such as Kwa-Zulu and BophuthaTswana,[42] what follows from that? How might such measures affect the balance between continuity and change, cohesion and consensus?

The promised program of self-government for the Bantu areas does not carry much conviction. The Transkei apart, the projected states are little more than divided rural reserves, interspersed with white-controlled areas in which border industries have been located in order to draw on migrant labor. As Stultz has pointed out, "under current policy Africans will always outnumber whites in so-called 'white' South Africa, even should every homeland obtain independence,"[43] and demographic indicators not only confirm the pattern but suggest its intensification.[44] The numerical preponderance of the African population is increasing throughout the republic as a whole, in which something like 40 percent of the population—black, white, Colored, and Indian alike—live as a single economic society in the urban industrial areas.[45] There is a gross and growing inequity, therefore, to a distribution that gives 70 percent of the land area to the white minority and 13 percent to the black majority—a fundamental and familiar ground of anguish. And where still, it can be asked, are the homelands for the Colored and Indian communities?

Why should there have been any hesitation, therefore, over current South African policies? Are they not a pretence, designed to mask the reality of white power? I think the hesitancy came from two sources. One was the uneasy belief that Pretoria may indeed buy time from the outside world—and time enough to stretch out into an unforeseeable future—by devolving power and producing the appearance of change while vigorously maintaining the substance of control. The other related source of doubt came almost certainly from a vague hope that perhaps South Africa might actually stumble by default, or necessity, or because events slide out of control, further than the government intends in the direction of devolution or federation or confederation or even toward that last terminus of partition. They will loosen the stones at the top of the slope and the avalanche will begin to sweep away existing structures. Remote parallels could be found with European decolonization on the rather absurd analogy that South Africa is by way of being an internal colonial power, or with India and Pakistan, or Palestine and Cyprus, in the sense that other opposed communities who were unable to live together had to be wrenched apart. Even in respect of South Africa, the extreme formulation of partition is not altogether new, although the practical design has always troubled those who advocate it.[46]

White Power: Cohesion without Consensus

There is always something very comforting in such distant views. They offer a remote prospect of fundamental change without raising awkward questions about the immediate steps to be taken. Because they promise a good deal, they encourage procrastination. Time is bought. And a pattern of change is laid up for the future which can be left to the future. My guess is that such heady ideas as federation or partition—for which the harbingers are said to be the visible relaxation of apartheid in sport, the easing of job reservation, independence for the homelands, and current proposals for revision of the constitution to provide some measure of multiracial (but non-African) representation—have immense appeal for Washington and London, which would like to believe in the reforming music of time if only to enable them, in the short term, to enlist South Africa against Rhodesia and, on a longer view, to put off the dreadful prospect of having to be concerned fully with the Republic. How else can one explain the disarray in Washington and London when, in the run-up to the 1977 election, the South African government beat down its critics in savage fashion? It restricted Mrs. Nelson Mandela, confined under house arrest Beyers Naudé of the Christian Institute, banned the European editor of the *Daily Dispatch*, detained Percy Qoboza of the *African World*, and imprisoned (until he died naked and chained) Steve Biko of the Black Consciousness movement. The consequence was that the United Nations imposed mandatory sanctions on the sale of arms to the Republic, but still the hope persisted in London and Washington of securing South African cooperation over Rhodesia and Namibia.

Nor do the present leaders of the Soviet Union display any marked enthusiasm for direct involvement. Very likely they, too, believe, or want to believe, that time is on their side in South Africa (as everywhere) and can be left to its own dialectic. Arms and the Cubans for Ethiopia and Angola or for the Patriotic Front, certainly: the investment is small, and the returns quite heartwarming. But involvement is not to be pushed too far against active displeasure in Washington, since détente and the vexed problems of the Middle East and Eastern Europe, and burdensome clients in Angola and Ethiopia, are quite enough to occupy them.

Is the most likely projection into the twenty-first century the continued "cohesion without consensus" of white power? Attempts at devolution hardly seem likely to slip into an avalanche of reform. There are too many restraints on them. Any major redistribution of power would require reform of the European parliamentary system, or the redistribution of land, people, and wealth. Each step along either road—toward the incorporation of all South Africans into one system, or toward their separation into distinct political communities—would mean sacrifices by the European minority which at present can scarcely envisage the costs or gauge the benefits. Moreover, power sharing, of whatever kind, would depend on its acceptance by the African majority, which may not like the idea at all: revenge is as powerful an emotion as self-interest, particularly when spurred by past injustice. Since a large part of the history of such internal transfers of power has been a record of too little too late, it hardly seems likely that South Africa would get it right.

Yet one cannot quite escape the fascination of number. Part of the bewilderment with which outsiders view South Africa reflects the size of the ruling white minority as much as the growing number of those controlled. Four million is a very substantial ruling class, more numerous than the entire population of, say, Jamaica or New Zealand or Israel or Eire. If only white South Africa were an island in a distant sea! One might pause a little at Israel and note its survival against much heavier odds, except that Israel has so far avoided total dependence on a large internal proletariat and South Africa lacks any direct external help comparable with that afforded Israel by the United States. It is true that 800,000 French Algerians quit Algeria in the 1960's. But can one really imagine the flight of four *million* Afrikaner and English South Africans? Or the internal boundaries of a divided Republic which combined political separation with economic interdependence among South African Africans, South African Whites, South African Colored, and South African Indians? By the year 2000 the total population of the Republic may be fifty million, including nearly seven million whites and forty million Africans. So at least the demographers have forecast.[47] Cohesion without consensus among so many? It would be as though the United States were ruled not by its "Caucassian majority" but by twice the number of its present black population in positions of greatly disproportionate wealth and power, having also to

White Power: Cohesion without Consensus

confront a Latin America recently liberated from black rule. A fantasy world indeed! But white power in South Africa is no fantasy.[48]

One's mind swings back and forth between one implausibility and another. If there *were* a total collapse, the international world would need to be drawn to their rescue—Britain by its history, the United States by its power, the Soviet Union by equal and opposite reaction, and China, too, along with the United Nations, the OAU, and many smaller states, including the helpless victims of the southern African region. They would have to try to put what was left together again in ways no one can possibly foresee. Even to sketch such vague fears is to try to see into a grossly uncertain future, and after each attempt to assess the irresistible momentum of revolution against the irremovable structures of control, I am none the wiser about the outcome. In trying to look at the changes that may reshape the southern part of the continent, we are not dealing with the set pieces of a jigsaw puzzle that can be assembled only in a certain fashion to produce a single picture. Arguments drawn from what appear to be present trends are much more like the fragments of a mosaic, the future design of which we cannot see, however much we try to place them together in a compelling way. That in itself is difficult enough, but there is the added certainty that we do not as yet have all the pieces or arguments from which to form the image of what may come.

6. The Darkling Plain: Literature and Politics

To move from the earthy concerns of politics to the imaginative world of the novel or of drama and poetry might at first be thought extravagant, even frivolous. Politics is often said to be the art of the possible, but can one turn sensibly to literature in order to add to an understanding of so practical a craft? The answer is surely yes, in respect of the past three or four decades in Africa since, in an age which is intensely political, writers will not escape its impulse, and they may offer a view which not only is intrinsically interesting but reflects a wider range of issues than are commonly looked at by historians and political scientists. They will, if they can, give expression to what they think is politically central to their time, and we too (if only indirectly) can share that experience through their poetry or novels. Consider, for example, the change in mood among writers during the period before and after independence. It has been very marked and must surely illustrate more than the writers' own sensibilities. What that sentiment is today might be expressed once again by the lines from Matthew Arnold quoted earlier:

> *for the world, which seems*
> *To lie before us like a land of dreams,*
> *So various, so beautiful, so new*
> *Hath really neither joy nor love nor light*
> *Nor certitude, nor peace, nor help for pain;*
> *And we are here as on a darkling plain*
> *Swept with confused alarms of struggle and flight*
> *Where ignorant armies clash by night.*[1]

Dover Beach is a world away from Africa in the twentieth century, but its note of inner melancholy is very close to the pessimism (or failed optimism) in a good deal of modern African literature. We might look therefore not only at committed poets and novelists but at writers who have tried to give dramatic force and shape to those inner problems of general concern to their own generation, for which politics are the outward expression. One may think especially of Yeats, who gave all the passionate intensity of his genius to his native country, Ireland—that former colony—and by doing so made it a "microcosm of the whole civilized world."[2] In England there were the radical poets of the 1930's who reflected (though often distortedly) an intellectual mood of the interwar years.[3] Are there such poets, novelists, and dramatists in Africa today, writing of their own country and creating a microcosm not of the whole world perhaps but of their continent at least? I believe there are, though none is as yet of particular genius, and I think they do mirror the fears and longings of their own intensely political age. For it seems they cannot avoid writing about politics—the politics of the old past or the politics of nationalism and the post-independence years. Between the past and the future they cry out today against the present, as if writing

> between two worlds, one dead
> The other powerless to be born.

Like most mirrors, literature will reflect only what is shone upon its surface. A prevailing mood is caught and returned. But that is not the whole story, for the literary mirror is also an active agent, more prism than mirror, and it is proper to ask in what sense a poet or novelist will portray the politics of an age. Is he not, as an African writer, bound more to the external world, however much he may seek to loosen its hold, than to those of his own compatriots who can scarcely read what he writes? And is there not a major difficulty about which language to use—a problem not only of an elite which is separated by art and taste from the masses but of an inherited or imposed language as against the spoken vernacular of the marketplace? Dependency takes many forms and a cultural dependence may chafe as painfully as its counterpart in politics or economics. The difficulties of African or Asian writers in this respect have not been ignored. Innumerable conferences have passed unfulfilled resolutions (in English or French) about the problem, but it is worth some comment here by way of introduction to a wider theme.

At one of the conferences of African writers, Per Wästberg gently pointed out that he, too, as a Swede, belonged to one of the smaller European communities, inhabiting (one might say) only a village in the global world of literature: fewer people spoke Finnish than Wolof, many more understood Yoruba than Norwegian.[4] Yet that had not prevented Ibsen's or Strindberg's speaking to the world through his national language. Many of the world's languages were "provincial" in relation to the major centers of culture, yet still there were Dutch or Greek or German or Scandinavian writers.[5] Was there no African writer eager to parallel, say, Tagore and the renaissance of Bengali literature?

But that is not the full measure of the problem facing the African novelist or poet. Whereas African artists can draw on tradition in sculpture or dancing or music, it seems doubtful whether a poet or novelist can write in his mother tongue out of a background of general illiteracy. Where would his audience be? I suppose it is possible that African legends might be recast today as epic poetry or used, like Celtic mythology, to begin a national literature, assuming that Hausa or Swahili or whatever language the writer was born to could be stretched to the task. There is said to be a continuing tradition of poetry in the Somali language, and Hausa epics are still recited in northern Nigeria. There have also been local attempts to recast village ceremonies in modern dramatic form, as in the Ogun plays among the Yoruba in Nigeria, or as Efua Sutherland has tried to do in village theaters among the Akan in Ghana. At every turn, however, the African writer is confronted not simply with illiteracy but with the prevalance of English or French or Portuguese. There is an educated minority which is yearly growing in number, and despite the substitution of Swahili for English as the national language in Tanzania, and of Malgache for French in the Malagasy Republic, the former metropolitan languages seem unlikely to be displaced as the main instruments of higher education and literary expression. Only in North Africa, which lies beyond my competence to discuss, is Arabic a powerful challenge to French and English. South of the Sahara the problem is a very real one for many writers and they have argued about it intelligently.[6] It is in one sense a problem of the cultural hegemony of the former colonial language which imposes patterns of words and thoughts to which the writer may not be able fully to respond; but it is also a question of the attractive power of a strong center of literary culture to which African writers reach out, eager for an audience of critical intelligence as well as for a market of commercial importance.[7]

It might be asked, particularly by an American audience brought up on Mark Twain, whether there will be a distinctive use one day of English by Africans: an Afro-English, or Afro-Saxon perhaps, and its equivalent in French? It may, I suppose, develop. But I do not think it is likely to extend all the way to that expressive idiom of pidgin English or Creole which has wide usage and great vigor but is unable to sustain a popular national literature, although attempts have been made to write a kind of demotic English by Amos Tutuola (for example) in *The Palm Wine Drinkard*, and its use in dialogue can add a marvelous local flavor:

Then a knock at the door and a young man in heavily starched white shorts and shirt comes in to offer his services as a cook.

"Wetin you fit cook?" asked Chief Nanga as he perused the young man's sheaf of testimonials, probably not one of them genuine.

"I fit cook every European chop like steak and kidney pie, chicken puri, misk grill, cake omlette...."

"You no sabi cook African chop?"

"Ahh! That one I no sabi am-o," he admitted, "I no go tell master lie."

"Wetin you de chop for your own house?" I asked, being irritated by the idiot.

"Wetin I de chop for my house?" he repeated after me. "Na we country chop I de chop."

"You country chop no be Africa chop?" asked Chief Nanga.

"Na him" admitted the cook. "But no be me de cook am. I get wife for house."

My irritation vanished at once, and I joined Chief Nanga's laughter. Greatly encouraged the cook added:

"How man wey get family go begin enter kitchen for make bitterleaf and egusi? Unless if the man no get shame."

The Darkling Plain: Literature and Politics

> *We agreed with him but he lost the job because Chief Nanga preferred bitterleaf and egusi to chicken puri—whatever that was. But I must say the fellow had a point too. As long as a man confined himself to preparing foreign concoctions he could still maintain the comfortable illusion that he wasn't really doing such an unmanly thing as cooking.* [8]

Too much, however, is more than plenty. The overextended use of any dialect can have the effect of baffling those outside its narrow range to the point of incomprehensibility.[9]

Are such novels themselves foreign concoctions? The dangers of mimicry are certainly there, though rarely (I hasten to add) in Mr. Achebe's novels. In the post-colonial relationship, perhaps the final grasp of imperialism will be its strongest, through the cultural dependency of an African educated minority on Europe and America. African politicians have been the easy prey of a simple Marxism, African academics of an American political science, and one may wonder whether African novelists and poets will be able to free themselves from the dominance of an imported culture which is all the more powerful because it is self-imposed. "In place of distaste for the English language, there developed a passion to command it. In the same way, our national attire came to be favoured and the dark suit was everywhere to be seen. So Africans were gradually persuaded to use the amenities which make vice agreeable.... They talked of such novelties as 'civilization' when really they were only a feature of their enslavement."[10] Mimicry can easily lead to banality, or to pastiche, or to misjudgment of words and sentiment as, for example, in what is surely a false echo of French symbolism:

> *Le coeur vaste comme un rêve*
> *un rêve d'enfant*
> *Souffrant ailleurs*
> *Voeux, pleurs*
> *Serments, leurres*
> *des heures*
> *d'antan.*[11]

Or of Wordsworth in Dei Anang's recollection of

> *untutored days*
> *when maid was ever chaste*
> *And lad abhorred unhallowed ways*
> *For fear of ancient gods.*

Or of an absurdity (which is rather endearing) as in the Zambian poet's description of "the slave's farewell":

> *Farewell, young trees of Africa*
> *And all the beasts of the continent*
> *Farewell to every creature, ant*
> *Snake, cow, goat, bird and all*
> *That dwell in its waters.*
> *This shipping shall be told to my generation*
> *Farewell souls of Africa*
> *Where animals nibble.*[12]

A borrowed language carries its trademark of foreignness, and in all but the most skillful hands it may never quite fit the home-grown use to which it is put. It may be not simply a matter of vocabulary or tone or competence but—at the deepset level—the resonance carried by the language. So, for example, Joyce made Stephen Dedalus lament the need to express himself in English: "The language in which we are speaking is his before it is mine. How different are the words *home, Christ, ale, master,* on his lips and mine! I cannot speak or write these words without unrest of spirit. His language, so familiar and so foreign, will always be for me an acquired speech. I have not made or accepted its words. My voice holds them at bay. My soul frets in the shadow of his language."[13] Yeats, too, professed to mourn the loss of a native idiom of speech and vocabulary: "Gaelic is my national language, but it is not my mother tongue."[14]

I cannot judge the extent of such feeling among African writers. Yeats could evoke an Irish sense of nationality, and yet become "certainly the greatest [poet of our time] in this language and so far as I am able to judge, in any language."[15] Joyce reduced the English language to a subconscious stream of imagery, but with great precision and beauty of expression when he wanted to. The Welsh have tried to keep alive a double tradition of Welsh and English poetry: the Eisteddfod alongside Dylan

Thomas and Alun Lewis. But the African writers I wish to put before you in order to mirror the politics of their generation have chosen to write in English or French, and the extent to which they speak for their own countrymen has to be taken to some degree on trust. They are an elite minority writing in a foreign language about the politics of nationalism; but the politics, too, are largely elite-dominated.

The writers themselves are surprisingly consistent. They have tended to take a common path covering three broad stages: (1) from protest within to rejection of the European colonial world; (2) an assertion of the values of a black African past and a willingness "to endorse any kind of 'ism' with a clear conscience"[16] if they thought it would help the nationalist movement; (3) an indictment of post-independence governments which are seen as corrupt and brutal. The categories are not neatly demarcated. As the independent states exhibited different identities, some more ugly, some more venial, the novelists and poets reacted differently. But the general theme today has become one almost of total disenchantment not only with the leaders whom the writers now distrust, but with the idealism that they themselves once tried to express.

They began with protest. Like much else in the world shaped by a European imperialism, the instruments of the written word, as primary agents of political control, were turned against their users. Just as the colonial state produced the anticolonial movement, so its metropolitan language became the medium of protest against its rule, and it is at the point where African writers began trying to do something about colonialism that we need to begin.

Mild at first was the literature of protest, more prose than poetry, more tract than fiction, and more sorrowful than angry. At its best, it took on a semivisionary character, of which *Ethiopia Unbound* by the Ghanaian, Ephraim Casely Hayford, was an eponymous example.[17] "Africa shall arise and her sons and daughters will fly like eagles."[18] No disrespect was intended in those times "to the Throne or Person of the King Emperor," or to the one and indivisible French Republic. It was simply asserted that Africa needed to take its place in full equality with the rest of the world within the British or French Empire. Ethiopia, a fabled land, would then join the comity of nations.

By the 1930's, a decade later, the protests were more accusatory. There was no upholding now of Empire but the condemnation of imperialism. The Marxists (among others) had got at them. It was a peculiar form of Marxism, stressing race rather than class, and the colonized African rather than the proletariat of the world, but it was no less appealing for that.

"The African trumpet shall sound and we shall all be changed." Such was the start of the literature of *négritude* and of restoring value to the African past. Since the colonial state was now objected to, and the nation-to-be was still unclear, it was understandable that the first direct protest against European rule should take as its themes "being black" and "being African." After all, the colonial empires had thought continentally—why should the African intellectual not think of a zone of black power stretching out from Africa to the New World? Historically (though the actual history hardly mattered now) it is true that the Pan-African movement had grown the other way around in the 1900's and 1920's, from the West Indies and black America back to Africa, under Marcus Garvey (originally from Jamaica) and W. E. B. DuBois of the United States. (The latter lies buried in Accra; the former was buried in Highgate cemetery in London —an irony of juxtaposition, since one feels that Garvey should somehow have got to Africa and that DuBois would have been happier with Marx in Highgate.)[19] The masterful exponent of *négritude* after 1954, however, was Léopold S. Senghor, a black Frenchman and a Francophone African who was a deputy and minister in the French National Assembly between 1946 and 1958, and president of Senegal after 1960. The term itself first appeared in print in a long autobiographical poem, *Cahier d'un retour au pays natal* by Aimé Césaire, the Martinque poet, published in Paris in 1939. It caused little stir at first, being overborne by much weightier events. But when it was reissued in 1947, with an introduction by André Breton, the times were propitious, and *négritude* was then taken up as a cultural protest in Paris and Dakar not under any direct political banner, since the movement toward self-government was just beginning to take direction in British West Africa and was quite dormant in the French territories. As Senghor wrote some years later, "Paradoxically it was the French who forced us to seek the essence of

Négritude when they imposed the policy of assimilation and thus deepened our despair. . . . We had been able to assimilate mathematics and the French language but we could never strip off our black skins nor root out our black souls."[20] Senghor, Césaire, and Alioune Diop (editor of the Paris-based magazine *Présence Africaine*) gave force in this way to a new notion, the negro-African world, elusive in definition and purpose but emotive and symbolic. It was intended, said Diop, as "a vindication of the dignity of persons of African descent," a revealing phrase in the sense that it was very much an intellectual need, or certainly more strongly expressed at an educated urban level than in the villages where birth and custom reinforced a pride in descent.

Négritude was a very French term. But in one form or other the cry of "black Africa" was taken up on both sides of the colonial frontier. It was the basis of a large number of assertive poems:

> *Femme Nue, femme noire*
> *Vêtue de ta couleur qui est la vie, de*
> *ta forme qui est beauté!* [21]

and

> *O ma Lionne ma Beauté noire*
> *ma Nuit noire ma Noire ma Nue!*[22]

and

> *Your breasts of black satin, full and glistening. . . .*
> *Rousing in me tonight*
> *The rhythms with which our sisters*
> *Black and nude in the land of Guinea*
> *Intoxicate themselves.*
> *And makes rise in me this night*
> *The heavy dusk of my passion*
> *Because the soul of the black country*
> *Where our ancestors sleep*
> *Lives and speaks this night*
> *In the restless power of your curving loins.* [23]

The Darkling Plain: Literature and Politics

To be black, and assertively so, was a form of cultural protest against the arrogance of colonial rule, but it joined forces with a new pride in being nationalist. Both evoked deep emotion, to which writers responded full of hope. The nationalist fervor beginning to stir across the continent could exert its appeal without having to be specific: it simply pointed forward to an age that would bring a common purpose to all who joined together. There were parallels in other decades:

Come then, companions. This is the spring of blood
Heart's hey-day, movement of masses, beginning of good.[24]

But the African renaissance was far broader, if similar in sentiment. Under a wide cluster of beliefs it combined pride in being black with being African, and being African with the delight of being nationalist. Moreover, it knew that independence would bring a new age of freedom with prosperity. English writers found a title for such aims as a rough equivalent to, and more focused than, négritude—the assertion of an African Personality. The titles of a key number of books spanning several years had already evoked the dream: J. de Graft-Johnson's *Towards Nationhood* (1928), Nnamdi Azikiwe's *Renascent Africa* (1937), Kenyatta's *Facing Mount Kenya* (1938), R. E. G. Armattoe's *The Golden Age of West African Civilization* (1946), J. C. de Graft-Johnson's *African Glory* (1954). Indeed the extravagance of such sentiments about being African, though hardly more exaggerated than the dark savagery of Africa commonly portrayed in European tales,[25] reached back a very long way. More than a century ago J. A. B. Horton—"Africanus Horton"—was claiming that Africa had been "the nursery of science and literature" because "Origen, Tertullian, Augustine, Clemens Alexandrinus and Cyril, who were fathers and writers of the Primitive Church, were tawny African bishops of Apostolic renown."[26] By the end of World War II more elaborate ideas were abroad. It began to be argued that African societies were gifted with the knowledge of life: they held values which were "essentially informed by intuitive reason"; and "a sense of communion, the gift of rhythm" were to be found throughout "the negro-African world."[27] The independent African nations would retain such qualities, since "we of Africa belonging neither to the East nor the West, are fundamentally observers, penetrating observers, relying more on intuition than on the process of reasoning. We excel neither in mysticism nor in science and technology, but in the field of human relations."[28] In verse, the argument became:

Those who have invented neither gunpowder nor the compass
Those who have tamed neither gas nor electricity
Those who have explored neither the seas nor the skies . . .
They abandon themselves, possessed, to the essence of all things,
  ignoring surfaces but possessed by the movement of all things.
Heedless, taking no account, but playing the game of the world.
                                    (Aimé Césaire)

One must remember that the 1950's and '60's were still periods of colonial struggle, and of a defensive insistence on the right of national independence. Anticolonialism, Pan-Africanism, national liberation, négritude, a sovereign African independence, were all parts of a redemptive creed of national salvation, and they were still powerful ideas to those who wanted to dissolve the colonial world. Many writers at the time found the call for a social and national upheaval, which would cleanse the continent and their own country of a colonial corruption, immensely exciting. Some were drawn intellectually to violence and the community of revolution. The Congress of Negro Artists and Writers, in Paris in 1956 and in Rome in 1959—forerunners of later conferences in Dakar, Kampala, Dar-es-Salaam, and Lagos—paralleled the Pan-African meetings of heads of state and party leaders for whom the poets and novelists tried to express their support. For some, Marx was to be redressed in African cloth, for others philosophy was to be reformulated, history rewritten, and literature brought to the service of the nationalist movement. Often enough, there was an admonitory note to the novels of the time, as in *A Wreath for Udomo* in 1956, by the South African Colored writer Peter Abrahams, some months before the independence of Ghana. The plot is simple enough, and convincing; the descriptions of party nationalism during an election campaign for self-government are vivid. Udomo, the nationalist hero (obviously Nkrumah), triumphantly leads his country to independence only to discover that the necessities of politics oblige him to sacrifice first his principles and then his friends. Even so, he does not escape, and the novel ends with his assassination by the tribal forces of the interior. There is no moral, but it tells a warning story.[29]

On the other side of the continent, James Ngugi, a Kenyan Kikuyu, was still arguing a decade later that the artist in his writings is not exempted from revolutionary struggle—that he should give moral direction and vision and take up the crisis of conflict between the emergent African bourgeoisie and the African masses. His novels, *Weep Not Child* (1964) and *A Grain of Wheat* (1967), were awkward attempts to explore such themes; but they were interestingly assertive of the need for revolution and the difficulties of the nationalist hero in times of acute political change. Similarly, James Kariuki proclaimed his part in the Mau Mau uprising, writing that "the soldiers of the forest were neither 'hardcore terrorists' nor 'murderers' but the noblest fighters for freedom."[30] The West African novelist Yambo Ouologuem also defended the duty of violence throughout the 1960's. His *Lettre à la France nègre* and the novel *Devoir de Violence* (Bound to Violence) were a "demonstration of inescapable bondage . . . to violence" in order to achieve freedom. Awarded the Prix Renandot, the novel describes the "sickening sexual misadventures of incest and sodomy" which befall and degrade the assimilated "half-whitened nigger" Raymond and there is a good deal of "high-flown banter" about the need of ruthlessness in politics. Whatever its appeal in French-speaking Africa, it was also intended (one suspects) for a Paris audience half in love itself with violence and revolution.[31]

But for those who were still able to see the nationalist movements as belonging to a heroic period when a colonized society would be baptized by violence and reborn, Frantz Fanon was preeminently the articulate and ferocious guide. Writing out of the savagery of the Algerian war, Fanon insisted that "National Liberation, national renaissance, the reconstruction of nationhood . . . or whatever heading is used . . . is always a violent phenomenon. . . . The naked truth of decolonization evokes for us the searing bullets and bloodstained knives which emanate from it. . . . The colonized races, those slaves of modern times, are impatient . . . but for such colonized people violence invests their characters with positive and creative qualities. The politics of violence binds them together as a whole."[32] Novelists and poets who lacked the material for such views in their own country—and it is commonly forgotten that Fanon was writing out of a settler society of a very peculiar kind—were able to express their militancy by writing symbolically on behalf of black Africa as a whole, or in support of revolutionary leaders such as Edouardo Mondlane or Agostinho Neto, who were actually engaged in armed struggle but found time to express their beliefs in poetry that made up in revolutionary and often mystical zeal what it lacked in verse.[33]

At popular level, too, the 1960's were rich in market ballads and political pictures of the heroes—especially the martyred heroes—of the nationalist movements. At the river crossing into eastern Nigeria at Onitsha there were dozens of market stalls and little shops full of booklets hawked and sold to the barely literate. Lumumba was the cult hero, along with Jomo Kenyatta, Kwame Nkrumah, Nnamdi Azikiwe, and near-legendary figures outside of Africa—"How John Kennedy Suffered in Life and Died Suddenly." There were postcards, too, of dignified Africans in colored robes representing the ancient splendors of the continent, or of "Kenyatta Receiving the Blessing," and adaptations of the Creed or the Lord's Prayer to sanctify the nationalist movement.[34]

If the naiveté of such popular literature was rather endearing, and if the poetry of négritude was often interesting, it was also true that political interests began to appear behind such concepts which were much less palatable. The invocation of the past was now used to disguise the present under an African mask, as if tradition could be made into a kind of séance to conjure up protective spirits. Senghor, for example, was still talking of the virtues of négritude and of the "racist-anti-racialism of the movement" at the World Festival of Negro Arts in Senegal in 1966 while the prisons were filling up with political detainees, including those in Dakar. Pseudo-doctrines were proclaimed of *commaunocracie*, or *conscientisme*, or *Bourguibisme*, or *Mobutisme*, or *Nkrumaism*, while single-party rule, military rule, presidential rule, republican rule, and the search by lawyers and politicians for autochthony and authenticity were all pressed into the celebration of an African awakening. The consequence, at least for the novelists, poets, and dramatists, was that the dream began to fade. It turned into a nightmare, ugly and disturbing. The African world had changed, not for the better; and one by one the articles of faith advanced in the 1950's and '60's fell away. The literature of protest continued, but the targets changed from the colonial government to the corrupt regimes that had inherited the colonial past. Once upon a time, David Diop had evoked the colonial sufferings of the poor negro:

> *Souffre, souffre, pauvre Nègre*
> *Le fouet siffle*
> *Siffle sur ton dos de sueur et de sang*
> *Souffre, pauvre Nègre!* ...
> *Tes enfants ont faim*
> *Faim et ta case est vide*
> *Vide de ta femme qui dort*
> *Qui dort sur la couche seigneuriale*
> *Souffre, pauvre Nègre!*
> *Nègre noir comme la Misère.* [35]

But after 1960 the whip was held by African governments, and the party leaders slept (not alone) on the seigneurial bed. And still the children went hungry and the squalor remained. There was less talk now of an intuitive reason or of communal values amid the coups, torture, and collective tyranny of single-party or military rule. Africa was no longer the land of laughter that it was once romantically said to have been.[36] "If," said Davidson Nicol, "the West African intellectual does not become too English, if he does not become too French, he is very tempted to become very chauvinistic, that is to say, he moves towards intense and sometimes erratic manifestations of African civilisation. He makes wild claims for which there is no basis.... That is wrong.... He must not overlook the intense feeling of being independent because it is through this that proof of personality takes place, that people are able to hold their heads up [but] his loyalties have become confused ... because religion, tribe, politics all pull against each other."[37]

Clearly the mood was changing. Romantic Africa was dead and gone; it was with the past, and the past, too, needed proper respect. Already Wole Soyinka, Africa's leading playwright (as Bernth Lindfors properly calls him), had begun to mock the pretense that tradition could be used as a means to justify the present under whatever form a particular government chose to adopt. In *A Dance of the Forests*, a search is started by the Council to find and bring back "the direct descendants of our great forefathers" for the great occasion of independence and "the gathering of the tribes":

Find them. Find the scattered sons of our proud ancestors. The builders of empires. The descendants of our great nobility. Find them. Bring them here. If they are half-way across the world, trace them. If they are in hell, ransom them. Let them symbolise all that is noble in our nation. Let them be our historical link for the season of rejoicing.

They are found and brought, and a sorry set they are, neither noble nor proud. In fact, they are just like us, and it is no help to the present to pretend otherwise. Other plays followed, and in 1967 Soyinka published *Kongi's Harvest*, a burlesque of an independent African state whose ruler, Kongi, exalts himself foolishly and destructively above his followers and the gods. He governs by the principles of "enlightened ritualism," he is commemorated by the Kongi Airport, Kongi University, the Kongi Dam, the Kongi Calendar, and he holds in preventive detention Oba Danlola (a traditional religious leader) who eventually agrees to honor him as a god—until, like Caesar, he is persuaded (despite forebodings) that there is nothing he need fear, with the result that his violent downfall is ensured.[38]

Still, the fact remained that, below the absurd and fictitious historiography, there had been African traditional societies in which men and women lived out their lives in comedy and tragedy within familiar laws until they were distorted by colonial rule. The two novels by Achebe, *Things Fall Apart* (1958) and *Arrow of God* (1964), are romantic tales, but they are also tragic accounts of the tensions introduced into Ibo society by the coming of the white man. I quote from the conclusion of the second of the two novels. The story is of the fate of the High Priest Ezeulu, who remains faithful, as he sees it, to Ulu the God of his people in the village of Umuaro, despite the sudden intrusions into its customs (including that of the New Yam Feast) of the colonial administration and the Christian Mission Church

The Darkling Plain: Literature and Politics

and school. He remains faithful despite the tribulations brought by the new colonial order including his own imprisonment, and despite the sufferings he feels obliged to impose on his people because of that loyalty. His own community, however, does not see it that way and would be prepared to compromise. Then his son Obuka dies of a heart attack (even then, it seems, no man was immune!) while running and carrying the night spirit (*Ogbazulobodo*) through the district. The body is brought to the father before the first cock crows:

The first cock had not crowed. Ezeulu was still in his obi. The fire still glowed on the big logs but the flame had long gone out. Were those footsteps he was hearing? He listened carefully. Yes, they were getting louder, and voices too. He felt for his matchet. What could this be?

"Who?" he called. The footsteps stopped, and the voices. For a moment there was silence, heavy with the presence of the strangers outside in the dark.

"People," said a voice.

"Who is called people? My gun is loaded, let me warn people."

"Ezeulu, it is me, Ozumba."

"Ozumba."

"Eh."

"What brings you out at this time?"

"An abomination has overtaken us. Goat has eaten palm leaves from off my head." . . .

At any other time Ezeulu would have been more than equal to his grief. He would have been equal to any grief not compounded with humiliation. Why, he asked himself again and again, why had Ulu chosen to deal thus with him, to strike him down and cover him with mud? What was his offence? Had he not divined the god's will and obeyed it? When was it ever heard that a child was scalded by the piece of yam its own mother put in its palm? What man would send his son with a potsherd to bring fire from a neighbour's hut and then unleash rain on him? Whoever sent his son up the palm to gather nuts and then took an axe and felled the tree? But today such a thing had happened before the eyes of all. What could it point to but the collapse and ruin of all things? Then a god, finding himself powerless, might take to

his heels and in one final backward glance at his abandoned worshippers cry:
   If the rat cannot flee fast enough
   Let him make way for the tortoise!
... But in destroying his priest he had also brought disaster on himself, like the lizard in the fable who ruined his mother's funeral by his own hand. For a deity who chose a time such as this to destroy his priest or abandon him to his enemies was inciting people to take liberties; and Umuaro was just ripe to do so. The Christian harvest which took place a few days after Obika's death saw more people than even Goodcountry could have dreamed. In his extremity many an Umuaro man had sent his son with a yam or two to offer to the new religion and to bring back the promised immunity. Thereafter any yam that was harvested in the man's fields was harvested in the name of the Son.

pp. 284-287

But where did the blame lie for the misfortunes, not before colonial rule, but after independence? If the retraditionalization of society and its rulers led to the Emperor Bokassa and General Amin, perhaps the past should be allowed to bury the past: but who could be held responsible for the present?[39] At that conference outside Stockholm in 1963, Soyinka had raised the disturbing question whether the non-South African writer may not "begin to envy the South African the bleak immensity of his problem. For the South African writer has still the right to hope, and this prospect of a future as yet uncompromised by failure on his part is something which has lately ceased to exist for other African writers." Very clearly indeed did Soyinka spell out the problem at the Stockholm conference. First, there had been a

united opposition by the colonised to the external tyrant. Secondly, victory, of sorts, came and the writer submitted his integrity to the monolithic stresses of the time. For this any manifesto seemed valid, any -ism could be embraced with a clear conscience. With few exceptions the writer directed his energies to enshrining victory, to re-affirming his identification

> with the aspirations of nationalism and the stabilisation of society. (Wästberg, p. 16)

> The third stage, the stage at which we find ourselves, is the stage of disillusionment, and it is this which prompts an honest examination of what has been the failure of the African writer, as a writer.... Isolated by his very position in society, he mistook his own personal and temporary cultural predicament for the predicament of his entire society and turned attention from what was really happening in that society. He even tried to give society something that the society had never lost—its identity. (Wästberg, p. 16)

So it came about, said Soyinka, that the writer turned to "the war-cry of cultural separatism ... I refer of course to negritude," only to find that when he

> woke from his opium dream of metaphysical abstractions, he found that the politician had used his absence from earth to consolidate his position.... He was in any case still blinded to the present by the resuscitated splendours of the past. When he is purged from the long deception and has begun to express new wisdoms, the gates of the preventive-detention fortresses open up and close on him. He becomes an exile, impeccable in his dark suit in the offices of the UNO or UNESCO, or resorts to new weapons of violence. (Wästberg, p. 19)

It is a sombre picture, heavy with the impending tragedy of civil war in Nigeria, where (as Soyinka said) writers had actually made "every effort to protect their own existence by remaining articulately watchful," where "at no stage was a level of suppression reached comparable to what existed in Ghana before Nkrumah's fall or exists now in Malawi." Those who listened were not at all in agreement with Soyinka. James Ngugi went on talking about the need for revolution. But there was at least a growing understanding not only that "the African writer needs an urgent release from the fascination of the past" but that to try to base a literature on race, or the mumbo-jumbo of négritude, or the mystical values of a Golden Age, would be sterile, although Senghor continued to press its claims. Négritude had

The Darkling Plain: Literature and Politics

served its minor turn. But if it was sterile in relation to literature it was all too fertile in politics; it bred charlatans.[40] Ezekiel Mphahlele had left South Africa as an exile, lived in London and Paris, taught extramurally in Nigeria, was one of the founders of the Mbari (Cultural Club) of Ibadan, and had worked in Kenya and Zambia. His Pan-African credentials were impeccable. But in 1962 he wrote:

In my struggle to overcome the artistic difficulty that arises when one is angry most of the time . . . I have never thought of calling my negritude to my aid, except when writing protest material. But is this not elementary protest—shall I call it "underdoggery"?—that Senghor is talking about? Even he must know, however, that his philosophy will contain his art only up to a point: it won't chain his art for long. He must know that his negritude can at best be an attitude, a pose, where his art is concerned, just as it was a pose in my protest writing.[41]

And ten years later:

I still think that in the African context, negritude has overplayed itself and that negritude, purely as a cultural front against colonialism and white culture, is now something that has succeeded in what it set out to do, and now that the African is independent . . . I don't think that negritude is necessary. . . . It romanticizes the past, it is a yearning for the past, and a past which has gone, which has long gone.[42]

What was the African writer to take as his theme in such times? Lewis Nkosi was skeptical about social commitment. Commitment to what? To gun-running and seizing radio stations? No. The writer's task, said Nkosi, was to write, since he had the gift of eloquence and "can communicate the anguish of his situation"; but he is not a maker of policies or a legislator or even a visionary. Reactionary views have been held by good poets, progressive views by bad novelists. "Gun-running and holding up radio stations have very little direct relationship to literature" (Wästberg, p. 47). Writers have a function: it is perhaps "to mirror their societies, be bad tempered, grumble and protest, but there is not very much they can do about the real direction of society."⁴³ Nkosi was answered by a fellow South African, Dennis Brutus who (at Stockholm) "had come from prison to live as a free man in a castle" while others were still "facing imprisonment because they have published my poetry." Writers in many parts of Africa, he insisted, were inescapably caught up in events. "In South Africa, commitment is not a problem. You do not have to be a hero to be committed, you are compelled to be committed... in a situation so fraught with evil that you are brought into collision with it.⁴⁴

The argument gave point to Soyinka's agonized recognition that at least the black South African knew who he was, and what his predicament was, whereas in independent Africa violence had lost its way and was running wild. It might perhaps one day cleanse South Africa—at least one could hope it would and even write about it. But in the 1960's and '70's violence divided Nigeria and the Sudan, Mali, Ethiopia, Rwanda, and Burundi by civil war not between settler and colonized peoples but between African governments and rebel citizens, and between one Nigerian community and another. Violence also divided governments from people, and the black jailer was no less cruel than the white prison warder. At the end of 1976 the film *3002*, Ethiopia's official entry at the Black Arts Festival in Lagos, was screened in the absence of its director, Tefferi Buzuaychu, who was in London seeking asylum. A general manager of the theater and a television producer in Addis Ababa, Tefferi said that he had already been jailed arbitrarily for four months in 1975, and the following year a close colleague in the Ministry of Culture had been assassinated. "I am convinced that if I were to return to Addis I would be killed."⁴⁵

For some, of course, the heroic age was returning, but there was a terrible doubt about its price. In the poems and appeals that came out of Biafra (as it used to be called) and from Bangladesh,⁴⁶ the note of defiance, and of what was seen as a new *patria*, were very similar, though it ended in defeat in one case and victory in the other. For many writers, however, particularly in Nigeria, the struggle posed a very different moral choice from that of the earlier protest against colonial rule or apartheid:

> *I hope some day*
> *Intent upon my trade of living to be checked*

In stride by your apparition in a trench,
Signalling, I am a soldier....
But .... do you friend, even now, know
What it is all about?[47]

A similar unresolved questioning runs through Ali Mazrui's ingenious play *The Trial of Christopher Okigbo*[48] and through many of the short stories and novels that tried to grapple with the violence of the conflict. *The Last Duty* (London, Longmans, 1976), a novel of the civil war by Isidore Okpewho, ends with the bemused comment of the soldier administrator who has had to face the unpleasant duties of military control in an occupied zone:

Isaac Okutubo is a damn good soldier, the tough no-nonsense kind. I respect him. No doubt he'll hold this post well. As I hand over my command now, I have just this wish for him: that he has sense enough to tell there's more to a soldier than his gun, and better luck than I've had. But—if I had the same chance, if I was to hold this bloody post again, Allah, I'd make the same mistakes all over! (page 243)

More recently still, the pendulum has swung from disquiet to despair and to an almost total rejection of the politics of independence. Satire, parody, abuse, and disgust are brought together in a sweeping condemnation of politics as the muckheap of independence. Hence Jagua Nana, the heroine of Cyprian Ekwensi's novel, tells her former boyfriend when he returns from England to stand for election:

Politics not for you, Freddie. You got education. You got culture. You're a gentleman, an' proud. Politics be game for dog. And in dis Lagos, is a rough game. De roughest game in de whole worl'. Is smelly an' dirty an' you too clean an' sweet.
(page 137)

Freddie persists and is murdered, and Jagua is sick at the thought of "how ordinary people she knew became transformed by this strange devil they call politics."[49] Similarly, Ngugi expresses his disenchantment with the politics of independence in his latest novel, *Petals of Blood*, while retaining an intense interest in the corrupting effect of power on the people of his imaginary city of "New Ilmorog."[50]

The despair of the artist confronted with a society of which he disapproves, of which he is a member, and for which he can see no salvation, is not of course peculiar to Africa. When are writers at ease in a world they never made? If the times are out of joint, many authors become Hamlets. They curse fate and the age in which they are born:

> *Pour quoy est si obscurs le temps,*
> *Que li uns l'autre ne cognoist,*
> *Mais muent les gouvernements*
> *De mal en pis, si comme on voit?*
> *Le temps passé trop mieulx valoit.*
> *Que règne? Tristesse et Ennuy;*
> *Il ne court justice ne droit;*
> *Je ne scé mais desquelz je suy.*

Translation:

> *Why are the times so dark*
> *That men do not know each other,*
> *But governments move*
> *From bad to worse as we see?*
> *The past was much better.*
> *Who reigns? Affliction and Annoyance;*
> *Justice nor law are current;*
> *I know no more where I belong.*[51]

The lament was written five hundred years ago in Europe. But it would not be out of place in Africa today, in the "fat-dripping, gummy, eat-and-let-eat" regimes of Achebe's novels, regimes "which inspire the common saying that a man could only be sure of what he put away safely in his gut or, in language ever more suited to the times: 'you chop, me self I chop, palaver finish.'" Nor is it simply the tragic case of hero turned villain. Society at large is as much to blame. The decencies of the village are swallowed up in the filth of national politics. In his novel *A Man of the People*, as in the earlier volume *No Longer at Ease*, Achebe sets his characters down amid the moral degeneration of a system of national politics in which the venality of the leader is matched by the hypocrisy of his followers, who once knew and lived by the rooted customs of the village but who are now rootless and lost in the nation-state. His commentary on the successful staging of a coup in Nigeria (the incident in the novel antedates the actual event) does not exonerate the masses:

Overnight everyone began to shake their heads at the excesses of the last regime, at its graft, oppression and corrupt government: newspapers, the radio, the hitherto silent intellectuals and civil servants—everybody said what a terrible lot; and it became public opinion the next morning. And these were the same people that only the other day had owned a thousand names of adulation, whom praise-singers followed with song and talking-drum wherever they went. Chief Koko in particular became a thief and a murderer, while the people who had led him on—in my opinion the real culprits—took the legendary bath of the Hornbill and donned innocence. (page 167)

Why should there be this guilt? Because, Achebe suggests, there are no restraints on public morality at a national level. In the village, where a trader had tried to steal a medicine stick from the blind man, what could be seen as "public opinion" asserted itself. The trader Josiah had gone too far—he "had taken enough for the owner to see" and was shunned. But there were no limits in national politics:

"Koko had taken enough for the owner to see," said my father to me.... My father's words struck me because they were the very same words the villagers of Anata had spoken of Josiah, the abominated trader. Only in their case the words had meaning. The owner was the village, and the village had a mind; it could say no to sacrilege. But in the affairs of the nation there was no owner, the laws of the village became powerless.
(page 98)

I used the word "filth" a little earlier. It is not excessive, certainly not in respect to the remarkable novels by the Ghanaian writers Ayi Kwei Armah, *The Beautyful Ones Are Not Yet Born*

(1969) and Kofi Awoonor, *This Earth My Brother* (1972). They are far removed from earlier protests against colonial rule or running up a flag of négritude, or from the novels of social conflict. Personally, I find them distasteful, but there is no denying their power; they are vitriolic denunciations of postindependence politics. Cameron Duodu had already attacked the politicians in Accra in his novel *The Gab Boys* (1967) as a thieving set of hypocrites.[52] Now all Ghanaian society is covered in filth. The plot of *The Beautyful Ones Are Not Yet Born* (a phrase common enough on the mammy-trucks which run up and down the country) is once again the politics of a coup and its consequences.[53] Nothing in fact alters; there is only

a change of embezzlers and a change of the hunters and the hunted. A pitiful shrinking of the world from those days Teacher still looked back to, when the single mind was filled with the hopes of a whole people. A pitiful shrinking, to days when all the powerful can think of is to use the power of a whole people to fill their own paunches. Endless days, same days, stretching into the future with no end anywhere in sight. (page 98)

Intrigue follows intrigue. Only "the man" (the anonymous hero) is honest enough to stand aloof from what is happening, although he, too, is drawn by family obligations into helping the deposed minister find a way of escaping, by bribing the soldiers who intervened to put an end to corruption. The big fish get away, for

The net had been made in the special Ghanaian way that allowed the really big corrupt people to pass through it. A net to catch only the small, dispensable fellows, trying in their anguished blindness to leap and to attain the gleam [money] and the comfort the only way these things could be done. And the big ones floated free, like all the slogans. End bribery and corruption. Build Socialism. Equality. Shit. A man would just have to make up his mind that there was never going to be anything but despair and there would be no way of escaping it, except one. That could wait. Meanwhile the days could go on and on like this. A man could learn to live with many, many things before the end. Many, many things. (page 27)

For a final comment on this novel of despair, I turn again to Keith Panter Brick:

Such pessimism makes depressing reading, and the symbolism of filth which is to be found on almost every page makes it even more unpleasant. The all pervasive corruption is matched by that of filth—"unconquerable filth." Big money—"gleam"—is the key to cleanliness, but that is denied to all but the big men. So the reader is treated to pages of filth—of dirt-caked banisters, overflowing refuse bins, blocked wastes, and above all latrines and their stinking deposits. One is thankful for the slight comic relief provided by the manner of the Minister's escape from the man's house—through the hole of the latrine, described, needless to say, in considerable detail. Yet even this episode is, I suppose, deadly serious: the big fish merely slip through the filth: the others have to endure it.[54] *(page 81)*

What are we to make of it all? The wealth of African writing over the past two or three decades is incontestable, and it holds up a rich mirror of observation to the poverty of African politics. Is it—to return to Matthew Arnold's phrase—representative of its time? More than ten years ago, Wole Soyinka raised the question whether the novels and poetry being written reflected only "the predicament of the writer's accidental situation which he tries to stretch to embrace his society and race, or the fundamental truths of his community which inform his vision and enable him to acquire a prophetic insight into the evolution of that society." It is difficult to collate elite and popular views, and there is always likely to be a sense in which the novelist and poet feel the anguish of their times more deeply than ordinary people. I am tempted to say that just as it was the educated elite who insisted on emphasizing an Africanism which the population at large had never ceased to exhibit and experience, so the present expression of despair in a novel like *The Beautyful Ones Are Not Yet Born* is likely to be seen as exaggerated—outside Uganda or the Central African Republic or South Africa—by those who are primarily affected only by their domestic concerns and the day-to-day existence of life. Perhaps, then, the writer should distance himself a little from too direct a concern with politics and look not into the mirror of society but into the dark mirror of his own being? He might remember Yeats's dictum[55] that "State and Nation are the work of the intellect and when you consider what comes before and after them, they are, as Victor Hugo said of something or other, not worth the blade of grass God gives for the nest of the linnet." Yet Yeats, too, gave a great deal of his time to state and nation. The African writer has been drawn into their making by the times in which he lives, and I do not believe that he has been far removed from the general mood of his own society.

There is the fleeting suggestion in the quotation from Kwei Armah on page 158 that there may be a way—but only one way —of escaping from despair. It is not elaborated upon, but Panter Brick ventures the opinion very tentatively that what may be implied is "the need for salvation . . . through total regeneration— washing off the filth by a moral purification." Perhaps. I am sure there is a need to get away from abuse and preaching, which are very different from "commitment," being an exasperation of the spirit. It would add force to that other saying of Yeats, that "we make out of the quarrel with others, rhetoric, but of the quarrel with ourselves, poetry" (Jeffares, p. 46). African writers have quarreled too much perhaps with others and not enough with themselves. But when so much that passes for political science is arid or obscure and often both, we can be grateful that a rich source of observation is available. The novels, plays, and poetry that have taken politics as their theme may not be high literature, but they have certainly lifted the level of interpretation. Nor is it hard to understand why there should be that note of "despair and anguish."[56] What else but sombre can one be in the face of present events, whether it is the conflict between racially entrenched minorities and those they rule, or the approach of international conflicts which threaten a new partition of Africa, or the crowding out of individual rights by regimes murderously intolerant of dissent, or the perplexity of what might be fair-minded governments if it were not for the weight of communal or financial problems which press upon them?

In fairness to many of the African governments, one must acknowledge that they have shown a degree of tolerance not commonly found among politicians toward those who write disparagingly of them. The three Anglophone countries principally concerned—Nigeria, Kenya, Ghana—are still fairly open societies, although West African writers have also been protected by the rapid succession of leaders, each regime being quite willing to entertain criticism of its predecessors. It is also the case that no African writer has yet offered his services as apologist for those in office. There were sycophantic writers during the nationalist years, but hardly any worth considering today. It is surely just as well, since state control would probably be the end of any hope of a national literature: novelists, like certain species of animals which refuse to breed in captivity, need a large element of freedom from direction. How long will the tolerance and the freedom last? As African governments grow more fearful, the probability must increase that they, too, in common with regimes in other troubled areas of the world, will want to curb what is a distinct literature of protest.[57] Perhaps it is then that an external market and foreign publishers will be seen to have their use by way of sales abroad or recognition abroad or asylum? But how much more dangerous are the politics of the worst! A primitive totalitarianism is taking hold of a number of African countries, and it is impossible to believe that any form of creative writing can survive in a society whose rulers will murder a playwright not because he is hostile but simply because he is an intellectual. There are no novelists or poets or theater to be heard in Uganda today. The glass held up by literature to politics has been brutally smashed. In July 1977 the manager and two leading actors in the National Theatre in Kampala were taken away and shot by Amin's soldiers. No wonder that the once mild alarm voiced by writers about the *dictat* of the overseas market has been eclipsed by fear of the power of African dictators. Is it a justified fear, and is the squalid picture that the novelists, poets, and dramatists draw of even the more tolerant regimes a true portrait? Perhaps Uganda is the ghastly exception? If past hopes of a nationalist paradise were dupes, may not present fears prove liars? They may be so. But there are sombre and general grounds for concluding that the writers we have looked at are (to turn back to Arnold's phrase) representative of their time and that they have good reason to be apprehensive of the future not only for themselves but for the societies to which they belong in their own half-liberated continent.

Appendix

The African states became independent as follows:

Libya	24 December 1951
Sudan	1 January 1956
Morocco	2 March 1956
Tunisia	20 March 1956
Ghana	6 March 1957
Guinea	2 October 1958
Cameroon	1 January 1960
Togo	27 April 1960
Mali	20 June 1960
Senegal	20 June 1960
Madagascar	26 June 1960
Zaire (formerly Belgian Congo)	30 June 1960
Somalia	1 July 1960
Benin (formerly Dahomey)	1 August 1960
Niger	3 August 1960
Upper Volta	5 August 1960
Ivory Coast	7 August 1960
Chad	11 August 1960
Central African Republic	13 August 1960
Congo (Brazzaville)	15 August 1960
Gabon	17 August 1960
Nigeria	1 October 1960
Mauritania	28 November 1960
Sierra Leone	27 April 1961
Tanzania (as Tanganyika)	9 December 1961
Rwanda	1 July 1962
Burundi	1 July 1962
Algeria	3 July 1962
Uganda	9 October 1962
Zanzibar (now part of Tanzania)	10 December 1963

Appendix

Kenya	12 December 1963
Malawi	6 July 1964
Zambia	24 October 1964
The Gambia	18 February 1965
Botswana	30 September 1966
Lesotho	4 October 1966
Swaziland	6 September 1968
Equatorial Guinea	12 October 1968
Guinea-Bissau	10 September 1974
Mozambique	25 June 1975
Cape Verde	5 July 1975
São Tomé and Príncipe	12 July 1975
Angola	11 November 1975
Djibouti	27 June 1977

Bibliography

The following titles have been chosen for their general interest as well as for particular themes. They are also among the more readable books on African politics. Length has been designated (L), (M), or (S), but there is no necessary correspondence between quality and quantity.

Chapter 1

Arrighi, G., and J. Saul, eds., *Essays on the Political Economy of Africa.* New York, Monthly Review Press, 1973. (L)
Cohen, Sir Andrew, *British Policy in Changing Africa.* London, Routledge and Kegan Paul, 1959. (S)
Dumont, René, *False Start in Africa.* London, André Deutsch, 1966. (M)
Fanon, Frantz, *The Wretched of the Earth.* London, Penguin Books, 1967. (S)
Fortes, Meyer, and E. E. Evans-Pritchard, eds., *African Political Systems.* London, Oxford University Press, 1970. (M)
Gupta, Anirudha, *Government and Politics in Africa.* Delhi, Vikas, 1975. (M)
Gutteridge, W. F., *Military Regimes in Africa.* London, Methuen, 1975. (S)
Huntington, S. P., *Political Order in Changing Societies.* New Haven, Yale University Press, 1968. (L)
Kasfir, Nelson, *The Shrinking Political Arena.* London, University of California Press, 1976. (L)
Lee, J. M., *African Armies and Civil Order.* London, Oxford University Press, 1969. (M)
Leys, C., ed., *Politics and Change in Developing Countries.* Cambridge, Cambridge University Press, 1969. (L)
Lofchie, M. F., ed., *The State of the Nations: Constraints on Development in Independent Africa.* Berkeley, University of California Press, 1971. (L)
Mair, Lucy, *African Kingdoms.* Oxford, Oxford University Press, 1977. (S)
Mayall, James, *Africa: The Cold War and After.* London, Elek Books Ltd., 1971. (M)

Bibliography

Minogue, M., and J. Mulloy, eds., *African Aims and Attitudes*. Cambridge, Cambridge University Press, 1974. (L)
Mphalele, Ezekiel, *The African Image*. London, Faber, 1962. (M)
Nwabueze, B. O., *Constitutionalism in the Emergent States*. London, C. Hurst, 1973. (M)
Padmore, George, *Pan-Africanism or Communism?* London, Dobson, 1956. (M)
Robinson, Kenneth, *The Dilemmas of Trusteeship*. London, Oxford University Press, 1965. (S)
Rotberg, R. I., and A. A. Mazrui, *Protest and Power in Black Africa*. New York, Oxford University Press, 1970. (L)
Wolfers, Michael, *Politics in the Organisation of African Unity*. London, Methuen, 1977. (M)

Chapter 2

Austin, Dennis, *Ghana Observed*. Manchester, Manchester University Press, 1976. (M)
Awolowo, Obafemi, *Awo*. Cambridge, Cambridge University Press, 1962. (L)
Azikiwe, Nnamdi, *Zik*. Cambridge, Cambridge University Press, 1966. (S)
Bello, Sir Ahmadu, *My Life*. Cambridge, Cambridge University Press, 1962. (M)
Bretton, Henry, *The Rise and Fall of Kwame Nkrumah*. New York, Praeger, 1967. (M)
Brick, Keith Panter, *Soldiers and Oil: The Political Transformation of Nigeria*. London, F. Cass, 1978. (L)
Busia, K. A., *Africa in Search of Democracy*. London, Routledge and Kegan Paul, 1967. (S)
Clapham, Christopher, *Liberia and Sierra Leone: An Essay in Comparative Government*. Cambridge, Cambridge University Press, 1976. (S)
Dudley, B. J., *Politics and Crisis in Nigeria*. Ibadan, Ibadan University Press, 1973. (M)
Kirk-Green, A. H., *Crisis and Conflict in Nigeria*. London, Oxford University Press, 1971. (L)
Luckham, Robin, *The Nigerian Military*. Cambridge, Cambridge University Press, 1974. (L)
Markowitz, Irving L., *Senghor and the Politics of Négritude*. London, Heinemann, 1969. (L)
Morgenthau, Ruth S., *Political Parties in French-speaking Africa*. London, Oxford University Press, 1964. (L)

Nkrumah, Kwame, *Ghana: Autobiography*. London, Nelson, 1957. (L)
Ojukwu, C. O., *Biafra: Random Thoughts*. New York, Harper and Row, 1969. (L)
Senghor, L. S., *Nationhood and the African Road to Socialism*. London, Pall Mall Press, 1964. (M)
Zolberg, Aristide, *One Party Government in the Ivory Coast*. Princeton, Princeton University Press, 1964. (M)

Chapter 3

Amsden, Alice H., *International Firms and Labour in Kenya 1945-1970*. London, F. Cass, 1971. (L)
Buijtenhuis, Robert, *Mau Mau Twenty Years After*. The Hague, Mouton, 1974. (M)
Clapham, Christopher, *Haile Selassie's Government*. London, Longmans, 1969. (S)
Cone, L. Winston, and J. F. Lipscombe, eds., *The History of Kenya Agriculture*. Nairobi, University Press of Africa, 1972. (L)
Gertzel, Cherry, *The Politics of Independent Kenya*. London, Heinemann, 1970. (M)
Kariuki, James, *Mau Mau Detainee*. London, Oxford University Press, 1963. (S)
Kenyatta, Jomo, *Suffering without Bitterness*. Nairobi, East African Publishing House, 1968. (M)
Lewis, I., *A Pastoral Democracy*. London, Oxford University Press, 1967. (L)
Leys, Colin, *Underdevelopment in Kenya: The Political Economy of Neo-Colonialism 1964-1971*. London, Heinemann, 1970. (M)
Martin, David, *General Amin*. London, Faber, 1974. (M)
Nyerere, Julius, *Freedom and Unity 1952-1965*. London, Oxford University Press, 1966. (M)
——*Freedom and Socialism 1965-1967*. London, Oxford University Press, 1968. (M)
——*Freedom and Development 1968-1973*. London, Oxford University Press, 1973. (M)
Odinga, Oginga, *Not Yet Uhuru*. London, Heinemann, 1967. (M)
Pratt, Cranford, *The Cultural Phase in Tanzania 1945-1968*. Cambridge, Cambridge University Press, 1976. (L)
Twaddle, Michael, ed., *Expulsion of a Minority: Essays on Ugandan Asians* London, Athlone Press, 1975. (S)

Bibliography

Chapter 4

Davidson, Basil, *In the Eye of the Storm, Angola's People.* London, Penguin Books, 1972. (S)
Dayal, Rajeshwar, *Mission for Hammarskjold.* London, Oxford University Press, 1977. (L)
Duffy, James, *Portugal in Africa.* London, Penguin Books, 1962. (S)
Gibson, Richard, *African Liberation Movements.* London, Oxford University Press, 1972. (M)
Good, Robert C., *U. D. I.: The International Politics of the Rhodesian Rebellion.* London, Faber, 1973. (M)
Hatch, John, *Two African Statesmen.* Chicago, Henry Pegueoy, 1974. (M)
Hoskyns, Catherine, *The Congo since Independence.* London, Oxford University Press, 1965. (L)
Kaunda, Kenneth, *Zambia Shall Be Free.* London, Heinemann, 1962. (S)
Mondlane, E., *The Struggle for Mozambique.* London, Penguin Books, 1968. (S)
Mulford, D., *Zambia: The Politics of Independence.* London, Oxford University Press, 1967. (L)
Sithole, Ndabaningi, *Roots of a Revolution: Scenes from Zimbabwe's Struggle.* London, Oxford University Press, 1977. (S)
Spínola, Antónia Sebastão Ribeiro de, *Portugal and the Future.* London, Heinemann, 1974. (M)
Tordoff, William, ed., *Politics in Zambia.* Manchester, Manchester University Press, 1974. (L)
Wheeler, D. L., and René Pelisser, *Angola.* London, Pall Mall Press, 1971. (M)
Windrich, Elaine, *The Rhodesian Problem: A Documentary Record 1923-1973.* London, Routledge and Kegan Paul, 1975. (M)

Chapter 5

Barber, James, *South Africa's Foreign Policy 1945-1970.* London, Oxford University Press, 1973. (M)
Brotz, Howard, *The Politics of South Africa.* London, Oxford University Press, 1977. (S)
Davidson, B., ed., *Southern Africa: The New Politics of Revolution.* London, Penguin Books, 1976. (S)
Heard, Kenneth, *General Elections in South Africa 1943-1970.* London, Oxford University Press, 1974. (M)
Heribert, A., *South Africa: Sociological Perspectives.* London, Oxford University Press, 1971. (M)

Jones, Arthur Keppel, *Friend or Foe?* Pietermaritzberg, Shuter and Shooter, 1949. (S)
Kuper, Leo, *An African Bourgeoisie: Race, Class, and Politics in South Africa.* New Haven, Yale University Press, 1965. (M)
Laurence, Patrick, *The Transkei.* Johannesburg, Ravan Press, 1976. (S)
Luthuli, Albert, *Let My People Go.* London, Collins, 1962. (S)
Mandela, Nelson, *No Easy Walk to Freedom.* New York, Basic Books, 1965. (M)
Matanzima, Kaiser, *Independence My Way.* Pretoria, Foreign Affairs Association, 1976. (S)
Nolutshungu, Sam, *South Africa in Africa.* Manchester, Manchester University Press, 1974. (L)
Potholm, C., and R. Dale, eds., *Southern Africa in Perspective.* New York, The Free Press, 1972. (L)
Stultz, Newell, *Afrikaner Politics in South Africa 1934-48.* Berkeley, University of California Press, 1974. (L)
Temkin, Ben, *Gatsha Buthelezi.* Johannesburg, Purnell Press, 1977. (L)
Thompson, L., and J. Butler, eds., *Change in Contemporary Africa.* Berkeley, University of California Press, 1975. (L)
Verwoerd, H. F., *Verwoerd Speaks: Speeches 1948-1966.* Johannesburg, APB Publishers, 1966. (M)

Chapter 6

Abrahams, Peter, *A Wreath for Udomo.* London, Faber, 1956. (M)
Achebe, Chinua, *Things Fall Apart.* London, Heinemann, 1958. (S)
——*No Longer at Ease.* London, Heinemann, 1960. (S)
——*Arrow of God.* London, Heinemann, 1964. (S)
——*A Man of the People.* London, Heinemann, 1966. (S)
Amadi, Elechi, *The Concubine.* London, Heinemann, 1966. (S)
Armah, Ayi Kwei, *The Beautyful Ones Are Not Yet Born.* London, Heinemann, 1972. (M)
Awoonor, Kofi, *This Earth My Brother.* London, Heinemann, 1972. (S)
Bown, Lalage, *Two Centuries of African English.* London, Heinemann, 1973. (M)
Bowra, C. M., *Poetry and Politics 1900-1960.* Cambridge, Cambridge University Press, 1966. (S)
Echeruo, Michael, *Joyce Carey and the Novel of Africa.* London, Longmans, 1973. (M)
Ekwensi, Cyprian, *Jagua Nana.* London, Hutchinson, 1961. (M)
——*People of the City.* London, Heinemann, 1963. (M)
Laye, Camara, *The Radiance of the King.* London, Collins, 1955. (M)

Bibliography

Mazrui, 'Ali, *The Trial of Christopher Okigbo*. London, Heinemann, 1971. (S)
Mphahlele, Ezekiel, ed., *African Writing Today*. London, Penguin Books, 1967. (M)
Ngugi, James, *Weep Not Child*. London, Heinemann, 1964. (S)
——*A Grain of Wheat*. London, Heinemann, 1967. (S)
Nicol, Davidson, *The West African Intellectual Community*. Ibadan, University of Ibadan Press, 1962. (M)
Okpewho, Isidore, *The Last Duty*. London, Longmans, 1976. (M)
Ouologuem, Yambo, *Bound to Violence*. London, Heinemann, 1971. (M)
Senghor, L. S., *Anthologie de la Nouvelle Poésie Nègre et Malgache*. Paris, Seuil, 1948. (M)
——*Nocturnes*. London, Heinemann, 1974. (S)
Soyinka, Wole, *Idanre and Other Poems*. London, Oxford University Press, 1967. (S)
——*A Dance of the Forests*. London, Oxford University Press, 1963. (S)
——*Kongi's Harvest*. London, Oxford University Press, 1967. (S)
Tam'si, Tchicaya U, *Selected Poems*. London, Heinemann, 1966. (S)
Thiong'o, Ngugi Wa, *Petals of Blood*. London, Heinemann, 1977. (M)
Udoyeop, Nyong J., *Three Nigerian Poets*. Ibadan, Ibadan University Press, 1975. (S)
Wästberg, Per, ed., *The Writer in Modern Africa*. Uppsala, Scandinavian Institute of African Studies, 1968. (S)
Wright, Richard, *Black Power*. London, Dobson, 1954. (M)

Notes

1. The Fallacies of Hope

1. "The great purpose of the British Empire is the gradual spread of freedom among all His Majesty's subjects in whatever part of the world they live. That spread of freedom is a slow, evolutionary process. In some countries it is more rapid than others. In some parts of the Empire, in the Dominions, that evolutionary process has been completed, it is finished. In some colonies like Ceylon the gaining of freedom has gone very far. In others it is necessarily a much slower process. It may take generations, or even centuries, for the peoples in some parts of the Colonial Empire to achieve self-government. But it is a major part of our policy, even among backward peoples of Africa, to teach them and encourage them always to be able to stand a little more on their own feet." Malcolm Macdonald, *Parliamentary Debate*, 13th December, 1939.
2. Cf. Harold Macmillan's use of the phrase "wind of change" to describe the force of African nationalism in his speech in Accra and Lagos and before the joint houses of the South African Parliament in 1960. It had been used earlier by Stanley Baldwin about Asia in a speech on the 1935 Government of India Bill. See K. Middlemas and J. Barnes, *Baldwin* (London, Weidenfeld and Nicolson, 1969), p. 713.
3. "The path to Commonwealth membership" lay "through the traditional gateway of responsible parliamentary government." N. Mansergh, *Commonwealth Perspectives* (Durham, N.C., Duke University Press, 1958), p. 34.
4. The U. K. remained the largest single supplier, but the value of U.K. imports as a percentage of total imports fell sharply:

	1959	1974
Into Kenya	36%	20.5%
Into Tanzania	31%	13.6%

    Source: Board of Trade, Report on Overseas Trade.

    Similarly in West Africa, the commonest taxi or private car in the 1950's was a British-produced Ford or Vauxhall or Morris. Now it is a Toyota or Volkswagen or Peugeot. "The British visitors . . . soon noticed that apart from the odd Range Rover and eccentric Mini, British cars cannot be seen in Lagos streets." *West Africa*, 25 (April 1977).

5. *La Conférence Africaine Française, Brazzaville* (Algiers, 1944), p. 35.
6. See below, Chapter 6.
7. M. Fortes and E. E. Evans-Pritchard, eds., *African Political Systems* (London, Oxford University Press, 1970), pp. 17–18.
8. The most recent accounts in a growing literature on clientalist policies in African peasant societies are Teodor Shanin, "Peasantry: Delineation of a Sociological Concept and a Field of Study," *Archives Européenes de Sociologie*, 12 (1971), and René Lemarchand, "Political Clientelism and Ethnicity in Tropical Africa," *American Political Science Review*, 66 (March 1972).
9. See below, chapter 2. A particular example: in the colonially formed administrative region of northern Ghana in 1954 a Northern People's Party was formed by the joining together of local communities many of which, antagonistic toward each other in earlier times, had become aware of being "northern" by virtue of their menial employment in the South, and because the South had become the power base of a new nationalist movement. When the NPP was regionally successful in the general election of that year, Nkrumah and the CPP immediately and rather absurdly, yet understandably, accused the new party of "tribalism." On the general question of what is meant by ethnic category, ethnic group, tribe, and nation, see R. Cohen and J. Middleton, eds., *From Tribe to Nation in Africa: Studies in Incorporation Processes* (Scranton, Pa., University of Pennsylvania Press, 1970).
10. Cf. Byron, that early apostle of nationalism:

> Once more upon the waters, yet once more
> And the waves bound beneath me as a steed
> That knows its rider. Welcome to their roar.
> Swift be their guidance, wheresoe'er it lead.

11. By survival I mean survival in politics, either as the government or as the opposition. In nearly every African state, however, there is usually only the simple choice (as Horace Walpole once remarked) between "Downing Street or the Tower." On the problems of an opposition see D. Austin, *Ghana Observed* (Manchester, Manchester University Press, 1976), chapter 8.
12. E.g. in the supply of Nigerian troops to the Tanzanian government in 1964 after British rescue forces were withdrawn, or of Guinean

troops to the Siaka Stevens government in Sierra Leone in 1967, or of Ethiopian help to southern Sudanese rebels and Sudanese help to Ethiopian rebels or Moroccan troops to Zaire.
13. One could, I suppose, argue that the French would have intervened to keep Houphouët-Boigny in office after 1960 had a serious threat developed to his rule: so many mutual interests would have been at stake. But there is no evidence that such help was needed.
14. A view strongly defended by T. L. Hodgkin in the little Penguin essay *African Political Parties* (London, 1961).
15. Recently renamed the *Chama cha Mapandazi* ("Revolutionary Party") after its merger with the Afro-Shirazi Party in Zanzibar.
16. Nkrumah was in office under the British from 1951 to independence in 1957, and from 1957 to 1966. Busia was prime minister only from 1969 to 1972. The first military council was formed in 1966 and withdrew voluntarily; the second is still under the control of General Acheampong.
17. There is an enormous literature on the military and its disposition to intervene. The best summary is by R. L. Luckham, "A Comparative Typology of Civil-Military Relations," *Government and Opposition*. 6 (1971), 5–35. See also Chapter 2. On the effect of corruption in Egypt and Morocco, where it is rife and may be critical, see J. Waterbury, "Corruption and Political Stability," *Government and Opposition*, 11 (1976), 426–445.
18. This is the main argument of the intelligent book by Maxwell Owusu, *Uses and Abuses of Power* (Chicago, University of Chicago Press, 1970), about a small town in West Africa.
19. See the interesting article by David Hilling in *African Affairs* (1976), pp. 397–424. which was based on a paper given at the School of Oriental and African Studies in London in November 1975. He chose four categories: the rich oil-rich, the poor oil-rich, the rich oil-poor, the poor oil-poor. Libya, Algeria, Nigeria, and Gabon might be said to belong to the second category and all other African states to the fourth.
20. Article III of the Charter runs as follows: "Member states adhere to the principles of sovereign equality, non-interference in internal affairs of member states (and) respect for territorial integrity. . . ." The following year the OAU Summit Conference adopted by acclamation a resolution by which member states pledged themselves "to respect the borders existing on their achievement of national independence." Such pledges were in sharp contrast to the 1958 Accra pan-African conference which "(a) denounces artificial frontiers drawn up by imperialist Powers to divide the peoples of Africa . . . and (b) calls for the abolition or adjustment of such frontiers at an early date."

Notes to Pages 27–31

21. Saadia Touval once recalled that "a politician from Niger actually invoked the Berlin Conference 1884-5 to defend his country's claim against Dahomey to the island of Lete in the Niger river, asserting that 'since 1885 the island had always belonged to Niger.' The politician forgot that the administrative entity of Niger was not yet in existence at that time." "Africa's Frontiers: Reactions to a Colonial Legacy," *International Affairs*, 42 (October 1966), pp. 202-237.
22. Many thousands of both communities were killed in the successful Wahutu uprising against the Tutsi in 1959-60 in Rwanda and during the 1966 civil war and invasion in Burundi. See the account by Helen Codere and her argument that Rwanda was a racist society in the sense that innate Hutu inferiority was taken for granted by most Tutsi (though not by the Wahutu), in *The Biography of an African Society: Rwanda 1900-1960* (Brussels, Tervureen, 1973). In Burundi on the night of 25 April 1972, the Hutu majority attacked the ruling minority of Tutsi, killing some 2000. Revenge was swift and terrible. It is said that the Tutsi killed between 100,000 and 150,000 Hutu and that very few educated Hutu escaped. It was "an elimination of the opposition elite by selective genocide." William Butler and George Obiozur, *The Burundi Affair* (Geneva, International Commission of Jurists, 1972); René Lemarchand and David Martin, *Selective Genocide in Burundi* (London, Minority Rights Group, 1974).
23. Bjorn Beckman, *Organising the Farmers, Cocoa Politics and National Development* (Uppsala, Scandinavian Institute of African Studies, 1976), p. 235.
24. Ibid.
25. Robert W. Clower and George Dalton, *Growth without Development* (Evanston, 1966). For the Ivory Coast and its rapid rate of growth since 1960, see Chapter 2.
26. Jean M. Due, "Development without Growth—The Case of Ghana in the 1960s," *Economic Bulletin of Ghana*, 3 (1973), pp. 3-15.
27. In 1973 only one country (Egypt) spent more than 10 percent of its per capita GNP on arms, placing it in the same category as the Soviet Union and Israel; three spent between 5 and 10 percent (Chad, Somalia, Nigeria), in roughly the same percentage bracket as the U.S. and the U.K.; most of the continent fell into the 2-5 percent group. Since 1973, however, it seems likely that proportionate arms expenditure has increased *pro tanto* with the rise in national and international disputes. See Robin Luckham, "Militarism = Arms and the Internationalisation of Capital," in *Imperialism: New Tactics.* Institute of Development Studies Bulletin, Sussex, 8, No. 3 (March 1977).

28. René Dumont, *False Start in Africa* (London, André Deutsch, 1966).
29. This is what I was told when inquiring after the disappearance of a student's father. See below, Chapter 3.
30. The exception (if it is that) is South Africa, and there the National Party has been in office continuously since 1948. The president of the Somali Republic was removed by an adverse vote in the Assembly in 1967; a coup followed in 1969. Elections are held in the single-party republics and individual ministers have been voted out. But for a change of government, ordinary people have to look to the army. Only in the Gambia—one of the oldest colonies—is there an opposition of the recognizably Western kind.
31. Frantz Fanon, *The Wretched of the Earth* (London, Penguin Books, 1963), p. 134.
32. R. H. Tawney, *The Attack: Christianity and the Social Revolution* (London, 1953), p. 165, quoted in Ross Terrill, *R. H. Tawney and His Times* (Cambridge, Mass., Harvard University Press, 1973), p. 138.
33. Régis Debray, *Strategy for Revolution* (London, Penguin Books, 1973), p. 18.
34. E.g. by B. J. Dudley, *Instability and Political Order: Politics and Crisis in Nigeria* (Ibadan, Ibadan University Press, 1973), p. 258.
35. Ethiopia is the only noncolonial African state—Liberia having been planted in Africa from outside. Egypt, of course, is a very ancient precolonial state, and Arab/Islamic culture gives a shifting historical identity to areas of north Africa. At the beginning of 1977 Col. Mengistu Haile-Mariam had succeeded three previous heads of state—The Emperor Haile Selassie, General Andom, and General Teferi Banti—whom he had executed or caused to be executed. The country was ringed by hostile states; the capital, Addis Ababa, was surrounded by hostile troops. The U.S. had armed the military, and the ruling Dergue (military junta) were beginning to turn to Moscow, while being opposed by an underground Marxist Revolutionary People's Party as well as by Eritrean, Tigrean and similar secessionist forces. There was also rumored to be a royalist party in the villages. What a nightmare of chaos!
36. "Politics in Asunafo," in D. Austin and R. L. Luckham, eds., *Politicians and Soldiers in Ghana* (London, Frank Cass, 1975), p. 206.

2. No Longer at Ease

1. There were eight territories in French West Africa (*L'Afrique Occidentale Française*): Mauritania, Senegal, Guinea, Mali, Ivory Coast, Upper Volta, Dahomey, and Niger; and four territories in French

Notes to Pages 37–47

Equatorial Africa (*L'Afrique Equatoriale Française*): Chad, Central African Republic, Gabon, and Congo (Brazzaville).
2. *Communist Manifesto* (London, Allen and Unwin, 1948 edition), pp. 124-125.
3. Philip Foster and Aristide Zolberg, eds., *Ghana and the Ivory Coast: Perspectives in Modernization* (Chicago, University of Chicago Press, 1971), p. 187.
4. Nkrumah paid a state visit to the Ivory Coast in April 1957 shortly after independence, and Houphouët-Boigny was reported as saying: "You are witnessing the start of two experiments. A wager has been made between the two territories, one having chosen independence, the other preferring the difficult road of building with the metropole [i.e., France] a community of equal rights and duties. . . . Let each of us undertake his experiment, and in 10 years we shall compare the results." But within ten years, Nkrumah was in exile in the neighboring capital, Conakry, and the Ivory Coast was independent.
5. Special Report on the Ivory Coast, *The Times*, London, 25 March 1977.
6. Amusement and criticism joined forces recently when it was reported that a new luxury hotel in Abidjan—a humid, tropical city—had installed an ice-skating rink for the benefit of its wealthy patrons. It was outdone, however, by Libreville, the fabulously expensive capital of Gabon—few in population, rich in oil—when President El Haji Omar Bongo had his marble palace defended by "two Cadillac security vehicles . . . six armored-plated secret service cars, 65 Mercedes and an unspecified number of Rolls Royces." (See the *Report* in the London *Times*, 27 July 1977.)
7. In 1976 a chicken in the local market was fetching $8.25, a bicycle cost $400-600, a Honda scooter $1,700-2,000. The average per capita income, as we have seen, was under $450. *Ghana Commercial Bank, Economic Review*, December 1976–July 1977. In May 1977 the university students rose in protest against the cost of living and the military closed all three institutions.
8. The treaty between the African, Caribbean, and Pacific countries (ACP) and the EEC followed earlier arrangements under Part IV of the 1975 Treaty of Rome and the subsequent Yaoundé Conventions of 1963 and 1969 between the six EEC governments and a number of French-speaking African/Caribbean states.
9. I have tried to explore the result of such a search in "Et in Arcadia Ego," *Minerva* (April 1976), pp. 352-389.
10. There has been a good deal of unease among OAU member governments over the action taken by Morocco and Mauritania, particularly since there is also an active guerrilla movement, known as the Polisario Front, which—supported by Algeria—demands independence for

their territory. See John Mercer, *Spanish Sahara* (London, Allen and Unwin, 1976), and John Gretton, *Western Sahara: The Fight for Self-determination* (London, Anti-Slavery Society, 1976).
11. The history of the census in Nigeria is farcical but understandable. Numbers are power in the democratic game of representation, and many Nigerians would like to have a parliamentary government. A census count, however, is likely to show that one political group—the "North" or the "South" or this or that particular group of states—has a disproportionate weight of population in relation to parliamentary seats.
12. It is rich only in the aggregate, however, since its wealth divided by number brings its per capita national income down to a miserable level of about $300, making it one of the *poorer* West African states. Cf. Gabon, with a per capita income of $2,000; Ivory Coast, $500; Ghana, $460; and Senegal, $370.
13. One must recall, though, that the rickety federation of Indonesia sought external distraction through aggressive demands on neighbors. About 824 million naira—one-seventh of its overall federal expenditure of 5,756 million naira—is presently allocated to defense.
14. See Robin Luckham, *The Nigerian Military 1960-67* (Cambridge, Cambridge University Press, 1971), and his "Comparative Typology of Civil-Military Relations" in *Government and Opposition*, 6 (1971), 5-35.
15. Luckham, *The Nigerian Military*, p. 54. There were several coups in West Africa in 1965-66—in Zaire, Dahomey, the Central African Republic, Upper Volta, and Ghana.
16. Ibid., p. 54.
17. Ibid., pp. 54-55.
18. Ibid., p. 43.
19. Ibid., p. 56.
20. Ibid., p. 76. The description "northern" is very general. As Luckham says, it included Hausa-Fulani and Kanuri of the Muslim emirates of the far North, as well as Muslims of the Niger Province, Bauchi, southern Zaria and Adamawa, Middle Belt peoples, and northern Yorubas (p. 77).
21. As in *Revolution and Counter-Revolution in Germany* (London, Lawrence and Wishart, 1933), p. 13, where Engels describes Germany in 1848 as having a multiplicity of social classes: the nobility, the bourgeoisie, the small-trading and shopkeeping class, the artisan class, and the peasantry.
22. Radio broadcast, 28 January 1966.
23. Radio broadcast, 2 August 1966.

24. Irving L. Markowitz, *Leopold Sedar Senghor* (London, Heinemann, 1969), pp. 147, 14.
25. L. S. Senghor, *On African Socialism* (London, Praeger, 1964), pp. 11-12.

3. E Pluribus Plures

1. The move by the Sultan of Omar from Arabia to Zanzibar in the 1830's amply reflected Arab power over the East African coast until 1890, when a British Protectorate was established. It is estimated that about two million Africans were "exported" as slaves until the trade was suppressed.
2. In a brief period between 1942 and 1947 Italian Somaliland, British Somaliland, and the Ogaden region of Ethiopia were united under British military administration. Then the pre-1939 boundaries of Ethiopia were restored.
3. Buganda expanded its influence under British protection, including its authority over areas of what had been part of Bunyoro, later to be known as the "lost counties" issue. Terminology is a little complicated. Bantu languages often alter the related meaning of words by changing the prefix. The root stock *Ganda* becomes *luganda* (= the language), *Baganda* (= the people), *Muganda* (one of the *Baganda*). *Uganda* is a colonial name for the whole territory, including other Bantu kingdoms and the northern Nilotic peoples. (Very likely, these people are confused by Britain, England, the United Kingdom, English, Scotch, Scots and so on!)
4. Cmd 1922, HMSO London, 1923, p. 9.
5. The story is well told by John Hatch, *Two African Statesmen* (Chicago, Regnery, 1976), and Cranford Pratt, *The Critical Phase in Tanzania 1945-1968* (Cambridge, Cambridge University Press, 1976).
6. The first African to be appointed to the Legislative Council was E. W. Mathu in 1955, but the decisive events were (long term) the growing number of educated Africans from places like the Alliance High School and (short term) the ugliness of the Emergency, including the deaths of African internees at Hola Detention Camp in 1959.
7. "Explicit ideologies arise when one wants to create a political system that is not supported by the implicit primitive beliefs of the population." Sidney Verba and Lucian Pye, eds., *Political Culture and Political Development* (Princeton, Princeton University Press, 1965), p. 546.
8. "The ideologies of the nineteenth century were universalistic, humanistic, and fashioned by intellectuals. The mass ideologies of Asia and

Africa are parochial, instrumental, and created by political leaders. The driving forces of the old ideologies were social equality and, in the largest sense, freedom. The imputations of the new ideologies are economic development and national power." Daniel Bell, *The End of Ideology* (New York, Collier, 1962), p. 403. One may cavil at the notion of "mass ideologies" in Africa, and demur in relation to a description of all "old ideologies" as being concerned with freedom; but there is something in the distinction drawn.

9. "In replacing market forces with planning a new constraint—the capability of the government to implement plans—joins the picture and in many less developed countries it supersedes the constraints imposed." T. Y. Shen, "Sectoral Development Planning in Tropical Africa," *East African Economic Review*, 7 (June 1975), 263-294. The judgment that "the governments in tropical Africa are not up to the tasks given to them in the development plans" was based on a study of twenty-two Development Plans adopted between 1965 and 1972. The main sectors examined were agriculture, education, health, housing, transport and communications, and housing in rural areas.

10. Milton Obote, quoted in Crawford Young, *The Politics of Cultural Pluralism* (Madison, University of Wisconsin Press, 1976), p. 268.

11. See Sir Edward Mutesa, *The Desecration of My Kingdom* (London, Constable, 1967).

12. The Protestant-based UPC came to power in alliance with the *Kabaka Yekka* (the "King Alone" party) in Buganda against a Catholic-supported Democratic Party under Benedicto Kiwanuka, a dissident Ganda leader. Uganda's politics have always been *very* complicated.

13. See Milton Obote, "Proposals for new methods of election of representatives of the people to Parliament," pamphlet headed "On the Move to the Left" (Kampala, Government Press, July 1970).

14. Amin was welcomed in place of Obote not only by the British and other western governments but by many in Uganda itself. After all, he had seized power allegedly to curb "the wealthy class of landowners who are always talking of socialism while they grow richer and the common man poorer," according to the first broadcast after the coup. The most sombre account is David Martin, *General Amin* (London, Faber, 1974). Less harrowing is Judith Listowell, *Amin* (Dublin, Irish University Press, 1973). There is of course a comic side to the tragedy. For example, it was announced by the Uganda Defense Council in June 1977 that Amin's full title was to be "His Excellency President for Life, Marshal Al Hadji Dr. Idi Amin, V.C., D.S.O., M.C., Conqueror of the British Empire in Africa in general and Uganda in particular."

15. See Michael Twaddle, ed., *Expulsion of a Minority: Essays on Ugandan Asians* (London, Athlone Press, 1975).
16. *Not Yet Uhuru* is the title of Oginga Odinga's autobiography (London, Heinemann, 1967). *Uhuru* means "self-rule."
17. Colin Leys, *Underdevelopment in Kenya* (London, Heinemann, 1975), p. 237.
18. Published in 1938 (London, Secker and Warburg). Kenyatta came to London in 1929 to plead the cause of land reform and female circumcision and to gain permission to found independent (nonstate, nonmission) schools. He returned to Kenya, then came back to London in 1931 and did not return until 1946, when he became principal of the independent Teacher's Training College. The following year he was president of the Kenya African Union (KAU) and on his tortuous road to power.
19. Notably Charles Rubbia, Waruru Kanja, and George Anyona.
20. Present contenders are said to be Arap Moi (who constitutionally assumes the office of president for ninety days after the death of Kenyatta); Mwai Kibaki, Minister of Finance; Mbiyu Koinange, Head of Security and the paramilitary General Service Unit; Dr. Njoroge Mungai; and (less plausibly) Mama Ngina, Kenyatta's wife.
21. *Land of Sunshine* is the title of an interesting early book by Muga Gicaru on the Mau Mau revolt (London, Lawrence and Wishart, 1958). See too James Kariuki, *Mau Mau Detainee* (London, Oxford University Press, 1963). The most intelligent commentary on Kenya, well illustrated by its full title, is Colin Leys, *Underdevelopment in Kenya: Economy of Neo-Colonialism 1964-71* (London, Heinemann, 1975); the most knowledgeable is Cherry Gertzel, *The Politics of Independent Kenya* (London, Heinemann, 1970); the most authoritative account of Kenya's key agricultural sector is L. Winston Cone and J. F. Lipscombe, *The History of Kenya Agriculture* (Nairobi, University Press of Africa, 1972). See also Alice K. Amsden, *International Firms and Labour in Kenya 1945-70* (London, Frank Cass, 1971), and Richard Sandbrook, *Proletarians and African Capitalism: The Kenya Case 1960-72* (Cambridge, Cambridge University Press, 1975). By far the best early survey is A. Clayton and D. Savage, *Government and Labour in Kenya 1895-1963* (London, Frank Cass, 1974).
22. Pratt, *The Critical Phase in Tanzania*, p. 217.
23. Ibid., p. 256.
24. Robert Martin, *Journal of African Studies*, 13 (1975), 528-532, review of *Socialism and Participation: Tanzania's 1970 National Elections* (Dar es Salaam, Tanzanian Publishing House, 1974).
25. Nyerere, quoted in Hatch, *Two African Statesmen*, p. 162.

26. Pratt's phrase, ibid., p. 184.
27. Nyerere, *Freedom and Unity: Uhuru na Umoja* (London, Oxford University Press, 1966), p. 312. By October 1966 the university students were in direct opposition to Nyerere. When they demonstrated against aspects of a newly introduced national science program, the government sent home nearly 400 of them under armed escort, including some 300 of the 380 Tanzanians at the college.
28. David Shub, *Lenin* (London, Penguin Books, 1967), pp. 377-378.
29. Pratt, *The Critical Phase in Tanzania, 1948-1968*, p. 263.
30. John Hatch, *Two African Statesmen*, pp. 198-99.
31. *Socialism and Participation*.
32. Pratt, p. 255.
33. There have been no elections in Zanzibar, though the present merger between TANU and the island's Afro-Shirazi Party to form the Chama cha Mapandizi (Revolutionary Party) may see elections in both parts of the union in 1980. In the October 1975 elections, two ministers and one junior minister lost their seats. Among those reelected was the Asian-born Amir Jamal, later minister for finance and planning. There is also a British-born nominated MP, L. D. Stirling, as minister for health.
34. Cf. the opinion, in the early 1970's, of a sympathetic critic, John Nellis, *A Theory of Ideology, The Tanzanian Example* (Nairobi, Oxford University Press, 1972): "there is an increasingly authoritarian response to increasingly critical problems ... balanced by the unusual and attractive personality ... of Nyerere" (pp. 95-96).
35. See Hamis Kunsanje, *Tanzania, Differences between Oscar S. Kambona and President Nyerere* (London, Debemoja, n.d.). The author was Dennis Phombeah, writing under a pseudonym since he too had fled from Dar es Salaam.
36. *Socialism and Participation*, p. 375.
37. Ibid., p. 367. "Despite several apparent efforts to revitalize the parliamentary institution, the very logic of the one-party system has ... led the National Assembly to political atrophy."
38. Address to the British Colonists in North America (1777), *Works* (London, Macmillan, 1803-13), IX, 211-212. Note the contrast to Lenin's much later diction that "No parliament can in any circumstances be for Communists an arena of struggle for reforms for betterment of the situation of the working class.... The only question can be that of utilizing bourgeois state institutions for their destruction." *Collected Works* (1929 edition), XXV, 566.
39. "Speech from the Throne," *Kenya Parliamentary Debate* (Nairobi Government Printer, 15 December 1963).

40. Kenya's External Trade: £ '000, 1967

	Exports to	Imports from
Tanzania	11,382	3,288
Uganda	14,796	10,165

Source: *Africa South of the Sahara 1971* (London, Europa Publications, 1971), p. 97.

41. The most sensible assessment is that of Roger Van Zwannenberg, "Neo-colonialism and the Origin of the National Bourgeoisie in Kenya between 1940 and 1973,"*Kenya Historical Review*, 1976, 210-242.
42. The case for and against is set out in the April 1967 Kenya government document "Kenya-Somali Relations" (Nairobi, Government Printer) and the Somali Government's reply, "Somali-Kenya Relations in True Perspective," (Mogadishu, Government Printer, September 1967).
43. The republic was formerly known as the Territory of the Afars and Issars, the population of some 220,000 Muslim pastoralists being divided almost equally between Afar- and Somali-speaking tribesmen. The present government consists of eight Somali, six Afars, and one Arab, led by Hassan Gulled, a Somali politician and former French National Assembly member, and an Afar President Ali Arif. But how long will such a sensible compromise be allowed to last?

4. The Middle Zone

1. There was provision in the 1910 South Africa Act for their incorporation into the Union.
2. MPLA = Popular Movement for the Liberation of Angola; Frelimo = Mozambique Liberation Front; UNITA = National Movement for the Total Liberation of Angola; FNLA = National Front for the Liberation of Angola.
3. For example: "Development means the structural transformation of the national economies which are industrializing in a world shaped by the colonial revolution . . . a world in which political independence continues with economic dependence, and when breaking with the international division of work is much more painful and risky than breaking with the political bonds of dependence." Paul Singer, "Dinamia de la problación y desarrollo," *Siglo XXI* (1971), 236-262.
4. According to René Pélissier, the nationalist guerrillas had pledged themselves to destroy the Cabora Bassa Dam before its first stage was com-

pleted in 1974, but failed to do so. *Africa South of the Sahara* (London, Europa Publications, 1971), p. 528.
5. A new rail link between Malawi and Mozambique was completed in July 1970 to Nacala, north of Beira.
6. See, particularly, Norman Sherry, *Conrad and His World* (London, Thames and Hudson, 1972).
7. 1957 Press Release of the Alliance des Bakongo, quoted in Crawford Young, *The Politics of Cultural Pluralism*, p. 163.
8. See *Standard Chartered Review* (January 1976), p. 4.
9. As argued by A. Hazelwood and P. D. Henderson, *Nyasaland: The Economics of Federation* (Oxford, Oxford University Press, 1960).
10. There are said to be some one hundred tribal identities, thirteen separate language groups, and four dominant ethnic solidarities.
11. But Kaunda was stern enough—or nervously determined enough—to use armed force against the separatist Lumpa church movement under Alice Lenshina in the North in 1965.
12. *Report and Statistical Handbook on Manpower, Education, Training and Zambianisation in 1965-66* (Lusaka, Government Printer, 1966), quoted in William Tordoff, "Zambia: The Politics of Disengagement," *African Affairs*, 76 (January 1977), p. 60.
13. Cmd 814, *Report of the Nyasaland Commission of Inquiry*, HMSO, 1959; chairman, Mr. Justice Devlin.
14. There were innumerable constitutional conferences on various stages of self-government in London and local colonial capitals between 1960 and 1964: for example, Kenya (January-February 1960), Nyasaland (July-August 1960), Tanganyika (March 1961), Zanzibar (March-April 1962), Kenya again (April 1962), Uganda (June 1962), Nyasaland again (November 1962), Kenya once more (September 1963).
15. Cmd 1148, *Report of the Advisory Committee of the Review of the Constitution of Rhodesia and Nyasaland*, HMSO, 1960; chairman, Lord Monckton.
16. Population:

	European	African	Asian	Colored
Rhodesia:	252,414	4,817,950	2,700	
South Africa:	4.2m	17.7m	0.7m	2.3m

17. The distribution of land in 1958 was as follows:

	Population		Land		
	African	European	African	European	Crown
S. Rhodesia	2,590,000	211,000	38%	51%	11%
Zambia	2,250,000	72,000	94.5%	2.5%	3%
Malawi	2,720,000	8,600	86.5%	4%	9.5%

Source: Africa Publications Trust 1960
18. (1) The principle and intention of unimpeded progress to majority

rule, already enshrined in the 1961 Constitution, would have to be maintained and guaranteed; (2) there would also have to be guarantees against retrogressive amendment of the Constitution; (3) there would have to be immediate improvement in the political status of the African population; (4) there would have to be progress toward ending racial discrimination; (5) the British government would need to be satisfied that any basis proposed for independence was acceptable to the people of Rhodesia as a whole; and (6) it would be necessary to ensure that, regardless of race, there was no oppression majority by minority or of the minority by the majority. The Conservative government agreed to the first five principles. The 1964-70 Labor Administration added the sixth, which came to be interpreted as NIBMAR: "No independence before majority rule."

19. "We could only guess what the outcome would have been had Joshua Nkomo tipped the balance to Sir Edgar Whitehead (in 1962) and entered Parliament himself at the head of a deputation of fifteen African nationalist representatives. Certainly in Parliament, Nkomo would have enjoyed substantial tactical advantages. . . . With the benefit of hindsight, Nkomo was foolish to have denied himself these opportunities [although] one suspects that racial confrontation would only have been postponed, not averted." Robert C. Good, *U.D.I. The International Politics of the Rhodesian Rebellion* (London, Faber, 1973), p. 40. The study is an excellent account of the whole affair, including the argument over the refusal by Britain to use force.

20. Harold Wilson held talks with Smith and his advisers on board HMS *Tiger* in Gibraltar in December 1965, followed by Lord Alport (former High Commissioner in Salisbury) in June 1967, George Thomson (Commonwealth Secretary) November 1967, Wilson again on HMS *Fearless* in Gibraltar October 1968, Lord Goodman April 1971, Sir Alec Douglas Home in Salisbury November 1971. Later that month, an agreement was actually signed in Salisbury between the Heath Conservative government and Smith, but it was dependent on "African acceptability" of the proposals. Lord Pearce led a commission to Rhodesia to gauge African opinion, and concluded that whereas whites, coloreds, and Asians favored the settlement, Africans opposed the terms in the ratio of 36 to 1. That dashed another European hope of settlement. See Good, *U.D.I.*, chapter XI.

21. Good, p. 41.
22. Martin Loney, *Rhodesia* (London, Penguin Books, 1975), p. 107. Chitapo was assassinated in Lusaka in 1975.
23. Richard Gibson, *African Liberation Movements* (London, Oxford

University Press, 1972), p. 183. See also S. E. Wilner et al., *Zimbabwe Now* (London, Rex Collings, 1973).
24. There were two Sitholes: Edison Sithole, aligned with Nkomo, and the Reverend Ndabaningi Sithole, who returned to Rhodesia in mid-1977 to join forces with Muzorewa. See Elaine Windrich, *The Rhodesian Record, 1923-73* (London, Routledge and Kegan Paul, 1975).
25. Loney, *Rhodesia*, p. 104. Most white Rhodesians could flee south to the Republic or to Europe and the United States—many with more than one passport. The worst victims of collapse would probably be Africans holding office under the present regime and the Asian minority.
26. See below, Chapter 5.
27. Holden Roberto had his great moment of glory in March 1962 when he proclaimed the existence of a Revolutionary Government in Exile (GRAE). The first government to recognize its authority was that of Ben Bella of Algeria. Others followed, and in July 1964 the OAU recommended approval. Thereafter it was downhill most of the way for Roberto, and the OAU withdrew its recognition in July 1971. There were endless maneuvers, coalitions, and protestations of unity, followed by bitter enmity, throughout the 1960's and 70's. The most recent account is Basil Davidson, *In the Eye of the Storm*, Part 3, (London, Penguin Books, 1972).
28. Ibid., p. 308.
29. Ibid., p. 309.
30. South Africa "is reported to have already furnished Zambia with considerable export credit facilities in addition to airfreight capacity directly to Lusaka." *Standard Bank Review*, March 1976.
31. *Standard Bank Review*, March 1976. A good detailed view is given in Charles Elliot, *Constraints on the Economic Development of Zambia* (London, Oxford University Press, 1971).
32. The 1977-81 Third Development Plan (Lusaka, Government Printer, 1977) includes a substantial component giving "priority to industries based on locally available materials . . . contributing substantially to import substitution."
33. *Annual Register*, article on Zambia (London, Longmans, 1965), p. 268.
34. The outcome of the fifth East and Central African Summit Conference in Lusaka in April 1969 which had condemned the notion of dialogue with South Africa while stressing the need for a peaceful solution, by agreement, of Rhodesian and South African problems.
35. I have relied heavily on Ralph Young's article on Zambia in these passages.

5. White Power: Cohesion without Consensus

1. Julius Lewin, "No Revolution Round the Corner," *Africa South* (October-December 1958). The itch to be optimistic still exists today, particularly in the security of exile. "All this [the circumstances of discontent] does not mean that the revolution is around the corner. It rather signifies that conditions for its unfolding are perhaps more favorable today than at any time this century." J. Slovo in Basil Davidson, ed., *Southern Africa: The New Politics of Revolution* (London, Penguin Books, 1976), p. 205.
2. Population: whites, 4.2m, Asians 0.7m, Colored 2.3m, black 17.7m (1974 estimate).
3. "Afrikaans is a highly streamlined version of the 17th century Dutch language brought to South Africa by its first permanent settlers." E. G. Malherbe, quoted in Potholm and Richard Dale, eds., *Southern Africa in Perspective* (New York, The Free Press, 1972), p. 341.
4. A vote in the South African parliament brought a victory by eleven votes in favor of declaring war on Germany, whereupon Hertzog resigned, Smuts took office again as prime minister, and South Africa entered World War II—a remarkable decision of immense value to the allies, including the United States, which was not brought into the conflict until December 1941.
5. The most thorough account of the fortunes of the political parties at elections since 1943 is Kenneth Heard, *General Elections in South Africa 1943-1970* (London, Oxford University Press, 1974). The most interesting interpretation of Afrikaner political history is Newell Stultz, *Afrikaner Politics in South Africa, 1934-1948* (Berkeley, University of California Press, 1974).
6. Arthur Keppel-Jones, *Friend or Foe?* (Pietermaritzburg, Shuter and Shooter, 1949), p. 77. (Rooinek = red-neck. Majuba refers to the battle at Majuba Hill, where the Boers defeated the British in 1881.)
7. On the importance of the Afrikaner belief in Christian National Education, see Deborah Lavin, "The Dilemma of Christian National Education in South Africa," *The World Today*, 21 (October 1965).
8. Quoted in David Carter, "The Defiance Campaign," *Societies of Southern Africa in the 19th and 20th Centuries*, No. 12, October 1970-June 1971 (London, 1971), p. 83.
9. Speech at the Rivonia Treason Trial, quoted in Nelson Mandela, *No Easy Walk to Freedom* (London, Heinemann, 1965), pp. 82-83. Cf. Albert Luthuli, *Let My People Go* (London, Collins, 1962); see, too, Mary Benson, *The African Patriots: The Story of the African National Congress of South Africa* (London, Faber, 1963).
10. These people had drawn together to force the repeal of the pass laws,

the Group Areas Act, Separate Representation of Voters Act, the Suppression of Communism Act, the Bantu Authorities Act, and the Compulsory Cattle Culling Policy.
11. H. Strauss, "Underground African Politics, " *Societies of Southern Africa in the 19th and 20th Centuries,* 3 (London, Institute of Commonwealth Studies, 1972), p. 132.
12. Ibid.
13. Mandela, *No Easy Walk to Freedom,* p. 164.
14. The main ethnic divisions among the African population (1970 estimate) are: Xhosa, 3,570,000; Sotho, 4,000,000; Zulu, 3,500,000; Venda, 350,000; Ndebele, 400,000; Tsonga, 500,000; Swazi, 400,000; other, 300,000. In a detailed examination of the 1952 Defiance Campaign in the Eastern Cape and the Transvaal, David Carter was able to show that the movement differed from region to region. "The presence on the Rand of members of all the principal ethnic and linguistic groups living in South Africa . . . contrasts sharply with the position in the Eastern Cape where in the main centres, Africans are almost entirely Xhosa speaking . . . Resistance leaders of the Eastern Cape were able to draw together in common protest the different segments of the Xhosa community, and they made good use of the common Xhosa identity and traditions . . . when encouraging involvement in the campaign." Carter, "The Defiance Campaign," p. 76. Other factors, too, played their part; "the Fingo, who comprised the first Cape African voters, form a major element of the population of the Peddie district which was an important centre of resistance during the campaign and by far the most significant area of rural opposition." *Societies of Southern Africa,* p. 84.
15. Strauss, "Underground African Politics," p. 131.
16. See Harold Wolpe, "Class, Race and Occupational Structure," *The Societies of Southern Africa in the 19th and 20th Centuries,* Vol. 2, October 1970–June 1971, No. 12, London, 1972, and J. Slovo, "South Africa—No Middle Road," in Davidson, ed., *Southern Africa,* pp. 118-149. The most intelligent discussion of the question is H. J. and R. E. Simons, *Class and Colour in South Africa 1850–1950* (London, Penguin Books, 1969).
17. Stanley Trapido, "South Africa in a Comparative Study of Industrialization," ibid., p. 54.
18. Eschel Rhoodie, "Southern Africa: A New Commonwealth," Potholm and Dale, *Southern Africa in Perspective,* p. 276.
19. Ibid.
20. H. Bhengu, quoted in C. R. Hill, "Separate Development in South Africa," Potholm and Dale, p. 67.
21. *Report of the Commission for the Socio-Economic Development of*

Notes to Pages 120-125

the Bantu Areas within the Union of South Africa, Pretoria, 1955. The Tomlinson Commission included the then British High Commission Territories of Basutoland, Swaziland, and Bechuanaland as part of the Bantu Areas.

22. A third possibility, arising from the growth of economic factors, is discussed on page 123.
23. Once again a new Afrikaner Party was formed—the *Herstigte* (Reconstituted) National Party of Dr. Albert Hertzog—as "a party which is unashamedly Afrikaans . . . and . . . based on the infallible word of God." The best guides to South Africa's "outward movement," each from a rather different standpoint, are Sam Nolutshungu, *South Africa in Africa* (Manchester, Manchester University Press, 1974), and James Barber, *South Africa's Foreign Policy 1945-1970* (London, Oxford University Press, 1973).
24. Max Gluckman, "The Tribal Area of South and Central Africa," in Leo Kuper and M. G. Smith, eds., *Pluralism in Africa* (Berkeley, University of California Press, 1971), p. 376.
25. Leo Kuper, *An African Bourgeoisie: Race, Class and Politics in South Africa* (New Haven, Yale University Press, 1965), p. 6.
26. Gluckman, p. 387.
27. Harold Wolpe has described how, in the garment industry, the proportions of the labor force were laid down in 1960 as 19 percent white, 37 percent Colored, and 44 percent African, with additional labor being permitted only in the ratio of 25 percent white, 37½ percent Colored, and 37½ percent African; but "the 1969 statistics showed . . . that the acutal composition of the labour force was 9% white, 32% coloured and 60% African." "Class, Race and the Occupational Structure," p. 116.
28. Trapido, "South Africa in a Comparative Study of Industrialization," p. 50. The evidence does not, in my view, fully support the argument except where racial divisions are concerned. The expansion of the South African economy plus Afrikaner nationalism did see a transfer of political-economic power from the English-speaking community to the Afrikaner.
29. Ibid.
30. An argument developed by Sam Nolutshungu, *South Africa in Africa*.
31. The United Party was formally dissolved in June 1977, splitting Left and Right. Parliamentary seats were National Party 123, United Party 30, Progressive Reform Party 12, South Africa Party (formed as a right-wing break away from the UP) 6. The UP seemed likely to reform under a different name, as a pale shadow of its heroic past.
32. Kuper and Smith, *Pluralism in Africa*, p. 278. In 1976, for example,

the budget increased pensions and disability grants. Whites were awarded an extra R.8 a month, Coloreds and Asians an extra R.4.50, and Africans an extra R.3.50. The monthly totals were R.72, R.34-R.38.50, and R.15-R.18.50; the ratios were Whites 100, Colored and Asians 53½, African 25¼. *Financial Mail,* Johannesburg, 9 July 1976.
33. Kuper and Smith, *Pluralism in Africa,* p. 180.
34. Ibid.
35. Ibid., p. 272. "In 1961 the Nationalist government finally decided that it could not expect South African-born Indians to expatriate themselves to India . . . and granted them a status that could be described as 'pariah citizenship'" (p. 270).
36. Whites, 3.8 million; nonwhites, 17.6 million; Africans, 15 million; non-Africans, 6.4 million (1970 census figures).
37. C. W. deKiewiet, *The Anatomy of South African Misery* (London, Oxford University Press, 1956).
38. *South African Digest,* 5 November 1976 (Pretoria, Government Printer), p. 9.
39. Newell M. Stultz, "Transkei Independence in Separatist Perspective," unpublished paper, 1976. See also Patrick Laurence, *The Transkei* (Johannesburg, 1977); Kaizer D. Matazima, *Independence My Way* (Pretoria, 1977); and Ben Temkin, *Gatshu Buthelezi: Zulu Statesman* (Johannesburg, 1977).
40. According to Stultz (ibid.), "There are . . . one million Xhosa-speaking Africans who are legally speaking Transkei citizens [under the Republic's *Status of the Transkei Act* 1976] but are permanently absent in the Republic. It is inconceivable that they could ever be accommodated in Transkei."
41. There are unusual features to Namibia's struggle toward self-government. Once a German colony, it was later administered under League of Nations mandate by South Africa, which objected in 1945 to its transfer to the United Nations. A huge amount of litigation at the International Court at The Hague went first this way and then that: the United Nations decided that South Africa should not administer the area; the South African government at first refused, and then yielded to, local demands for independence. SWAPO objects to the kind of independence worked out at Windhoek, but a number of local communities, including the once famous Herero, seem disposed to accept; and in May 1977 the white electorate voted substantially in favor.
42. The present intention is to establish nine homelands. Bophuthatswana was pronounced independent on 6 December 1977 as a divided state of 6 units islanded among a sea of white-dominated areas. Of its

2,000,000 prospective citizens, nearly two thirds live and work outside its territory. Of the 800,000 who actually live in the new state, about a quarter are ethnically distinct from the Tswana majority.
43. Stultz, "Transkei Independence in Separatist Perspective" (unpublished paper).
44. The rate of increase between 1960 and 1970 increased the numerical preponderance of the African population:

	1960 Census	%	1970 Census	%	% Increase
White	3,100,000	19.3	3,800,000	17.7	+ 24.4
Asian	477,000	3.0	614,000	2.9	+ 28.7
Coloured	1,510,000	9.4	1,996,000	9.4	+ 32.3
African	10,900,000	68.3	14,893,000	70.0	+ 36.3

From Howard Brotz, *Politics of South Africa* (London, Oxford University Press, 1977), p. 93.
45. Some 43 percent of all African men in the republic—that is, some one-and-a-half million—are estimated to be migrant workers. If we add roughly 260,000 African women to the total, the economy contains about one-and-three-quarters million African migrants. *African Bureau Document Paper*, March/April, 1977. About half a million Africans are prosecuted annually for infringing the pass laws, which still oblige every African aged 16 and over to carry a "reference book."
46. "The first explicit and extended consideration of the idea was probably provided by Dr. R. F. Alfred Hoernle in lectures given at the University of Cape Town in 1939 and later reproduced in his book *South African Native Policy and the Liberal Spirit*" (Stultz, "Transkei Independence in the Separatist Perspective"). By 1974 Chief Gatsha Buthelezi was giving the Hoernle Memorial Lecture, proposing a federation of three constituent states—one African-dominant, one white-controlled, one multinational.
47.

	1974	2000	2020
Whites	4.2	6.8	9.2
Asians	0.7	1.2	1.6
Coloreds	2.3	4.1	7.7
Africans	17.7	37.3	62.8
	24.9	49.9	81.3

Population in millions. (*Economist*, 1 January 1977).
48. There is, to be sure, the difference Vorster insists on vis-à-vis the United States: "The U.S. black man is an American in every sense of the word. The only difference is the colour of his skin. He has lost his language, his culture and identity. The black man in South Africa, however, was never a slave. He was a proud man of his nation." A telling argument; but as *The Guardian* (which printed part

of Vorster's speech) commented, "Mr. Vorster's attempt to preserve and dignify . . . every group in South Africa might meet with more sympathy if it did not invariably redound to the benefit of the whites" (21 May 1977).

6. The Darkling Plain: Literature and Politics

1. Matthew Arnold, *Dover Beach.* Arnold himself, in a very different context, believed that his poems represented "the main movement of mind in the last quarter of a century" and that "they will have their day as people become conscious to themselves of what that movement of mind is." Letter to his mother, 1869, quoted in Basil Willey, *Nineteenth Century Studies* (London, Chatto and Windus, 1949), p. 251, who also observed: "Not only his poems, but all his works have this representative character. . . ."
2. Maurice Bowra's phrase in *Poetry and Politics* (Cambridge, Cambridge University Press, 1966), p. 57.
3. See Robin Skelton, *Poetry of the Thirties* (London, Penguin Books, 1964).
4. Per Wästberg, ed., *The Writer in Modern Africa* (Uppsala, Scandinavian Institute of African Studies, 1968).
5. There was even a flourishing school in the 1960's of Afrikaner writers.
6. Notably in *Transition*, the journal once based in Uganda which moved first to London, then recently to Ife in Nigeria under its new title *Ch'Indaba*, edited by Wole Soyinka. There was also a good deal of erudite nonsense at one time by Sartre and others who sought to recreate Africa as a country of the mind where it was safe for them to be radical: "since the oppressor is present even in the language they speak, they will speak the language to destroy it. The European poet of today attempts to dehumanize words in order to return them to matter; the Black herald is seeking to de-Gallicize them. He smashes them together . . . and it is only when they have disgorged their whiteness that he adopts them." Jean Paul Sartre, *Black Orpheus* (Paris, Gallimard, 1949), p. 26, originally published as *Orphée Noire*, preface to Léopold Senghor, *La Nouvelle Poésie Nègre et Malgache* (Paris, Plon, 1946).
7. There is a sensitive exploration of such difficulties in E. Shils, *The Intellectual between Tradition and Modernity: The Indian Situation* (The Hague, Mouton, 1961). See too Bernth Lindfors, *Folklore in Nigerian Literature* (New York, Holmes and Meier, 1973), for an intelligent discussion of the relationship between African oral tradition and written English, and attempts to bridge the two. Lindfors has also argued

Notes to Pages 139–141

(p. 173) that "there are at least two distinct tribal prose styles in African literature in English, the Yoruba and the Ibo."
8. Chinua Achebe, *A Man of the People* (London, Heinemann, 1966), pp. 51-52.
9. The problem of dialect English is discussed by Vincent Naipaul in *The Overcrowded Barracoon* (London, André Deutsch, 1972). There is, however, the rather different attempt (largely I suspect artificial, but used to good effect) to write what purports to be a transliteration of traditional speech, as by Kipling (say) in *Kim* and by most African writers when describing conversation between non-English-speaking characters.
10. Tacitus, *Agricola*. I have of course changed both ruler and ruled, from Romans and British, to British and Africans. For "English," read "Latin"; for "dark suit" read "toga." The missing phrases are: "So the British were gradually persuaded to use the amenities which make vice agreeable—arcades, baths and sumptuous banquets." A wider array of technical marvels was left behind by the Europeans in Africa, among which public sanitation was perhaps the most valuable and the least observed.
11. Birago Diop, quoted in Wästberg, *The Writer in Modern Africa*, p. 68. Note the comment, too, by Gerald Moore on the poems of Tchicaya U Tam'si: "he has developed a profoundly esoteric style much influenced by surrealism and by the magic conjunctions of Rimbaud and Aimé Césaire": see R. Rotberg and 'Ali Mazrui, *Protest and Power in Africa* (New York, Oxford University Press, 1970). I find U Tam'si's poetry wholly obscure.
12. George Musowe in *The Jewel of Africa*, 1 (Lusaka, 1968), p. 16.
13. *A Portrait of the Artist as a Young Man* (London, Penguin Books, 1976), p. 189.
14. William Butler Yeats, " A General Introduction for My Work," in A. Norman Jeffares, ed., *Yeats, Selected Criticism* (London, Macmillan, 1973), p. 265. "I know . . . that I owe my soul to Shakespeare, to Spenser and to Blake, perhaps to William Morris, and to the English language in which I think, speak and write, that everything I love has come to me through English; my hatred tortures me with love, my love with hate" (ibid., p. 263).
15. T. S. Eliot, *Poetry and Poets* (London, Faber, 1957), p. 262.
16. Wole Soyinka's phrase in Per Wästberg, *The Writer in Modern Africa*, p. 14.
17. J. E. Casely Hayford, *Ethiopia Unbound* (London, C. M. Phillips, 1911). See, too, the famous passage in the sermon by Dr. Aggrey of Achimota School in the Gold Coast in 1926: "My people of Africa, we were created in the image of God, but men have made us think

we are chickens and we still think we are; but we are eagles. Stretch forth your wings and fly! Don't be content with the food of chickens." Quoted in Lalage Bown, *Two Centuries of African English* (London, Heinemann, 1973), p. 64.
18. Hayford, *Ethiopia Unbound*, p. 46.
19. Garvey's body was later removed to a place of honor in Jamaica.
20. Quoted in I. L. Markowitz, *Senghor and the Politics of Negritude*, p. 51. At no point does Senghor seem to have pondered the question whether language and its uses are fundamental to the soul of a man.
21. L. S. Senghor, *Chants d'ombre* (Paris, Seuil, 1945).
22. Ibid.
23. Quoted in Sartre, *Black Orpheus*, p. 28.
24. Rex Warner, *Hymn*, printed in Robin Skelton, ed., *Poetry of the Thirties* (London, Penguin Books, 1964).
25. These ranged from the very bad, e.g. *Cannibals and Headhunters of the Dark Continent*, through the *Sanders of the River* stories, to the marvelously evocative *King Solomon's Mines* which so influenced Graham Greene. For an interesting account of the mythology of the Negro in English history, see Edna Steeves, "Négritude and the Noble Savage," *Journal of Modern African Studies*, 2 (1973).
26. Horton was born in Sierra Leone in 1835, educated by missionaries, and trained as a doctor in London. Appointed Staff Assistant Surgeon with the British army in West Africa, by 1880 he was in charge of the Army Medical Department in the Gold Coast. See Bown, ed., *Two Centuries of African English*, and Martin Minogue and Judith Mulloy, eds., *African Aims and Attitudes* (Cambridge, Cambridge University Press, 1974). The quotation is from Bown, p. 77.
27. Senghor again, in K. Kirkwood, ed., *St. Antony Papers*, No. 15 (London, Oxford University Press, 1953). See too L. S. Senghor, *On African Socialism* (London, Praeger, 1964). There is a kind of parody of Henri Bergson in many of these assertions about intuitive reasoning.
28. Dunduzu Chisiza, of Malawi, "The Outlook for Contemporary Africa," *Journal of Contemporary African Studies*, 1 (March 1963); Chisiza was killed in a motor car accident in 1962—a victim of European technology. See too Camara Laye, *Le Regard du Roi* (Paris, Plon, 1955; translated as *The Radiance of the King*, London, Collins, 1955), a story of the attempt by a white man, Clarence, to find salvation at the court of the African king.
29. In rather different vein, Richard Wright (a black American) wrote *Black Power* (London, Dobson, 1954) as an account of his visit to Ghana before independence. The book is as revealing about his

reactions to black Africa as it is of African politics, but it ends with a warning appeal to Nkrumah to "be merciful by being stern," without being explicit about the advantages such a policy would bestow.
30. Conclusions to his semi-autobiography, *Mau Mau Detainee* (London, Penguin Books, 1963).
31. *Devoir de Violence* was published in 1971 (London, Heinemann). The quotations are from Keith Panter Brick's interesting review, "Fiction and Politics in Africa," *Journal of Commonwealth and Comparative Politics*, 13 (March 1975), pp. 79-86.
32. Frantz Fanon, *The Wretched of the Earth* (London, Penguin Books, 1967), translated by Constance Farrington from *Les Damnés de la Terre* (Paris, Présence Africaine, 1963).
33. I can read Neto's poetry only in translation, which does not perhaps do it justice. See Mario de Andrade, *Antologia da Poesia Negra de Expressão Portuguesa* (Paris, Oswald, 1958), or *La Poésie Africaine d'Expression Portugaise* (Paris, Oswald, 1971), and Agostinho Neto, *Sacred Hope*, the book of poems published by the Tanzania Publishing House, Dar es Salaam, 1974.
34. There has always been a widespread popular literature of the *Amelia's Promise* kind of love fiction. See Ulli Beier, "Public Opinion on Lovers: Popular Nigerian Literature Sold in Onitsha Market," *Black Orpheus*, 14 February 1964; K. W. J. Post, "Nigerian Pamphleteers and the Congo," *Journal of Modern African Studies*, November 1964; and Bernth Lindfors, "Heroes and Hero-Worship in Nigerian Chapbooks," *Journal of Popular Culture*, Summer 1967. An early example of political creeds: "I believe in the Convention People's Party, The Liberty of the Masses, The Progress of the Nation, The Resurrection of Ghana, and Freedom Everlasting ... Amen."
35. *La Nouvelle Poésie Nègre et Malgache* (Paris, Seuil, 1948).
36. Chisiza's phrase, in "The Outlook for Contemporary Africa."
37. Davidson Nicol, *The West African Intellectual Community* (Ibadan, Ibadan University Press, 1962), p. 34. Dr. Nicol was then principal of Fourah Bay College, Sierra Leone.
38. See the perceptive article by Bernth Lindfors "The African Politician's Changing Image in African Literature in English," *Journal of Developing Areas*, 4 (October 1969), pp. 13-28. John Pepper Clark's *Ozidi* (London, Heinemann, 1966) also followed oral tradition not simply in paying homage to the past but in giving structure and form to his own writing. I have not attempted any critical appraisal of particular African writers. An excellent interpretation of three of the most important poets will be found in Nyong J. Udoyeop, *Three Nigerian Poets: Soyinka, Clark and Okigbo* (Ibadan, Ibadan University Press, 1975). There are, of course, interesting African novels by

non-African writers, of whom the most outstanding is Joyce Cary. See Michael J. S. Echeruo's critical commentary, *Joyce Cary and the Novel of Africa* (London, Longman, 1973).
39. 'Ali Mazrui argued the case of "Soldiers as Traditionalizers: Military Rule and Re-Africanization of Africa," with particular reference to Amin, in *World Politics*, 28 (January 1976), 246-272.
40. Wästberg, ed., *The Writer in Modern Africa*, p. 19. Jean Paul Sartre, in *Black Orpheus* (p. 64), wrote what purported also to be literature: "Negritude is the content of the poem; it is the poem as thing of the world, mysterious and open, indecipherable and suggestive; it is the poet himself. It is necessary to go still farther. Negritude, triumph of Narcissism and suicide of Narcissus, tension of the soul outside of its culture, words and every psychic fact, luminous night of non-knowledge, deliberate choice of the *impossible* and of that which Bataille names the 'torture,' intuitive acceptance of the world and rejection of the world in the name of the 'law of the heart,' double contradictory postulation, exacting recantation, an expanding generosity, negritude is, in its essence, poetry. Upon this one occasion at least, the most authentic revolutionary program and the purest poetry derive from the same source."
41. "We begin to realise now that the beginnings of negritude were after all in the Caribbean and the Western Hemisphere generally, so negritude proper was an expression, the outcry of an alienated people, people who couldn't go back to Africa and recapture their African roots because they were complete exiles, and this is why negritude found its most poignant expressions in this area: it was a natural beginning for negritude. But how different with the African: an African who feels alienated can always go back to Africa if he wants to, and if he has a mind to it; he can go back and recapture his roots . . . because, after all, a good deal of Africa is still very traditional, and all he needs to do is go back to his people and make the contact again, while the negro in America and the negro in the Caribbean could not do that. So we begin to realize, all the more now, that it is a Western Hemisphere negro phenomenon more than an African one . . . because they are culturally in a state of siege, they are besieged by a formidable white culture which is threatening to suck them in, on its own terms; and the African is not in this situation at all. He is not in a state of siege." Ezekiel Mphahlele, *The African Image* (London, Faber, 1962), p. 47.
42. Extracts from an interview by Cosmos Pietersee, ed., in *African Writers Talking* (London, Heinemann, 1973), reprinted in Minogue and Mulloy, *African Aims and Attitudes*, p. 237.
43. Lewis Nkosi, quoted in Wästberg, *The Writer in Modern Africa*, ch. 3.

Notes to Pages 154-155

The most powerful expressions of Southern protest are to be found in Athol Fugard's trilogy of plays: *The Island, Sizwi Banzi is Dead*, and *After an Arrest under the Immorality Act*; and in black South African poets, Mongane Serote, Oswald Mtshali, and others. See Nadine Gordimer, *The Black Interpreters: Notes on African Writing* (Johannesburg, Spro. Cas/Ravan, 1973).

44. Nkosi, quoted in Wästberg, ch. 3.
45. Report in the London *Sunday Times*, 16 January 1977.
46. *Poems from Bangla Desh, The Voice of a New Nation*, translated by Pritish Nandy, selected by Tambimuttu (London, Lyrebird Press, 1971).
47. From the poem "Civilian and Soldier" in Wole Soyinka, *Idanre and Other Poems* (London, Heinemann, 1967), quoted as the epigraph to Robin Luckham, *The Nigerian Military* (Cambridge, Cambridge University Press, 1971).
48. I cannot do better than give Panter Brick's summary in *Journal of Commonwealth and Comparative Politics*: "'Ali Mazrui's *The Trial of Christopher Okigbo* [London, Heinemann, 1971] is set in After-Africa, the land of African dead, where continental space is still a reality but not time. After-Africa remains interested in what happens in Africa—which is said to lie under the curse of many tripartite divisions—and anyone who perpetuates that curse, even unwittingly, may find himself on trial. 'Death is an exercise in Panafricanism.' Christopher Okigbo is accused of having betrayed his poetic gifts, which he held in trust for the whole of mankind, in favor of a soldier's death in defence of the Ibo community. His case is argued by opposing counsel, one for Damnation and the other for Salvation. The two counsel are themselves also on trial, their performance being used as a test for their fitness for immortality (as distinct from the state of being deceased). As they and the defendant are judged, so are the public causes which they represent. Those who defended the Biafran cause are found guilty of miscalculation; those who opposed it are found not guilty. In the case of Biafra itself the verdict is 'not proven' so Okigbo 'must travel through the ages wondering: Was it worth it?' One cannot but admire the ingenuity of this interplay of public and private judgements, the dialectical skill of counsels' arguments and the imaginative use of analogy, for instance, the calling of Lord Byron as a witness for the defence. Okigbo himself, as a person, is left in shadow—only his poetry is cited to reinforce some point or other."
49. Ngugi is no longer James but Ngugi Wa Thiong'o, Chairman of the Department of Literature in The University of Nairobi, having spent three years in The University of Leeds and a year at Evanston,

Illinois. The themes of the novel are taken from Yeats's poem "The Second Coming." New Ilmorog is a boom town on the Trans-African highway, and the novel tells of the effect of violence, drunkenness, and power on the four main characters who have become involved in the murder of three African directors of a foreign-owned brewery. A novel of current social content?

50. Cyprian Ekwensi, *Jagua Nana* (London, 1961). There is a good account of the novel in Bernth Lindfors, *Journal of Developing Areas* (16 October 1969), pp. 21 ff.
51. Eustace Deschamps, writing in fourteenth-century Burgundy.
52. See Lindfors, *Folklore in Nigerian Literature*, pp. 19-20.
53. Slogans painted on buses and passenger trucks are a familiar part of Ghanaian travel: e.g., "God Will Provide," or "A Beautiful Woman Cannot Stay with One Man," or (the one I rather like) "Fear Women and Grow Old."
54. Panter Brick, pp. 80-81, who also discusses Kofi Awoonor's novel, *This Earth My Brother*.
55. In "A General Introduction for My Work," A. Norman Jeffares, p. 269.
56. Soyinka, in Wästberg, *The Writer in Modern Africa*, p. 21. "The despair and anguish which is spreading like a miasma over the continent..."
57. Ngugi wa Thiong'o was arrested and detained by the Kenya authorities on 31 December 1977 following his part-authorship of a new play (written in Kikuyu) which opposed the village poor to the new land-rich élite—a theme unlikely to appeal to authority in Kenya.

Index

Abubakar, Alhaji, overthrown, 21, 53
Achebe, Chinuah: *A Man of the People* quoted, 25, 138-139, 156-157; *Arrow of God* quoted, 149-151
Afrikanerdom, 110-113, 109-133 *passim*
Aggrey, J. E. K., quoted, 183
Amin, Field Marshal Idi, 6, 12; bloody seizure of power, 31, 68-69, 161; titles, 179
Anang, Dei, quoted, 139-140
Angola, 83-107; rail and economic links, 86-88; guerrilla war, 99-100, 182, 185
Armah, Ayi Kwei, quoted, 157-158
Armies, 51-52; Nigerian coups, 53-54; East African mutinies, 67; per capita GNP expenditure, 174
Arnold, Matthew, quoted, 90, 135-136, 159, 191
Asquith Commission, cited, 37

Banda, Hastings, 7, 20, 21; consolidation of power, 92-93
Biko, Steve, murdered, 131
Blake, William, quoted, 50
Boigny, Houphouët, 6, 14; quoted, 23; wager with Nkrumah, 41, 176
Bokassa, Emperor, described, 4
Bongo, El Haji Omar, 176
Botswana, 83; and Rhodesia, 103
Brutus, Dennis, quoted, 154
Burke, Edmund, quoted, 78, 181

Busia, K. A., 22, 39, 44
Byron, Lord, quoted 172

Cabinda, 47
Carter, David, quoted, 187
Carter, President Jimmy, 41; and South Africa, 119
Central African Federation: early history, 83-84; dissolution, 90-93; legacies, 103-107
Césaire, Aimé, quoted, 145
Chipembere, Henry, 20; and Hastings Banda, 92-93
Cocoa, 38-40
Conrad, Joseph, quoted, 88
Copper, 83-107; and Zambia economy, 104-105

Davidson, Basil, quoted on Angola, 102
Débat, Alphonse Massamba, 17; executed, 52
Debray, Régis, quoted, 32
Dependency: as a concept, 5-7, 30-31; cocoa, 38-41; copper, 103-105; cultural dependency, 139 ff.
Deschamps, Eustace, quoted, 156
Diop, David, quoted, 148
Djibouti, 81, 164, 182
Dunn, John, cited, 34

East Africa: and British trade, 13, 171; decolonization and disunity, 61-82
East African Community: early background, 64-65; disintegration, 78-79

Index

ECOWAS (Economic Commission for West Africa), 45, 49
EEC (European Economic Community), 13-14; Lomé Agreement, 45, 176
Ekwensi, Cyprian, quoted, 155
Ethiopia, 24, 61-82; US and USSR involvement, 80-81; oppressive rule, 154; tribal conflict, 175, 178

Fanon, Frantz: quoted, 32, 34; quoted on violence, 146
Fortes, Meyer, quoted, 15-16
Foster, Philip, cited, 41-42, 176

Gaddafi, Colonel, 24
Ghana: and cocoa, 38-40; inflation, 44, 176; resurrection creed, 194
Gluckman, Max, quoted, 122-123
Gowon, General, 23; aid policy, 49; resigns, 57
Gupta, Anirudha, 1, 165

Hatch, John, quoted on single-party rule in Tanzania, 75
Horton, J. A. B., "Africanus" quoted, 144

Ideology, 31-32; in East Africa, 65-66, 79-80; African writers, 135-161, 178-179, 181
Imperialism, 9-34; of trade and investment in East Africa, 64-65, in central Africa, 84-88
Ironsi, Major-General, 53; "Decree 34," 56-57
Ivory Coast, 41-44

Joyce, James, quoted, 140

Kapwepwe, Simon, 20; breaks with Kaunda, 91-92
Kariuki, J. M., murder of, 71
Karume, Abeid, 69

Kasavubu, 88-89
Kaunda, Kenneth, 6-7, 20, 22-23; independence struggle, 91-92; evil effects of UDI, 103-106; Lumpa church, 183
Kenya, 61-82, tribal factions, 27, 70-72; brief bibliography, 180; relations with Somalia, 182. *See also* Kenyatta
Kenyatta, Jomo, 11, 21, 64; politics of control, 69-73, 147, 180
Keppel-Jones, Arthur, quoted, 112
Khama, Sir Seretse, 22; and Rhodesia, 103
Kipling, Rudyard, quoted, 28
Kuper, Hilda, quoted, 125-126

Lenin, and political development, 75
Lesotho, 83; relations with South Africa, 120-121
Leys, Colin, quoted on tribalism, 70
Liberia, 24; growth without development, 31, 175
Lindfors, Bernth, 148; quoted, 191-192, 194
Looney, Martin, quoted, 184, 185
Luckham, Robin: cited, 51-52; quoted on Nigeria, 53-54, 173-174, 177
Lumumba, Patrice, 88; murdered, 89

Machel, Samora, 7; victory against Portugal, 99-101
Malawi, 83-84; rail and economic links, 86-88; and Mozambique, 103
Macdonald, Malcolm, quoted, 171
Malherbe, E. G., quoted, 186
Mandela, Nelson, quoted, 114, 116, 124
Margai, Albert, 23; overthrown, 52-53

Index

Markowitz, Irving, quoted, 58
Martin, Robert: quoted, 74; cited, 180
Marx, Karl, 7, 15; quoted, 36–37; paraphrased, 119, 145
Mazrui, 'Ali, 155
Mboya, Tom, 64; assassination, 70
Mobutu, Sese Seko, rise to power, 88–90
Mondlane, Edouardo, 100, 147
Mozambique, 83–107; guerrilla war, 99–100, 182
Mphahlele, Ezekiel, quoted, 153, 195
Mugabe, Robert, and guerilla war, 97
Musowe, George, quoted, 140
Muzorewa, Bishop Abel, 97

Namibia, 85–86; need for recognition, 107; and South Africa, 128–129, 189
Nationalism: as a revolutionary impulse, 19–20; problems of identity, 33; in Nigeria, 53–54; in Uganda, 67–68; in Kenya, 70–72; in Zambia, 91–92; in Angola, 101–102; divisive effect in Central Africa, 106, among Afrikaners, 110–113; and African writers, 135–161 *passim*
Négritude, 141–145; discarded by writers, 152–153
Neto, Agostinho: struggles in Angola, 100; position at independence, 101–103; as poet, 147
Ngala, Ronald, 64
Ngugi, James, 146, 152; *Petals of Blood*, 156; arrested, 197
Nicol, Davidson, quoted, 148
Nigeria, 2; power and influence, 48–49; 1966 coups d'état, 53–54; war, oil, and federal unity, 56–57; census, 177

Nkosi, Lewis, quoted, 153–154
Nkrumah, Kwame, 11, 21–22; compared with Houphouët Boigny, 23, 41, 176; severity of rule, 29, 44; compared with Nyerere, 76–77, 88, 147
Nkomo, Joshua, and UDI, 96–97
Nolutshungu, Sam, cited, 187
Nyerere, Julius, 7; resigns as prime minister, 73; political style as president, 74–77; quoted on *ujamaa*, 74

OAU (Organization of African Unity): early hopes, 18–19; later fears, 26; quoted, 173
Obasanjo, Olusegun, 57
Obote, Milton, 12; quoted on tribalism, 67; rise and fall, 67–68
Odinga, Oginga, 64; political life, 70–72
Ojukwu, C. O., and secession, 57, 167
Okpewho, Isidore, quoted, 155
Ouologuem, Yambo, 146
Owusu, Maxwell, cited, 173

Panter Brick, Keith, quoted, 146, 159–160, 196
Polisario, 176–177
Pope, Alexander, quoted, 56
Pratt, Cranford, quoted on Nyerere, 74–75

Rhodesia, 83–84; political economy, 85–87; politics of UDI, 94–98; population and land distribution, 183; "talks about talks," 184
Roberto, Holden, 99–100, 185

Sartre, Jean Paul, quoted, 191, 195
Savimbi, Jonas, 101–102
Senghor, L. S., 14, 22; quoted, 58; quoted on *négritude*, 142–143, 147

Index

Shen, T. Y., quoted, 176-177
Singer, Paul, quoted, 182
Sithole, Ndabaningi, 97
Slovo, Joe, quoted on revolution, 186
Smith, Ian, and politics of UDI, 94-98
Somalia: early history, 62; irredentism, 80-81, 178; relations with Kenya, 182
South Africa: as part of Central Africa, 86-88; intervenes in Angola, 101-102, 108, 109-133 *passim*; African National Congress and Pan-African Congress, 113-116; population distribution, 116, 186, 189-190; population ratios, 126; apartheid-into-Bantustans, 126-130, 189-190; Asians, 125-126; Afrikaans, 186; African communities, 187; partition, 190
Soyinka, Wole, 148; quoted, 149, 151-152, 154-155, 191, 197
Spínola, António de, 99
Strauss, H., quoted, 115, 117-118
Stultz, Newell, quoted, 189-190
Swaziland, 83

Tacitus, paraphrased, 139, 192
Tanzania: early history, 61-63; post-independence politics, 73-78; *ujamaa vijilini*, 75-77, 80; elections, 181
Tawney, R. H., quoted, 32
Telli, Diallo, imprisoned, 17
Thiong'o, Ngugi wa. *See* Ngugi
Tordoff, William, cited on Zambia, 91
Touré, Sekou, and 1958 referendum, 13, 20
Touval, Saadia, quoted, 174
Trapido, Stanley: quoted, 117, 123-124; cited, 187
Transkei, 127-129, 189-190
Tribal factions, 17-18, 27; in Rwanda and Burundi, 29; in Nigeria, 53-54; as ethnic solidarities, 55-56; in Senegal, 58-59; in Uganda, 67-68; in Kenya, 70-72; in Zambia, 91-92; in Rhodesia, 97; in Angola, 101-102; in South Africa, 116, 187; genocide in Rwanda, 174, in Ethiopia, 175
Tshombe, Moishe, rise and fall, 88-90

Uganda: early history, 62-64; under Obote and Amin, 67-69; brutality of regime, 162; terminology, 178
Ujamaa vijilini. See Tanzania
United States of America: and East Africa, 80-81; and Angola, 101-102; and South Africa, 120, 133, 190
USSR: and East Africa, 80-81; and Angola, 101-102; and South Africa, 120, 131-133

Vorster, John Balthazar, 97, 106, 109-133 *passim*; quoted, 190-191

Wästberg, Per, cited, 137
Wolpe, Harold, quoted, 188

Yeats, W. B., quoted, ix, 136, 160, 192
Young, Crawford, cited, 67, 179
Young, Ralph: quoted, 104-105; cited, 185

Zaire, 83-107; rail and economic links with Central Africa, 86-88; independence and civil strife, 88-90
Zambia, 83-107; breaks from Central African Federation, 83-84; political economy, 85-87; problems of independence, 91-92; problems of Rhodesian UDI, 103-106; and South Africa, 185
Zanzibar, 62-64, 69, 178, 181
Zimbabwe. *See* Rhodesia
Zolberg, cited, 41-42, 176